# CSR
# CORPORATE GOVERNANCE
# AND
# WORKPLACE PRACTICES
*A New Perspective*

# CSR
# CORPORATE GOVERNANCE
# AND
# WORKPLACE PRACTICES

*A New Perspective*

Dr. Anjana Hazarika

PENTAGON PRESS LLP

**CSR, Corporate Governance and Workplace Practices: A New Perspective**
*By Dr. Anjana Hazarika*

ISBN 978-81-942837-6-8

First Published in 2020



*Published by*
PENTAGON PRESS LLP
206, Peacock Lane, Shahpur Jat,
New Delhi-110049
Phones: 011-64706243, 26491568
Telefax: 011-26490600
email: rajan@pentagonpress.in
website: www.pentagonpress.in

Printed at Aegean Offset Printers, Greater Noida, U.P.

# Contents

# Preface

This book is an inquiry into the field of tri-junction of Corporate Social Responsibility (CSR), Corporate Governance and Workplace Practices. The author has made a humble effort to bring forth a new perspective on this contested terrain.

CSR is a complex subject. Indeed it has been ingrained with business since the beginning of mankind. Business and social responsibility are so intertwined that they can hardly be separated. However, there are different schools of thought which have been at loggerheads for centuries whether business enterprises should be involved in social and moral issues or not. On one spectrum of this debate, experts like Milton Friedman who won the Nobel Prize in Economics in 1976, pronounces that 'The business of business is business'. Following his gospel, many in later years, convincingly offered the proposition that the core responsibility of business is to conduct business sincerely. But with globalization, the legal, ethical and social accountability expectations from trade have risen to an unprecedented scale. Even much before that centuries old Indian business conglomerates, called as 'Shrenis', had substantially contributed to the growth and development of society and polity. Precisely, these Shrenis had provided an alternative form of governance to the ruling dispensations by taking care of a host of social and legal issues besides doing core business activities. Thus it can safely be argued that at this current juncture of global connectivity, even inchoate business groups carry out socially accountable activities not just to promote their business but also to share their utmost concern for society and community.

What the author argues is crystal clear. For a firm to be socially responsible is to first speak out and follow its responsibilities towards its own employees much before demonstrating the same for external stakeholders. Thus, highlighting the business firm's social responsibility, once Kumarmangalam Birla echoed: 'The days are long past when the business of business was just business. The idea that a corporation is merely a legal abstraction, devoid of heart and soul, no longer has legitimacy. The corporation may be an economic wunderkind, but it falls short and often falls apart if it does not meet the needs of society, or if it does not act with a conscience. Today, no stakeholder-be it a shareholder, an employee, the community or the Government-would accept a business whose rationale is limited to profits at any cost, or only to compulsions of its immediate business'. Henceforth, the book veers around the idea that business means social responsibility and accountability towards its stakeholders and creating a democratic environment at workplace so that the employees can voice their concerns and claim their legitimate rights.

Business to practice CSR in a democratic manner has to engage with its employee community in proactive way. The company needs to be responsible to all members of the employee community at all levels, be it the highest ranking official of the firm, or the lowest unskilled or may be the contractual workers. The company's responsibility towards all its employees should be equal. It is usually found that such responsibility does not percolate downwards. The author highlights the point that it is essential to establish a dialogue with employees to understand each other's problems better and find ways to resolve them.

Finally, the author in her course of navigating through the world of CSR, corporate governance and democratic practices have found that some of the top public sector organizations in India have also nearly perfected the art and practice of engaging in community work and offering democratic space to their employees besides delivering core business concerns. Therefore, it is not just business and making profit, but it is all about creating a positive environment for the stakeholders. Simply because, a business organization is purely a social entity as it wholly operates within the precincts of society and humanity.

# Acknowledgements

I am highly obliged to my late Professor Sharit K. Bhowmik at Tata Institute of Social Sciences (TISS), Mumbai who had always inspired me to pursue research in the field of Corporate Social Responsibility and Business Ethics. His kind words and guidance had not only helped me to conceptualize many intrigued debates and concepts but also shaped my future studies in this field.

I sincerely thank the library staff of Tata Institute of Social Sciences, Mumbai, O. P. Jindal Global University, Sonepat, Haryana and the Teen Murti Library, New Delhi. Without their cooperation and assistance, this work would have remained incomplete.

Apart from known sources, I have read and analyzed various anonymous authors for writing this book. I am immensely grateful to all these people for their rich works and seminal contributions.

Last, but not the least, I would like to thank my husband Dr. Makhan Saikia who had read and edited the entire book time and again, despite his busy schedule. I am grateful to my two daughters, Chitrangada and Yasudhara, who had to bear my odd working hours throughout the course of writing this work.

And very sincere thanks go to Rajan Aryaji for consenting to publish this book and expertly shepherding the work through the editorial production process with his team.

Needless to say, the shortcomings of the book are absolutely my own.

# 1

# Corporate Social Responsibility: Diverse Perspectives and Workplace Practices

Corporate Social Responsibility (CSR) is an integration of business with social and environmental concern. CSR is the point of convergence of various initiatives aimed at ensuring socio-economic development of the community in a sustainable manner. In fact, it is the alignment of business operations with social values. It takes into account the interests of stakeholders in the company's business policies and actions. The concept of CSR has a long history. The concern for social responsibility appeared in the 1920s and 1930s, but the modern era of social responsibility began from 1950s onwards. Earlier CSR was referred to as social responsibility, as the prominence of business sector has not occurred. It was Bowen's (1953) work on social responsibilities of business that started the modern period of CSR. According to him, large business firms were vital centres of power and decision making, and the activities of these firms touch the lives of common men at many points. That is why Bowen set forth the initial definition of social responsibilities of businessmen: "It refers to the obligations of businessmen to pursue those policies, to make those decisions, or to follow those lines of action which are desirable in terms of the objectives and values of our society" ( Bowen in Carroll, 1999: 270).

Keith Davis (1960) was concerned about the business–society relation, and stood for social responsibility in a managerial context. According to him, social responsibility refers to "businessmen's decisions and actions taken for reasons at least partially beyond the firm's direct economic or technical interest" (Davis, 1960: 70). Later on, Davis became popular, because of his view on the relation between social responsibility and business power. He argued that social responsibility and business power should be commensurate, and avoidance of social responsibility would lead to erosion of social power on the part of businesses. Therefore, businessmen cannot shun their social responsibilities, and only concentrate on profit.

Frederick stressed on the role of the economic system within business enterprises in the socio-economic welfare. Based on this belief, Frederick argued that "Social Responsibilities mean that businessmen should oversee the operation of an economic system that fulfills the expectations of the public and this means in turn that the economy's means of production should be employed in such a way that production and distribution should enhance total socio-economic welfare" (Frederick, 1960: 60). Frederick gave top priority to business's economic system, and its eventual benefit for the public. McGuire moved beyond economic and legal obligations, and stressed on social obligations. He stated, "The idea of social responsibilities supposes that the corporation has not only economic and legal obligations but also certain responsibilities to society which extend beyond these obligations" (1963: 144). Walton drew upon diverse models of social responsibilities, and said that "social responsibility recognizes the intimacy of the relationship between the corporation and society and realizes that such relationships must be kept in mind by top managers as the corporation and the related groups pursue their respective goals" (Walton, 1967: 18). He emphasized upon certain essential ingredients of the corporation's social responsibilities, i.e. a degree of voluntarism, as against coercion, an indirect linkage of certain other voluntary organizations to the corporation and finally, the acceptance of the fact that costs are involved because it may not be possible to gauge any direct measurable economic returns.

During 1970s, a different dimension of CSR ushered in. Heald's (1970) understanding of social responsibility was in the same vein as the thought process that developed during 1960s. He added certain new concepts to social responsibility of businesses: "meaning of the concept of social responsibility for businessmen must finally be sought in the actual policies with which they were associated" (Heald: X1). It implies that social responsibility should be practiced in the core policies of the organization. In the historical context, Heald argued that business people were preoccupied with corporate philanthropy and community relations. But in modern times, business organizations are moving towards incorporating social responsibility in policy making. Johnson (1971) presented the term "conventional wisdom" in reference to social responsibility of business. According to him, conventional wisdom implies a socially responsible firm, where the managerial staff who undertakes multiplicity of interests must look beyond its stakeholders profit and strive for initiatives for employees, suppliers, dealers, local communities and the nation. Johnson was trying to move beyond the stockholder paradigm to a stakeholder approach. Later on, he presented a second view of corporate social responsibility stating, "Social responsibility states that businesses carry out social programmes to add profits to their organizations" (ibid: 54), and social responsibility is perceived as a long-run profit maximization process. With the third view of social responsibility that he called utility maximization, the primary motivation of the business firms is utility maximization rather than only maximum profits, and finally, he presented a fourth view known as lexicographic view of social responsibility, whereby "The lexicographic utility theory suggests that strongly profit motivated firms may engage in socially responsible behavior" (ibid: 77) because once these firms attain profit, they act as if social responsibility was an important goal. Thus, social responsibility happens only when the profit motive of the firm is fulfilled. The firm's social responsibility endeavours to add to the firm's profit.

The Community for Economic Development (CED; 1971) noted that the social contract between business and society was changing in substantial ways. Business enterprises are asked to assume broader responsibilities to society and serve a wider range of human values. Besides profit, the business organizations have to recognize indispensability of human values. That is why, at the expense of profitability, the CED articulated three concentric circles of social responsibility: inner circle, intermediate and the outer circle. The inner circle includes the clear-cut basic responsibilities for the efficient execution of the economic function, the intermediate circle encompasses responsibility to exercise this economic function with a sensitive awareness of changing social value and priorities, and finally, the outer circle outlines newly emerging and amorphous responsibilities that business should assume to become owner broadly involved in improving the social environment (Carroll, 1999: 275). Another noteworthy fact is that the CED is composed of business people and educators, and thus reflects an important practitioner view of the changing social construct between business and society and businesses' newly emerging social responsibilities (ibid). In another development, it was put forward that business corporations are economic institutions, and social responsibilities have to be shared among the companies. Steiner (1971) stated that business must remain fundamentally an economic institution but it does have responsibilities to help achieve its basic goals and does, therefore, have social responsibilities, but all companies can assume some share of them at no cost and often at a short-run as well as a long-run profit. Business is recognized for its economic role, and it is its basic role. Of course, it can assume responsibilities towards the society, by sharing it with other business organizations.

Friedman's minimalist view or business-centric view of corporate responsibility is very important. According to him, "there is one and only one social responsibility of business to use its resources and engage in activities designed to increase its profits so long as it stays within the rules of the game which is to say, engage in open and free competition without deception or fraud" (Friedman, in Turner, 2006: 7). Friedman's legally binding responsibility is towards the business and its activities. It has no space for social responsibility, for he thought such responsibilities have to be handled by the state or state-run enterprises. If it does not happen so, then the very motive of the business enterprises is defeated. But a business cannot always shy away from its responsibilities towards society. The very fact that they are directly working and using the resources of the society makes their responsibility automatically mandatory.

Towards 1974, with Richard Eell's and Walton's ideas, a broader perspective of CSR set forth. They wrote at length on business history, the concept of the corporation, ownership and governance. New ideas and concepts evolved from social responsibility of businesses. Sethi (1975) placed corporate social performance along with CSR. He discussed different dimensions of Corporate Social Performance, and in the process made distinctions between various corporate behaviours, such as social obligation, social responsibility and social responsiveness. In Sethi's work, social obligation is a corporate behaviour in response to market forces or legal constraints, social responsibility goes beyond social obligation and social responsiveness is the adaption of corporate behaviour to social needs. He stated, "Social responsibility implies bringing corporate behaviour up to a level where it is congruent with the prevailing social norms, values, and expectations of performance" (Carroll, 1975: 62).

Thus, there was a shift from the concept of *corporate social responsibility* towards *public responsibility*. Preston and Post (1975) preferred the term public responsibility, because within public responsibility, the scope of management of a firm is limited, and it will be within the specific context of public life. They preferred public responsibility over social responsibility in order, "to stress the importance of the public policy process, rather than individual opinion and conscience, as the source of goals and appraisal criteria" (Preston and Post, 1975: 102) and defined the functions of organizational management within the specific context of public life. During this period, another body of literature evolved, focusing on the operationalization of CSR. Fitch (1976) looked at CSR in terms of solving problems. His problem-solving perspective on CSR was to identify and define first a social problem, and then, from an array of social problems, decide which ones to attack first. In this process, it has to make a distinction between social and non-social problems and then identify the methods for attacking the social problems.

In 1979, Carroll proposed four dimensions of CSR, embedded in a conceptual model of Corporate Social Performance. To him, "The social responsibility of business encompasses the economic, legal, ethical and discretionary expectations that society has to organizations at a given point in time" (Carroll, 1979: 500). Carroll stressed on the economic responsibility of business, because initially business institutions were the basic economic unit in the society. And all other business roles are dependent on the economic function of the business institution. He noted, "Just as society expects business to make a profit (as an incentive and reward for its efficiency and effectiveness, society expects business to obey the law. The law represents the basic rules of the game by which business is expected to function". Society expects business to fulfill its economic mission within the framework of legal requirements set forth by the society's legal system (ibid). Later on, Carroll stressed on the legal and ethical responsibility of business and finally, discretionary responsibilities. These discretionary responsibilities represent voluntary roles that business assumes and are left to individual managers and corporations' judgment and choice. This expectation is driven by social norms. Thus, it has been observed that corporate social responsibility has added new dimensions to it, such as the ethics, legal requirements, and public policy making.

From 1980s onwards, corporate social responsibility became more research and theme oriented. In this regard, Frank Tuzzolino and Barry Armandi (1981) developed a mechanism for assessing CSR by proposing a need hierarchy framework patterned after Maslow's need hierarchy theory (1954). They believed that it would help in facilitating the operationalization of CSR. This organizational need hierarchy suggested that organizations are like individuals and have some criteria's that needed to be fulfilled just as people do. Strand (1983: 92) too presented a system paradigm of organizational adaptations to the social environment that sought to illustrate how much related concepts social responsibility, social responsiveness and social responses are connected to an organization's environment model. His model was notable because it represented another model in a continuing stream of efforts to associate such concepts as CSR to other similar notions and to the organizational environment interface. Another significant line of thinking evolved in the 1980s with R. Edward Freemen's stakeholder perspective to corporate strategy. According to Freeman, stakeholders are "groups and individuals who benefit from or are harmed by, and whose rights are violated or respected by, corporate actions" (Freeman 1998: 174). Freeman recognized the contributions of other segments of the business enterprises, besides the shareholders. Freeman pointed that "in addition to shareholders, there are creditors, employees, customers, suppliers, and the communities at large" (Freeman in Branco and Rodrigues, 2007: 7), who are equally responsible for the growth of the enterprises. Freeman expanded the outlook of the businesses towards other contributors, and not just simply restricting to the owners of the enterprises. Therefore, a new strand of advocacy, i.e. the stakeholders, set forth the growth of strategic corporate social responsibility.

Drucker (1954), an ardent votary of performance-oriented business, centred his argument for social responsibility around three areas: relationship between private ethics and public ethics, the responsibility that the employer bears towards his employees by virtue of his power and wealth and the leadership responsibility of the businessman towards the community. To Drucker, profitability and compatibility in business are more important than anything else. And the new aspect in his contribution is that "business ought to convert its social responsibilities into business opportunities". That is why he argued, "But the proper social responsibility of business is to tame the dragon, that is to turn a social problem into economic opportunity and economic benefit, into productive capacity, into human competences, into well paid jobs, and into wealth" (Drucker, in Carroll, 1979: 286). To Drucker, all organizations in society are social organizations, whether it's an academic institute, a hospital or a business enterprise. The best social responsibility an organization can perform is scoring in its core functions. And, CSR can be pursued by businesses by sticking to its core competency, making it a profitable exercise for the company as well as the society.

In 1990s, the concept of CSR became the building block or point of departure for other related concepts and themes. Corporate Social Performance, stakeholder theory, business ethics and corporate citizenship took centre stage. Further, with the evolution of new theories, perspectives, dimensions and models of CSR, corporate social responsibility entered a new domain with new technologies and commercially viable application.

Although reference to CSR has occurred prior to 1950s, but Bowen's (1953) work on Social Responsibility marked the beginning of the modern era of CSR. Corporate Social Responsibility began to proliferate in the 1970s, and became very specific in its emphasis. Empirical examination of CSR started in the 1980s, with a strong emphasis on research and understanding of operationalization of CSR. Emphasis on alternative themes of CSR, like stakeholder, business ethics and corporate citizenship, took centre stage in the 1990s. Development took place towards the reconciliation of CSR practice and theory. Now, new realms are growing to capture the concerns for public regarding business and society relation, and, also towards strategic CSR, whereby CSR will be embedded in the corporate policies of the organizations.

## CSR from Diverse Perspectives

As we have observed, CSR as a concept evolved from crisis especially industrial crisis in the West. Later on, it took a reformative turn within business and outside. Value creation never remained within the shareholder fold, but it encompassed the entire gamut of stakeholders and their concerns. To arrive at the current ecology of CSR, businesses went through massive changes in their approach towards business–society relation.

The classical view of social responsibility of a business primarily stressed on the profit-making role of business. With the change in perspectives, and thought processes in business, constrained profit making evolved and later on, it became a part of the classical view.

Lantos (2001) has identified two perspectives in the classical view, i.e. the pure profit- making view and the constrained profit-making view. Carr focused on the pure profit-making view. The distinctive feature of this view is that some degree of dishonesty is acceptable because business people have a low moral standard than others. This low-moral standard permits businessmen to bluff, by consciously concealing important facts. Therefore for Carr, "a company has the legal right to shape its strategy without reference to anything but its profits, so long as it stays within the rules of the game legally set out by law" (Carr in Branco and Rodrigues, 2007: 6).

The proponent of the constrained profit making view was Friedman (1970). He believed that companies should behave honestly and they should not engage in deception and fraud. According to Friedman the only responsibility of business is to use its resources to engage in activities designed to increase its profits as long as it stays within the rules of the game. "As managers are agents of the shareholders they have a responsibility to conduct business in accordance with their interest" (ibid: 6). Friedman is of the opinion that as shareholders are the owners of the company, profits also belongs to them. And requiring the managers of the firms to pursue socially responsible objectives may be unethical, since it requires managers to spend money that belongs to other individuals. Theodore Levitt (1958), a conspicuous predecessor of Friedman believed that companies should be concerned with improving production and profits while abiding by the rules of the game, i.e. acting honestly and in good faith, and then the social problems should be left for the state to address. The classical profit-making view had many contemporary followers: Barry (2000), Coelho (2003), Henderson (2005), Jensen (2001), Sternberg (1997), and Sundaram and Inkpen (2004). But not all of them totally opposed the social responsibility actions of the companies. David Henderson (2005) in line with Friedmen contends that CSR adversely affects a company's performance. His argument against CSR primarily rests on the contention that it impairs the performance of business enterprises in their primary role and would make people in general poorer: "He does not attribute any social responsibility related function to companies" (Bronco and

Rodriques: 6). Jensen, Coelho, Sternberg, Sundaram and Inkpen defended the shareholder value maximization as the primary function of all companies, but they were not against the social responsibilities of the companies. These authors believed that value seeking should be a company's only objective and managers should not be allowed to pursue moral goals at the expense of profitability.

Even though these authors supported their predecessors, they were not necessarily against the social responsibility actions by companies.

According to Sternberg (1997), a company cannot afford to ignore any stakeholder concern that might affect its ability to generate long-term owner value. To Coelho (2003: 18), social responsibility actions might be used strategically by companies in seeking value maximization of the company. Even Carr (1968), in spite of defending the pure profit-making view, recognized that if a company wishes to take a long-term view of its profits, it has to consider or will need to preserve amicable relations with whom it deals

The classical view is justified mainly on the basis of neoclassical economic theory arguments using notions such as the free market, economic efficiency and profit maximization (Branco and Rodrigues: 7). Pure profit making and constrained profit making is no longer a universal phenomenon in business social responsibility. Even during the classical time, business ideas didn't correspond to this phenomenon in totality.

There is an inherent connection between power and position of business and its responsibility towards society. Davis (1960) was one of the first to explore the role of power that business has in society and also the social impact of this power. Davis introduced business power as a new element in the debate of CSR. According to him, business is a social institution and it must use power responsibly. It is an utmost reality that social responsibility arises from concern about the consequences of business acts, as they affect the interest of others. Business as such cannot make decisions that are solely economic because they are interrelated with the whole social system.

Davis formulated two principles that express how social power has to be managed: the social power equation and the iron law of responsibility. "The social power equation principle states that social responsibilities of business arise from the amount of social power that they have" (Davis, 1967: 48). The iron law of responsibility refers to the negative consequences of the absence of use of power, i.e. if a firm does not use its social power, it will lose its position in society because other groups will occupy it, especially when society demands responsibility from business (Davis, 1960). The equation of social power responsibility has to be understood through the functional role of business and managers.

Therefore, Davis rejects the idea of total responsibility of business as he rejected the radical free market ideology of no responsibility of business. His main concern was the social power of business and its impact on the society. Because, social power will assist business firms to be responsible towards the society, besides, being responsible towards business.

The social contract in business is based on a firm's indirect societal obligations and resembles the traditional social contract theory, which identified the reciprocal obligations of citizen and state. Originally, the social contract focused solely on economic responsibilities, and social progress and quality-of-life advancement were assumed to be a by-product of economic growth.

Donaldson, an adherent of this view, considered the business and society relationship from the social contract tradition, mainly from the philosophical thought of Locke: "He assumed that a sort of implicit social contract between business and society exists. This social contract implies some indirect obligations of business towards society" (Donaldson in Garriga and Mele, 2004: 56). But later on Donaldson and Dunfee (1994, 1999) extended this approach and proposed an "Integrative Social Contract Theory" in order to take into account the socio-cultural contexts and also to integrate empirical and normative aspects of management. According to Donaldson and Dunfee, there are two levels of consent: first, a theoretical macro-social contract appealing to all rational contractors, and second, a real micro-social contract by members of numerous localized communities. "According to these authors, this theory offers a process in which the contracts among industries, departments and economic spectrum's can be legitimate. In this process, the participants will agree upon the ground rules, defining the foundation of economics that will be acceptable to them" (ibid: 56).

The macro-social contract approach provides rules for any social contracting. These rules are called the hyper-norms. These hyper-norms are very much fundamental and they are discernible in a convergence of religious, political and philosophical thoughts (Donaldson and Dunfee, 2000: 441). The micro-social contracts are explicit or implicit agreements that are binding within an identified community, i.e. industry, companies or economic systems; the micro-social contracts that generate authentic norms are based on the attitudes and behaviours of the members of the norm-generating community and in order to be legitimate have to accord with the hyper-norms.

The corporate social contract is based on a firm's indirect societal obligations and resembles the traditional social contract theory that identified the reciprocal obligations of citizen and state. But the new social contract theory postulated that social progress should move equally with economic progress. The corporations as organizations have social responsibility and obligations tying them to a wider society.

The idea of the firm as citizen is not new (Davis, 1973), but a renewed interest in this concept among practitioners has appeared recently due to certain factors that have had an impact on the business and society relationship: "Among these factors, especially worthy of note are the crisis of the welfare state and the globalization phenomenon" (Garriga and Mele, 2004: 56). Crisis of the welfare state and the globalization phenomenon with the deregulation process and decreasing costs with technological improvements have shown that some large multinational companies have greater economical and social power than some governments.

In the 80s, the term "corporate citizenship" was introduced into the business and society relationship mainly from a practitioner's perspective (Altman and Vidaver-Cohen, 2000). Since the late 1990s and early 21$^{st}$ century, the term has become more and more popular in business. Corporate Citizenship or Corporate Social Responsibility deals with the interrelation of business and society. Business organizations are expected to exhibit ethical behaviour and moral management, among other things, by accepting some accountability for societal welfare (Asongu, 2007: 2). Business citizen, a similar development in the line of corporate citizenship, is also recent (Matten, 2003; Wood and Logsdon, 2002). Since this concept has connoted a sense of belonging to a community, it has become very popular among managers and business people and also makes clear that business needs to take into account the community where it is operating. Matten (2003) has distinguished three views of

"Corporate Citizenship": (1) a limited view, (2) a view equivalent to CSR and (3) an extended view of corporate citizenship. In a limited view, corporate citizenship is quite close to corporate philanthropy, social investment or certain responsibilities assumed towards the local communities. Regarding the equivalent to CSR view, Carroll (1999) believes that corporate citizenship is a new conceptualization of the role of business in society and largely overlaps with other theories on the responsibility of business in society. In the extended view of corporate citizenship (Matten, 2003), corporations enter the arena of citizenship at the point of government failure in the protection of citizenship. "This view arises from the fact that some corporations have gradually come to replace the most powerful institution in the traditional concept of citizenship, namely government" (Garriga and Mele, 2004: 57). The term citizenship is at the core of "Corporate Citizenship". According to Wood and Logsdon (2002), "business citizenship" cannot be deemed equivalent to individual citizenship; instead it derives from individual citizenship and is secondary to it (Wood and Logsdon, 2002: 86).

Even though there are some minor differences in the corporate citizenship theories, most of them converge on the strong sense of business responsibility towards the local community and also the environment.

Social responsiveness in the face of social issues within the organization was an approach that arose in the 1970s (Sethi, 1975). He distinguished between social obligation, social responsibility and social responsiveness. He argues that like all other social institutions, companies are an integral part of society and must depend on acceptance of role and activities for their existence, continuity and growth. When a difference between corporate performance and social expectations for such performance occurs, a legitimacy gap is created. The crucial issue here is that companies look out for legitimacy, and the critics doubt the legitimacy of the companies' actions. Social responsibility refers to congruence of corporate behaviour with prevailing social norms, values and expectations of performance and it is prescriptive in nature. The concept of social responsiveness suggests that what is important is not how a company should respond to social pressures, but what should be their long-term role in a dynamic social system. The crucial point is to consider the gap between what the organization's relevant publics expect its performance to be and the organization's actual performance.

These gaps are usually located in the zone that Ackerman calls the "zone of discretion (neither regulated nor illegal nor sanctioned) where the company receives some unclear signals from the environment (Ackerman, 1973: 92). The firm should perceive the gap and choose a response in order to close it (Ackerman and Bauer, 1976). Ackerman analyzed the relevant factors regarding the internal structures of organizations and integration mechanisms to manage social issues within the organization and the way a social objective is spread and integrates across the organization; he termed it as the process of institutionalization. Jones (1980) emphasized the idea of process rather than principles as the appropriate approach to CSR issues. He drew an analogy with the political process assessing that the appropriate process of CSR should be a fair process where all interests should get the opportunity to be heard. Jones stressed on inputs in the decision-making process rather than outcomes and has focused more on the process of implementations of CSR activities than on the process of conceptualization. Wartick and Rude defined the concept of issue management as "the processes by which the corporation can identify, evaluate and respond to those social and political issues which may impact significantly upon it" (Wartick and Rude, 1986: 124). According to them, issue management tries to minimize surprises that accompany social and political change by serving as an early warning system for potential environmental threats and opportunities.

Further, it spearheads more systematic and effective responses to particular issues by serving as a coordinating and integrating force within the corporation. Preston (1975) and Post (1981) were against the responsiveness. They accepted the term "public" rather than "social" to stress the importance of the public process rather than personal morality views or narrow interest groups and also defining the scope of responsibilities. Preston and Post found an appropriate guideline for a legitimate managerial behaviour within the framework of relevant public policy. They argued that "public policy includes not only the literal text of law and regulations but also the broad pattern of social direction reflected in public opinion, emerging issues, formal legal requirements and enforcement or implementation practices" (Preston and Post, 1981: 57).

Preston and Post analyzed the scope of managerial responsibility in terms of the primary and secondary involvement of the firm in its social environment. Primary involvement includes the essential economic task of the firm, such as locating and establishing its facilities, procuring suppliers, engaging employees, carrying out its production function and marketing products. It also includes legal requirements. Secondary involvements come as the consequence of the primary (Garriga and Mele, 2004: 59). They are also in favour of business interventions in the public policy process especially with regard to those areas where specific public policy is not yet clearly established or it is in a state of transition. While in practice discovering the content of the principle of public responsibility is complex and difficult and requires substantial management attention, if business adhered to the standards of performance in law and the existing public policy process, then it would be judged acceptably responsive in terms of social expectations (Garriga and Mele: 59).

Stakeholders are groups and individuals, who either contribute voluntarily or involuntarily, to the corporation, in its wealth-creating capacity and activities. Therefore, they are the potential beneficiaries as well as risk bearers. The stakeholder model is a reaction to Friedman's shareholder paradigm where no entity other than shareholders has a claim on the business (Lantos, 2001: 14). Stakeholder theory asserts that companies have a social responsibility that requires them to consider the interests of all parties affected by their actions. And then, the management should not only consider its shareholders in the decision-making process, but also anyone who is affected by business decisions.

Emshoff and Freeman (1978) presented two basic principles, which underpin stakeholder management. The primary goal is to achieve maximum overall co-operation between the entire system of stakeholder groups and the objectives of the corporation. And secondly, the most efficient strategies for managing stakeholder relations involve efforts, which simultaneously deal with issues affecting multiple stakeholders. Stakeholder relationship is more than just a relationship between agents who have fiduciary responsibility to a principal. There are also third parties to whom the corporation owes morally significant non-fiduciary obligations. "These duties exist because like stockholders, other stakeholders also make investments in enterprises, employees invest their time and intellectual capital, customers invest their trust on reputed business, communities provide infrastructure and education for future employees as well as tax support, and so on" (Graves, 2001: 17).

The goal of any company is or should be the flourishing of the company and all its principal stakeholders (Warhane and Freeman, 1999: 8). In other words, it implies that one has to go beyond profit maximization to trusteeship or the multi-fiduciary stakeholder relation.

It is envisioned that stakeholders exist at four levels: First is the systemic/ macro environmental/general environmental level, larger societal factors, including the entire business system, the social system, plus society at large that consists of institutions and forces. The second level of stakeholders is the corporation's micro-environment/operating/task environment, its unmediated environment, consisting of exchange relationships, partners (such as suppliers and distributors), plus competitors, customers, the local community, and the financial community (stockholders, bondholders, and creditor). A third level of stakeholders is found within the business organization, notably superiors, subordinates and other employees and unions. The final level of stakeholder is significant others of business decision makers, such as peers, family, friends etc. (Lantos, 2001: 14). Donaldson and Preston (1995) argued that stakeholder theory can be used in three different ways:

1. Descriptive/empirical, when it is used to describe, and sometimes explain, specific corporate characteristics and behaviour (ibid: 70).
2. The instrumental, when it is used to identify the connections, or lack of connections, between stakeholder management and the achievement of traditional corporate objectives (e.g. profitability, growth; ibid: 71).
3. The normative, when it is used to interpret the function of companies and identify moral or philosophical guidelines that should be followed with regard to their operation and management (ibid).

The normative approach to stakeholder theory regards stakeholders as end, whereas the instrumental approach to stakeholder theory views stakeholders' interest as factors to be taken into account and managed while the company is engaged in maximization of shareholders' wealth. Referring to the instrumental view, Jawahar and McLaughlin argue that the "ultimate objective of corporate decisions is market place success, and stakeholder management is a means to an end" (Jawahar and McLaughlin, 2001: 399).

Jensen (2001) argued that enlightened value maximization and enlightened theory are the same. Because the enlightened value maximization view uses stakeholder theory to consider that a company cannot maximize value if any important stakeholder is ignored.

There are many version of stakeholder theory and Freeman admits the existence of many normative cores. Some corporations are seeking corporate responses to social demands by establishing dialogue with a wide spectrum of stakeholders. Stakeholder dialogue helps to address the question of responsiveness to the generally unclear signals received from the environment (Garriga and Mele, 2004: 59). Therefore, stakeholder dialogue not only enhances a company's sensitivity to its environment but also increases the environment's understanding of the dilemmas facing the organization (Kaptein and Tulder, 2003: 208).

Carroll (1979) is believed to have introduced the "corporate social performance model". It consisted of an integration of three aspects:

1. A definition of social responsibility that fully addresses the entire range of obligations business has to society must embody the economic, legal, ethical, discretionary categories of business performance.
2. An identification of the social issues to which these responsibilities are tied such as consumerism, environment, employment, discrimination, product safety, occupational safety and health.
3. The philosophy of responsiveness, that is the philosophy mode or strategy behind companies, response to social responsibility and social issues—reaction, defense, accommodation and proaction; (Carroll in Branco and Rodrigues, 2007: 9).

Carroll went beyond the profit motive of firms, and argued that CSR encompasses four categories of social responsibilities, i.e. economic, legal, ethical and discretionary or philanthropic:

Economic responsibilities reflect the belief that companies have an obligation to produce goods and services that consumers need and want, and to be profitable in the process. Legal responsibilities indicate that companies are expected to pursue economic responsibilities within the confines of written law. Ethical responsibilities are a concern that company's meet society's expectations of business that are not codified into law, but rather are reflected in unwritten standards, norms and values implicitly derived from society (ibid: 9).

Wartick and Cochran (1985) extended and modified Carroll's approach that integrates three areas, the principles of CSR, the processes of corporation's social responsiveness and the policies developed to address social issues. Wood (1991) presented a model of corporate social performance composed of principles of CSR, processes of corporate social responsiveness and outcomes of corporate behaviour. She suggested that companies use three main kinds of processes to bring these principles into practice, i.e. environmental assessment, issues management and stakeholder management. She then presents the outcomes of bringing principles into practice within the economic, legal, ethical and discretionary domains, categorizing them in terms of social impacts both beneficial or negative social programme (which refer to the actions companies take to manage their social impacts in a favorable manner) and social policies (which emerge to guide decision making).

Again, Wood and Jones (1995) used a stakeholder framework to modify Wood's concept of corporate social performance as principles processes and outcomes. Stakeholders have three roles: they are the sources of expectation about what constitutes desirable and undesirable company performance, defining the norms for corporate behaviour; they experience the effects of corporate behaviours in terms of how they have met expectations and have affected the groups and organizations in their environment.

Thus, corporate social performance from a stakeholder perspective can be assessed in terms of company meeting the demands of its multiple stakeholder groups and companies' duty to satisfy their demands under any unavoidable circumstances.

A strong relationship between business and society requires a strong ethical standard. Ethical CSR implies a corporation's moral responsibility towards individuals and groups. An organization that doesn't adhere to ethical responsibilities would be acting as morally irresponsible agent. Although harms cannot be avoided, they should be minimized wherever feasible. In the context of ethical CSR, corporations are believed to have special moral obligations to their various stakeholders outside the organizations. Regarding ethical responsibility, Goodpaster, Mathews, Shaw and Barry stressed that it has three usages. First is the capability usage, where someone has the ability to accomplish something. Second is causal responsibility that means someone has caused something to happen and is therefore morally responsible and accountable for its consequences. Third is the role-related responsibility, the duties or proper behaviour that goes along with a given role or particular position within a social group or society (Solomon, 1994).

Ethical responsibilities are regarded as morally mandatory. It involves preventing or rectifying harm or social injuries, even if the company might not appear to have benefited from such endeavors. Rather, ethical responsibilities are required even if their fulfillment is detrimental to the company's profitability.

Prior to the 1960s, morality in business was not a major concern for the business people. It was left to theologians to discuss issues of fair wages, unfair labor practices and of course, morality of capitalism. Protestant work ethic taught people to work hard and be successful. And this was the essence of business social responsibility. Max Weber, a German philosopher worked on the relationship between religion, economy and society. After an investigative study, he found that an over-proportional number of Protestants owned capital, were entrepreneurs and higher qualified technical or sales personnel in modern business.

"With the arrival of Business Ethics as an articulated corporate practice, the conception of corporate social responsibility has gone well beyond the donor mentality. Business Ethics successfully merges social responsibility with the imperatives of corporate efficiency in a fashion that is hard nosed, pragmatic and bottom line oriented" (Gupta, 2006: 30). He stressed on the differences between morality and ethics. Morality is individualistic whereas ethics is a practical approach towards attaining goals in an environment that involves a number of people. Morality is basically about the self and attaining one's spiritual levels or other kinds of perfection. And ethics marks social interaction.

Gupta had proposed three principles of Business Ethics:

1. Standardization, i.e. all rules and norms following from business should be equally applicable to all.
2. Workable: Rules and norms be workable and show tangible benefits.
3. Driven from the top: The top management's complete commitment

is important to the Business Ethics programme of a firm, i.e. only when the top managers demonstrate their commitment to ethics, then only it is likely to work.

These three principles "make sense as a composite unity and not individually" (ibid: 43). It is strict adherence to Business Ethics that the corporate sector can best promote social responsibility.

Ethical responsibility of business also takes into account sustainable growth and development. The term sustainable development was used in 1987, when the World Commission on Environment and Development (United Nations) published a report known as "Brundtland Report". "This report stated that 'sustainable development' seeks to meet the needs of the present without compromising the ability to meet the future generation to meet their own needs" (World Commission on Environment and Development, 1987: 8). Even though sustainable development originally included the environmental factor, but later on it expanded its horizon to include the consideration of the social dimension. That is why sustainable development is regarded as a "process of achieving human development in an inclusive, connected, equitable, prudent and secure manner" (Gladwin and Kennelly, 1995: 876).

According to Wheeler, sustainability is "an ideal toward which society and business can continually strive, the way we strive is by creating value, creating outcomes that are consistent with the ideal of sustainability along social environmental and economic dimensions" (Wheeler 2003: 17). But the problem comes when the corporation has to develop the processes and implement strategies to meet the challenge of corporate sustainable development. Sustainability has developed as a unified way of addressing a wide array of business concerns about the natural environment, worker's rights, consumer protection and corporate governance as well as the impact of business behaviour on broader social issues, such as hunger, poverty, education, health care and human rights, and the relationship of all these to profit (Savitz and Karl Weber, 2006). One very powerful way to grasp the connection between sustainable development and how companies can become more profitable by doing the right thing is the concept of Triple Bottom Line (TBL), originally proposed by John Elkington, an advocate of sustainability. Elkington suggests that businesses need to measure their success not only by the traditional bottom line of financial performance (most often expressed in terms of profits, return on investment [ROI], or shareholder value), but also by their impact on the broader economy, the environment and on the society in which they operate (Elkington, 1998). In conducting their business, companies use not only financial resources (such as investment dollars and sales revenues) but also environmental resources (such as water, energy and raw materials) and social resources (such as community, employees time and talents and infrastructure provided by governmental agencies; Savitz and Weber, 2006: XIII).

A sustainable business measures a positive ROI on all three bottom lines: economic, environmental and social. The TBL captures the essence of sustainability by measuring the impact of an organization's activities on the world. The TBL focuses not just on the corporations' economic value, but also on the environmental and social value they add or they destroy.

Sustainability has moved beyond just making the environment green. The environmental revolution has crossed three decades of making and changing the way, the companies do business. In the 60s and 70s, corporations were in a state of denial regarding their impact on the environment. But now many companies have accepted their responsibility to do no harm to the environment. Production process has become cleaner. In the developed nations, more and more companies are going green because they have realized that if they reduce pollution, then profits will increase simultaneously. Beyond greening lies a huge challenge and an enormous opportunity. That challenge is to develop a sustainable global economy, i.e. an economy that the planet is capable of supporting indefinitely. Thus, companies will be offering solutions to the world's environmental problems. Hart (1997) argued that envisioning tomorrow's business, therefore, requires a clear understanding of those problems. To move beyond greening to sustainability, we must first unravel a complex set of global interdependence. In fact, the global economy is three different overlapping economies. They are the market economy, the survival economy and the nature's economy.

The market economy is the world of commerce comprising both developed nations and the emerging economies. About one sixth of the world population lives in the developed countries of the market economy. Those affluent societies account for more than 75 percent of the world's energy and resource consumption and create bulk of industrial, toxic and consumer waste (Hart, 1997: 68).

In the developed economies, in spite of use of energy and materials, the level of pollution is relatively low. There are factors that have accounted for such a paradox—stringent environmental regulations, the greening of the industry and the relocation of the most polluting activities to the emerging market economies. Therefore, the greening of the developed world is at the expense of the environment in emerging economies. The second economy is the survival economy: traditional, village-based way of life found in the rural parts of most developing countries (ibid: 69). This economy comprises more than 3 billion people, mostly African, Indian and Chinese, who are primarily subsistence oriented and they meet their basic needs directly from nature. The developing nations fall in the survival economy and they account for 90 percent of growth of this economy. Due to rapid expansion of the market economy, existence in the survival economy is becoming precarious. Extractive industries and infrastructure development have degraded the ecosystems upon which the survival economy depends. Women and children spend on average four to six hours per day searching for fuel wood (ibid: 69). But ironically such conditions encourage high fertility, so that in the long run children can assist the family to garner needed resources. The third economy is nature's economy that consists of the natural systems and resources that support the market and the survival economies. These economies consist of non-renewable and renewable resources. Non-renewable resources like oil, metals and other minerals are finite. Renewable resources such as soils and forests will replenish the non-renewable resources.

Hart (1997) argues that sustainability required putting business strategies to a new test. Companies must ask whether they are part of the solution to social and environmental problems or part of the problem. And such a vision is required to guide companies through three stages of environmental strategy:

**Stage I:** Pollution Prevention: The first step for most companies is to make the shift from pollution control to pollution prevention (ibid: 71), i.e. it focuses on minimizing or eliminating waste before it is created.

**Stage II:** Product Stewardship: This focuses on minimizing not only pollution from manufacturing but also environmental impacts associated with the full life cycle of a product (ibid).

**Stage III:** Clean Technology: Companies with their eye on the future can begin to plan for and invest in tomorrow's technologies (ibid: 73). This implies that the existing technology in many industries is not environmentally sustainable and that is why the companies should carefully work in this aspect.

Pollution prevention, product stewardship and clean technology all move a company toward sustainability (ibid). But all the three have to work in tandem within a framework known as sustainability portfolio. Sustainability portfolio according to Hart is an overarching vision of sustainability that gives direction to the company's activities, and also, to what extent a company has progressed through the three stages of environmental strategy, i.e. from pollution prevention to product stewardship to clean technology.

In order to move beyond greening, "a clear and fully integrated environmental strategy should not only guide competency development, it should also shape the company's relationship to customers, suppliers, other companies, policy makers and all its stakeholders. Companies can and must change the way customers think by creating preferences for products and services consistent with sustainability. Companies must become educators rather than mere marketers of products" (ibid: 75). Therefore, just making the environment green is not enough; it is important for the business corporations to pursue strategies for a sustainable world.

Strategic corporate social responsibility implies not just doing well to business but also to society. It incorporates the performance of the business organization based on the core competencies, harnessing the talents of the poor and making them capable buyers and choosing those social issues that the business organizations are competent at. From a performance management perspective, an institution's first social responsibility is performance of its function. Performance is the basis of a sustainability of the enterprise and the society does not gain but lose if the performance capacity of the institution in its own specific task is diminished. Until and unless an institution discharge its performance responsibly, it cannot discharge anything else and it will not be possible to create the capital for tomorrow's jobs and the opportunities for tomorrow's workers.

Business has an impact on the society. And these impacts should be avoided by business. Responsibility for social impacts is a management responsibility—not because it is a social responsibility, but because it is a business responsibility (Drucker, 2001: 55). Therefore, if the business has caused any damage, then it is best to convert the social problem into business opportunities. It is also essential for management to know the minimum profitability for the risk undertaken by the business and by its commitments to the future. But whenever a business has disregarded the limitation of economic performance and has assumed social responsibilities that it could not support economically, it has soon gotten into trouble (ibid: 59).

Drucker emphasized on the performance perspective of the business enterprises, managers and also on the limits of social responsibility. According to him, "any solution of a social impact or of a social problem except to make it into an opportunity for performance and results, creates social overhead costs". These costs cannot be borne out of profits, no matter what popular rhetoric may say. They are paid for either out of current costs, that is, by consumer or taxpayer, or out of capital, that is, by fewer and poorer jobs tomorrow and impaired standards of living. The only way to cover costs and to accumulate capital is through economic performance. All other satisfactions of society are being paid for, one way or another, out of the surplus between current production and current consumption, that is, out of the surplus of the economy (Drucker, 2004: 313).

Managers of enterprises face certain challenges, like what is the optimal balance between the need to take care of a social problem and also at the same time the need to preserve the performance capacity of the existing social institutions.

Drucker retorts, "Managers need to be able to think through the limits on social responsibility set by their duty to the performance capacity of the enterprise in their charge" (ibid: 313). The basic objective of an enterprise is to perform and then draw its limits on social responsibility, "whenever a business has disregarded the limitations of economic performance and has assumed social responsibilities which it could not support economically it has soon gotten into trouble" (ibid: 314).

The institutions' performance of its specific mission is also society's first need and interest. Besides, the management needs to know the minimum profitability required by the risk involved in the job, and its commitment for the future. Problem is whenever the management has assumed social responsibility by ignoring the economic consequence, it has usually got into trouble.

According to Drucker, a business can be socially responsible by staying within three limitations:

- The limits of competence
- Limits of authority
- When to say "no".

### The Limits of Competence

"An institution and especially a business enterprise have to acquire whatever competence is needed to take responsibility for its impacts. But in areas of social responsibility other than impacts, right and duty to act are limited by competences" (ibid: 314).

In other words, an institution should refrain from tackling issues which its value system does not permit. Management needs to know what it is competent at. The strength of businesses is accountability and measurability, and if they are lacking in these two principles, then they are outside their own value system. "Before acceding to the demand that it take this or that social responsibility and so to work on this or that problem, management better think through what, if any, part of the task can be made fit the competencies of its institution" (ibid: 316).

### Limits of Authority

According to Peter Drucker, the most important limitation on social responsibility is the limitation of authority. When business or any other institution of a society is asked to assume social responsibility for one of the problems, then the management should think through "whether the authority implied in the responsibility is legitimate. Otherwise, it is usurpation and irresponsible" (ibid: 31).

Drucker is of the opinion that all major institutions, including business enterprise, need, too, to concern themselves with serious ills of society. If at all possible, they should convert the solution of these problems into an opportunity for performance and contribution. At least they should think through what the problem is and how it might be tackled. They cannot escape concern; for this society of organizations has no one else to be concerned about real problems. In this society, managers of institutions are the leadership group (ibid: 63).

## When to Say "no"

Whenever business or any other institution is asked to take social responsibility beyond its own areas of performance, then it has to ask itself whether it possesses any authority in that area or not. Here, the bottom line is that "Management must resist responsibility for a social problem that would compromise or impair the performance capacity of its business (or its university or its hospital)" (ibid: 318). That is why it must resist when the demand goes beyond the institution's competence. It must stop when responsibility becomes illegitimate authority. Again, if the problem is genuine, then an alternative approach has to be applied.

According to Drucker, an all-developed society needs performing institutions with their own autonomous management. Organizations in a developed society are special purpose institutions. These organizations can take the greatest social responsibility by performing their functions accurately and adequately.

Traditionally, most business strategies are focused on targeting products at upper and middle-class people but most of the world population is poor or lower middle class (Garriga and Mele, 2004: 55). Prahalad (2002) analyzing the Indian experience has suggested some mindset changes for converting the poor into active consumers. The first of these is seeing the poor as an opportunity to innovate rather than as a problem or to make profit out of poverty. He proposes that business, government and donor agencies stop thinking of the poor as victims and instead start seeing them as resilient and creative entrepreneurs as well as value-demanding consumers. He also stressed that there are immense benefits to multinational companies who choose to serve these markets in ways responsive to their needs. After the Cold War, Russia, China, India and Latin America opened their closed markets to foreign investments in a varied fashion. This significant economic and social transformation has offered new economic opportunities for MNCs but has not percolated to all sections of the society. First, the prospect of millions of middle "class" consumers in developing countries clamouring for products from MNCs was widely oversold. To make matters worse, the Asian and Latin American financial crises have greatly diminished the attractiveness of emerging markets (Prahalad and Hart, 2002).

MNCs' emerging market strategies over the past decade have not changed the magnitude of the opportunities. Even the wealthy few in the developing world or the emerging middle class are not the real source of market promise. But it is the aspiring poor, joining the market economy for the first time, who are the most important driving force behind an economy's market standard. That is why it is the time for multinational corporations to look at globalization strategies through a new lens of inclusive capitalism, companies with the "resources and persistence to compete at the bottom of the world economic pyramid, the prospective rewards include growth, profits and incalculable contributions to humankind" (ibid: 2). But countries that still don't have the modern infrastructure are an "ideal testing ground for developing environmentally sustainable technologies and products for the entire world" (ibid: 3). Prahalad has divided the world economy into four Consumer Tiers 1,2,3 and 4, where Tier 1 is "a cosmopolitan group composed of middle and upper-income people in developed countries and the few rich elites from the developing world. In the middle of the pyramid in Tier 2 and 3 are poor customers in developed nations and the rising middle classes in developing countries" (ibid: 3). Tier 4 comprises 4 billion people who live in abject poverty and are at the bottom of the pyramid. Each of these four elements demands innovation in technology, business models and management processes, and business leaders must be willing to experiment. Collaborate, empower locals and create new sources of competitive advantage and wealth" (ibid: 3).

According to Prahalad, helping the world's poor elevate themselves above the desperation line is a business opportunity to do well and also do good. And in order to do so, two interventions are very important, i.e. providing access to credit and increasing the earning potential of the poor. He has also developed four principle strategies for the bottom of the pyramid. These principles are Price Performance, Sustainability, Views of Quality and Profitability. Price Performance includes product development, manufacturing power and distribution. Sustainability will examine reduction in resource intensity, recyclability and renewable energy. Quality will assess new delivery formats and the creation of robust products for harsh conditions (heat, dust etc.). Finally, profitability stressed on investment intensity, margins and volume of products.

With these, Prahalad drew a commercial infrastructure at the bottom of the pyramid. This includes the following:

(1) **Shaping aspirations:** Sustainable product innovations that was initiated in Tier 4 and promoted through consumer education. It will positively influence the choices of people in the bottom of the pyramid and also reshape those in Tier 1, "will not only positively influence the choices of people at the bottom of the pyramid but may ultimately reshape the way Americans and others in Tier 1" (ibid: 8).

(2) **Improving access:** Since Tier 4 communities are often physically and economically isolated, better distribution systems and communication links are essential to the development of the bottom of the pyramid.

(3) **Tailoring local solutions:** World's top 200 MNCs are contributing to 30% of total world gross domestic product. But the Third-World countries have offered absolute stagnation or decline. If the MNCs are to thrive in the 21st century, then they must broaden their economic base and share it more widely: "They must play more active role in narrowing the gap between rich and poor. This cannot be achieved if these companies produce only so-called global products for consumption primarily by Tier 1 consumers. They must nurture local markets and cultures, leverage local solutions and generate wealth at the lowest levels on the pyramid. Producing rather than extracting wealth from these countries will be the guiding principle" (ibid: 10).

(4) **Creating buying power:** Roughly one-third of the world's workforce is either underemployed or has very low-pay jobs. Neither can these people support themselves or their families (World Employment Report, 2001, in Prahalad and Hart, 2002: 6). Thus, helping the world's poor elevate themselves above the desperation line is a business opportunity to do well. And, in order to effectively conduct it, two interventions are crucial: "providing access to credit and increasing the earning potential of the poor" (ibid).

The four elements of the commercial infrastructure, creating buying power, shaping aspirations, improving access and tailoring local solutions, are interlinked. It is found that innovation in one leads to innovation in the others: "Corporations are only one of the actors MNCs must work together with NGOs, local and state governments and communities" (ibid: 11). Therefore, a huge opportunity lies in linking the poor and the rich across the world in a market organized around the concept of sustainable growth and development.

In strategic CSR, firms believe in giving back to their constituencies because they believe it to be in their best financial interests. Strategic philanthropy grew popular around mid-1980s (Jones, 1997). While being socially responsible, it may often entail short-run sacrifice and even pain, but ultimately results in the long-run gain. The long-term benefits might not be visible or show up on a firm's financial returns, but in due course of time, it will benefit the company and its shareholders.

Mutual dependence of corporations and society implies that both business and social policies must follow the principles of shared values. Therefore, choices must benefit both business and society to put the broad principles into practice; a company must integrate a social perspective into the core frameworks it already uses to understand competition and guide its business strategy (Porter and Kramer, 2006: 60).

Porter and Kramer identified some points of intersection between a company and society. These are as follows:

1. **Inside-out linkages:** A company impinges upon society through its operations in the normal course of business. Every activity within the firm creates either positive or negative social consequences. A company's impact on society also changes overtime, as social standards evolve and science progresses.
2. **Outside-in linkages:** External social conditions also influence corporations for better or for worse. Since companies operate within a competitive context, it significantly affects its ability to carry out its strategy, especially in the longrun. Social conditions form a key part of this context. Competitive context is more important than value chain impacts because it has greater strategic importance for both companies and societies.

Competitive context can be divided into four broad areas:

- First, quantity and quality of available business inputs—human resources or transportation infrastructure.
- Second, the rules and incentives that govern competition such as policies that protect intellectual property, ensure transparency, safeguard against corruption and encourage investment.
- Third, the size and sophistication of local demand, influenced by such things as standards for product quality and safety, consumer rights, fairness in government purchasing.
- Fourth, the local availability of supporting industries, such as service providers and machinery producers (ibid: 60).

Another important aspect is that companies should choose which social issues to address. No business can solve all of society's problems or bear the cost of doing so. Rather, each company must select issues that interest its particular business. Categorizing and ranking social issues is just the means to an end, i.e. to create an explicit and affirmative social agenda which looks beyond community expectations to opportunities, in order to achieve social and economic benefits simultaneously. It moves from mitigating harm to finding ways to reinforce corporate strategy by advancing social conditions.

At the core of any strategy is a unique value proposition or a set of needs a company can meet for its chosen customers that others cannot. The most strategic CSR occurs when a company adds a social dimension to its value proposition, making social impact integral to the overall strategy.

Integrating business and social needs requires good intentions and strong leadership. It requires adjustments in organizations, reporting relationships and incentives. Some companies have engaged operating management in processes that identify and prioritize social issues based on their silence to business operations and their importance to the company's competitive context. But companies must shift from a fragmented defensive posture to an integrated, affirmative approach. The focus must move away from an emphasis on image to an emphasis on substance.

Efforts to find shared value in operating practices and in the social dimensions of competitive context have the potential not only to foster economic and social development but also to change the way companies and society think about each other.

According to Porter and Kramer, there should be a shift in the thinking of governments, NGOs and companies from corporate social responsibility to corporate social integration. And, corporations are not responsible for all the world's problems, nor do they have the resources to solve them. Rather, each company can identify the particular set of societal problems that is best equipped to help resolve and from which it can gain the greatest competitive benefit.

Strategic CSR refers to "A business that is integrated with core business objectives and core competencies of the firm, and from the outset is designed to create business value and positive social change and is embedded in business culture and operations" (McElhaney, 2009).

McElhaney prescribed few strategies to make CSR strategic—senior leadership and management of the firm, including the board, must make an authentic, firm and public commitment to CSR. It implies that CSR needs to be embedded within the firm and should reflect the core values of the firm. It has to be linked to the mission, vision and values of the organization. It should be treated and managed as a core business strategy just like the strategies of marketing, R&D, talent management etc. And CSR should report to the top-level leaders in the company. Determine the top three business objectives and priorities of the company, and develop a CSR strategy that will contribute to the achievement of those business objectives (ibid: 32). Align CSR with the firm's core competencies (ibid: 33). Fully integrate CSR into the culture, governance and strategy—development efforts of the company, and into existing management and performance system (ibid). Develop clear performance metrics or key performance indicators, to measure the impact of CSR strategics. There should be clear internal CSR performance metrics, i.e. reputation achievements, gains in market share, brand perception, increased sales, decreased operational expenditure, employee satisfaction, as well as external, focused on society and the environment,. And, if there is no performance metrics in place, there will be no way to prove that the strategy was effective, which means that the strategy will not be sustainable over the long haul (ibid: 34).

This approach promotes the development of the knowledge base, skills and networks of the firm that help to increase medium- to long-run profit, while fulfilling a social responsibility to society. Strategic CSR can serve to develop competitive advantages (Porter and Kramer, 2006), create dynamic capabilities (Hart, 1995) or penetrate new medium to long run goal (Ramani & Mukherjee, 2010). According to McElhaney, CSR is "A business value and positive social change, and is embedded in day-to-day business culture and operations" (McElhaney, 2009: 31).

Effective CSR initiatives are believed to be those derived from careful analysis of each organization's unique culture, competencies and strategic opportunities.

## Democratic Practices at Work

Applicability of democratic principles in a workplace is a complex issue. Group or community identification, collective actions, compliance are symptoms of democracy at workplace.

Now, participation in the workplace may increase group and community identification through a formation of shared interests, as well as increased legitimacy granted to collective actions and compliance with them. Thus, individuals are expected to be willing to cooperate in work and as a result in arenas besides work, and accept the system in which they are members. It is therefore necessary to provide individuals with fora that replicate the grand political process to the greatest extent possible, and where they will be able to engage as equals in decision-making processes in exchange of interests and ideals.

Democracy in workplace is characterized by few major components. First, it assumes the existence of a community. Second, it requires a participatory process that secures an equal distribution of effective power among the constituents, and finally, it acknowledges the need for substantive rights to protect individuals and groups from unwarranted use of power by others. Why is the existence of a community very essential for considering democracy for institutions? Scholars argue that the organizations of the work are instrumental in the democratic practice in the workplace. But the workplace community is different from the nation-state and also resists at first the application of democratic practices. Democracy is embedded in a social, political and economic environment and the constituents are intrinsically limited in the spectrum of decisions in which they can decide. It takes part in a competitive market and is therefore measured in its ability to compete according to the dictates of the market. It is also a part of a broader economic system in which rules of entry are based on who is loyal to whom.

Mundlak (2013) believed that in spite of the fact that the workplace can sustain democratic practices associated with territorial communities, it is the fuzzy boundaries of the workplace that have become a critical factor in the gradual disappearance of the democratic workplace. Even similar processes may have taken place within the public and private spheres, i.e. at the state or at the private economic organization (Schuller, 1980).

It is important to rethink about the institutions associated with democracy, regardless of the community in which it takes place. With the community, a democratic constitutional order must prevail. A constitutional order prescribes the rules of the game and is therefore, process oriented (Mundlak, 2013: 11).

The principle that prescribes the rules of the game may be found in the company's bylaws, especially in external regulations (such as, for example, laws that mandate co-determination on the board or work councils within the firm), or in collective agreements (e.g. basic agreements that set up employee participation). Whether it is industrial, national, occupational, the rules here are different, in form and substance, from the typical constitutional order of the state that is enshrined in formal constitutional documents. The public firm is the shareholder democracy. And then, when the same organizations are regarded as workplace democracy, it tends to increase the horizons of the people. To understand the interest of the employees, it is necessary to study the way in which management is made accountable to a more extensive set of interests.

Another important principle of a democratic order is that each individual or constituency should have the same degree of power to affect the outcome of the firm's decision-making processes at all levels of decision making. Here, power implies both forms of negative power ("exercising power over") and positive power (the "power to act collectively"; Sabel 1997).

One person, one vote (OPOV) may be adequate for institutional adaptation of democracy at work, but it is more likely to work in small cooperatives. It can also be argued that voting is one form of negative power in which some succeed in overriding the power of others. But some studies also show that in small co-operatives, sometimes negative power relations exist. Then voting can be a viable method of self-governance, but it cannot capture the actual distribution of effective power in the community. Even power dynamics are more difficult to even out in plural workplace communities where OPOV has to withdraw in favour of multi-dimensional formulas of effective power. Now, collective power of a constituency or community intertwines with the distribution of individual power with the constituency or community. Voting also is one of the institutional methods to exert power over others.

Similarly applying principles of subsidiary to democracy is also to encourage an active democratic environment. Again, a similar conclusion can be reached by observing the need to complement the negative use of power with positive form of power that encourages individuals and groups to recognize each other's interest, deliberate and come together in action (Lukes, 2005 [1974]).

Communicative action is an important step towards participation in the public sphere. It shifts the enterprises from the alienation of individuals merely engaging in production, to an environment in which men and women interact together, working toward a goal they have defined themselves. Communicative action provides free flow of information. It redefines the nature of the workplace community and consequently of the individuals constituted by it (Stanby, 1992).

Mundlak believes that workplace democracy may require considering the fundamental values of democracy, instead of adhering to any single institutional form as the most essential of democracy.

This includes form of participation, empowerment, and equality of status within and across the boundaries of the workplace. Considerations of democracy should be included in each and every level—the design of production, the division of labor and work processes, organizational structures and political representations.

Democracy normally engages with the additional substantive layer of fundamental rights that protect individuals and collectivities from the tyranny of majority. The democratic process should be reflexive and outcomes must be constantly assessed. Once the democratic ideal is disconnected from simple rules, such as OPOV, its experimental design requires a bill of rights to prescribe the contours of experimentation (Mundlak, 2013: 14)

Basic rights are significant in the workplace. These are legitimate and enforceable claims to some desired treatment, situation or resource. Rights are a form of power[1] and the distinction between the process-based component of the democratic order and the substantive protection of rights should not be overstated. Both have negative implications. Functionally, they are in different situations and are part and parcel of the democratic order. They are instruments that aid in adjusting between due process and just outcomes.

The sources of the constituent rights are varied. There are sources exogenous to the workplace itself, and sources within. To the former, we can attribute general legislation, industrial custom, collective bargaining agreements applied at the national or sectoral level, and the like.

Unless an elaborate mechanism for the enforcement of rights exist outside the workplace, these rights need to be protected by an internal mechanism. Authoritative rights that are imposed from outside but are not legitimated by the constituent of the workplace community are likely to be defacto weaker than intended, and a greater discrepancy is expected between the formal constitutional order and order in action (Pollert, 2012).

The community deliberative process and rights are important aspects of workplace democracy. They aid in highlighting democratic qualities and deficiencies in existing institutions. But the feasibility of workplace democracy with the interplay of these three aspects only cannot be carried too far, due to the emergence of marketization and globalization.

Marketization accounts for emphasis on undisturbed markets as the most preferred institutional form. It is primarily associated with efficiency and economic adaptability. With regard to the organization of workplace, it refers to the gradual change in stable work communities, and growing reliance on peripheral, secondary and precarious workplace, as well as a growing reliance on disparity between the primary and secondary workplace. It involves rising labor market inequality, declining mobilization, and growing insecurity (Fudge, 2012).

However, with the Fordist percept of production system, an image of democratic stability, with an internal labor market wages, mutual lock-in, code of behaviour and almost seamless integration of local residence, economic dependence, social rights and cultural obligations increased.

The term Fordism was developed by Italian Marxist Antonio Gramsci as part of his theory of hegemony. For Gramsci, hegemony refers to the political and moral leadership by which the capitalist class incorporates the working class into society.

For Gramsci (1971), Fordism referred to a new form of work organization based on Taylorism. Gramsci saw the new forms of work organization whether Taylorism or mechanization as highly divisive. Taylorism signified a strict separatism between the organization of the production process, which was the task of technical offices, and the execution of standardized and formally prescribed tasks.

Fordism is not only an organization of production but also a regime of accumulation or macro- economic pattern of growth. Fordist mass production made possible mass consumption, generating a new norm of middle-class consumption, based on relatively high wages and the production of relatively inexpensive standardized products. The Fordist regime of accumulation included public insurance and public assistance (such as the US Social Security programme) and a system of collective bargaining which generalized the class compromise of relatively high and growing wages in return for labor peace throughout the core of the economy.

Gramsci (1971) tried to recall the history of Fordism. According to him, America does not have great historical and cultural traditions. This is one of the main reasons (and certainly more important than its so-called natural wealth) for its formidable accumulation of capital which has taken place in spite of the superior living standard enjoyed by the popular classes compared with Europe. The non-existence of viscous parasitic sedimentations left behind by past phases of history has allowed industry and commerce in particular, to develop on a sound basis. It also allows a continued reduction of the economic function of transport and trade to the level of a genuinely subaltern activity of production. Indeed, it has led to the attempt to absorb these activities into productive activity itself (Lipietz, 1997).

Gramsci recalled the experiments conducted by Ford and the economics made by the firm through direct management of transport and distribution of the product. These economies affected production costs and permitted higher wages and lower selling prices. And these preliminary conditions were rendered rational by historical evolution, as it was relatively easy to rationalize production and labor by a skillful combination of force (distribution of working-class trade unionism on a traditional basis) and persuasion (high wages, various social benefits, extremely subtle ideological and political propaganda) and thus succeed in making the whole life of the nation revolve around production. According to Gramsci, hegemony is born in the factory and requires for its exercise only a minute quantity of professional political and ideological intermediaries (Vidal, 2011).

In the world of production, these words like quantity and quality mean nothing more than satisfaction or failure to satisfy the basic needs of the popular classes and a tendency to raise or lower their standard of living. In a nation, an enterprise has at its disposal a large labor force and amount of raw material; the word quality implies the intention of employing a lot of labor on a little material, perfecting the product to the maximum. Thus, it means specialization for a luxury market (Gramsci, 1971: 284).

Taylorism[2] produces a gap between manual labor and human content of work. In the past, in professions like reproduction of texts for publication or other forms of diffusion and transmission, the process of adaptation to mechanization has been very difficult. But why? Because it is so hard to reach the height of professional qualification when this requires of the worker that he or she should "forget" or not think about the intellectual content of the text one is reproducing. Conversely, one's qualification is commensurate with one's lack of intellectual interest, i.e. the extent to which one has become mechanized. Mechanization takes toll on one's intellect and he or she might lose interest in work.

The Fordian ideology of high wages is a phenomenon derived from an objective necessity of modern industry when it has reached a certain stage of development. Why high wages and not lower wages? Then again why should a worker prefer lower wages than those paid by Ford?

The instability of the labor force demonstrates that as far as Ford is concerned, the normal conditions of the workers competing for jobs (differentials) are effective only to a limited degree. The different level of average wages is not effective, nor the pressure of the reserve army of the unemployed. The Ford industry requires qualifications, in its workers, which other industries do not yet call for, but that does not justify the weariness and exhaustion the workers face. And the given conditions of society and the wages that are paid to the workers are not sufficient to compensate. By now, it is established that the material and moral pressure of society and the state leads to the mass psycho-physical transformation of the workers, so that the average type of Ford workers becomes the average type of workers in general.

Ford's method[3] can be rational. But that requires a long process during which a change must take place in social conditions. And, here coercion alone is not enough, but self-discipline with persuasion should be there. Persuasion should also take the form of high wages which offer the possibility of a better standard of living or perhaps, the possibility of realizing a standard of living which is adequate to the new method of production and work which demands a particular degree of expenditure.

That is why to build up a well-articulated and skilled labor force in factory or a team of specialized workers has never been easy. Once the labor force or the team has been built up, its components or a part of them sometimes not only finishes up enjoying monopoly wages, but is also dismissed from work in the event of a temporary check in production. That is why it would be not economic to allow the elements of an organic whole so loosely built up to be dispersed because it would be almost impossible to bring them together again. While on the other hand, reconstructing it with new elements chosen haphazardly would involve inconsiderable effort and expense.

Fordism as a system of production came into crisis in the late 1960s and early 1970s. It is also argued that the Taylorist division of labor ran into its own limits, as it could not meet the new demands for organizational flexibility or to realize increased production through ongoing extreme fragmentation of tasks or rigidly hierarchical relations.

Even in the Fordist regime, far from the normative benchmark of the democracy, there was a defined community, some power sharing (example, collective bargaining) and a certain level of workers' rights enshrined in collective arguments and/or statues. But there was an absence of direct treatment for those who were left outside the workplace polity, the radical discussion of democracy at the workplace.

The post-Fordism period is based in the sense of dislocation and unease. The period after Fordism is characterized by an increasing discontent between traditional welfare, industry, and labor market policies, between labor progress and employment relations. The central problem is that employers cannot commit to workers' licenses of procedures from the broader competitive environment, especially from credit markets, with great emphasis on shareholder value.

Now, too much marketization has changed the institutionalized forms and the democracy in the workplace (Freeman, 2006). The regulation and distribution are guided by private consideration. The public or the nation-state guides the private by the set of substantive standard like employment standards and only to a limited degree by an establishment of labor, market, institutions and interventions in the labor process.

Besides, the workplace is also affected by globalization, both private and public spheres.

Fordism also implies Taylorism plus mechanization. Taylorism signified a strict separation between the organization of the production process, which was the task of the technical offices, and the execution of the standardized and formally prescribed tasks. According to this principle, the involvement of direct labor was not supposed to be necessary in carrying out the prescriptions of the technical office. As a macro-economic structure (or regime of accumulation, or social structure of accumulation), Fordism implies that gains in productivity resulting from the organizational principles would have their counterpart partly from an increase in financial investment from profits, and partly from the increased purchasing power of wage laborers. Besides, as a system of rules (or mode of regulation) Fordism implied a long-term contractualization of the wage relationship, with rigid controls over redundancy, and a monitored increase in salaries indexed to prices and general productivity. In addition, a vast socialization of revenue through the welfare state assured in permanent income for wage laborers.

Crisis in Fordism started from the demand side of the economy. Demand side, was dominated by salaries set in the domestic market of the each developed country. External constraints were limited by the coincidence of growth in different countries, with less importance given to the growth of the international trade relative to the growth of the domestic markets and by the hegemony of the economy of the developed nations.

The first most obvious reason was the competitiveness that appeared between the United States, Europe and Japan. The search for economies of scale induced internationalization of productive process and of the markets between developed counties.

Price increases for primary commodities imported from the South (particularly oil) stoked up the competition for exports at the start of the 1970s. In the end, firms from Fordist countries increasingly sought ways to overturn labor regulations by sub-contracting production to non-Fordist countries.

The supply side crisis of Fordism lies in erosion of Taylorism. So full employment, the elimination of the intellectual capacities of direct labor in carrying out production in contemporary society is irrational. An alternative can be responsible autonomy on the part of the workers, and the result would be a superior organizational principle particularly when putting new technologies into operation.

In fact many large firms in Japan and Germany and in Scandinavian countries resorted to these practices; in these firms, the unions and other traditional organizations opted for negotiated involvement or commitment of the workers to fight against the crisis of Fordism.

It was found after much inquiry that liberal flexibility and negotiated involvement might be one form of post-Fordism. Involvement can be negotiated individually and augmented with bonuses, but it is also limited by the collective character of the involvement required in most co-operative production processes. Involvement can be negotiated firm by firm, between the management and the unions. In such a case, the company and the workers reap the benefits of specific schemes accumulated in the course of a process of collective process. Also, involvement can be negotiated at the spectral level. Here, the external labor market has a high chance of being better organized, although on the whole more rigidly. Involvement can be negotiated at the level of the whole society, unions, employees association–negotiated social priorities and the distribution of profits at the national or the regional levels, with the basic understanding that the unions watch over what "their people" do both at the shop floor and at the office.

## Integration of CSR and Workplace Practices

Workplace practices are dominated by a whole lot of institutional and worker relations. When we talk of workplace democracy, it is more or less associated with worker-owned economy, worker co-operatives or the employee stock ownership. There is a long history to workplace practices, the shifting of production from home to the factories, and the subsequent changes that took place inside the factories and then the centralized factory system led to new form of employee–employer relation.

The centralized factory system began to dominate the workers and the workers traded for independence. But eventually the labors had to comply with work rules and structures that others determined (Parks, 1995: 20). Then the relation between the workers and the firms changed and an element of coercion crept in. The production system created a lot of problems for the workers. In fact the workers' condition forced the owners to change the strategy of business, and make the workplace congenial for them to work. So from a dominant relation, employer and employee moved into a collaborative relation. To boost the relation, technology came to aid. Technology also altered the workplace landscape.

CSR evolved in business in the West with worker concern especially after the Industrial Revolution. Many issues emerged in the factory system mostly related to women and children (Wren, 2005). So business changed its strategy and concentrated on improving the workers' lives so that production remained uninterrupted. Hence, business's initial social concern or social responsibility was directed towards its employees, giving them a better standard of living, though it was for corporate benefit. From then onwards, It was also recognized that to maintain a democratic environment in the workplace, compromise, negotiation and accommodation are primary keys. This set a new motion for workplace practices.

A democratic trend started in the workplace. But applicability of democratic principles in a workplace is a complex issue. It is understood that workplace can sustain democratic practices associated with the territorial communities, but indistinct boundaries in workplaces might not allow such practices to grow (Mundlak 2013: 12). But one should not lose hope, rather workplace should include different forms of participation, empowerment and enforce equality of status for all employees within and outside the boundaries of the organization. Such democratic practices in the workplace will form the Corporate Social Responsibilities of the organization with regard to the workers. To perceive the workplace as a domain of practicing democracy is not far from impossible. Rather, it can form the right ground for democratic practices. Also, CSR to be democratic in the workplace, should endorse governance mechanism which would facilitate social responsibility inside the organization and assess its impact outside.

## NOTES

1. Richard Edwards emphasizes individual rights in the workplace. These individual rights are also open to group rights, because in a workplace both are very significant. (See Richard Edwards, 1993, Rights at Work: Employment Relations in the Post Union Era. Washington, DC: Brookings Institution, Chapter 2.)
2. Frederick Taylor and his scientific management theory stressed on workman's initiative and its absolute uniformity. In this system, besides the workers, the managers also assume new burden of gathering together all of the traditional knowledge which in the past has been possessed by the workmen, and then of classifying tabulatory and reducing this knowledge to rules and laws which are helpful to the workmen in doing their daily work. The most significant single element in modern scientific management is the task idea. The work of every workman is fully planned out by the management at least one day in advance, and each man receives in most cases complete written instructions, describing in detail the task which he is to accomplish, as well as the means to be used in doing the work. And, as the work is planned in advance, the task is a joint effort of the workman and the management. Whenever the workman succeeds in doing his task right, within a specified time, he receives an additional 30 to 100 percent hike in his ordinary wages. These tasks are carefully planned so that both good and careful work are called for in their performance, but it should be clearly understood that in no case is the workman called upon to work at a pace which would be injurious to his health. Therefore, the task is regulated so that the man who is well suited to this job will thrive while working at this rate for a long term and grow happier and more prosperous instead of being over-worked (See F.W. Taylor, 1910, The Principles of Scientific Management: 1-2.)

3. It calls for a new type of qualification, a form of consumption of labor power and a quality of power consumed in average hours which are the same numerically, but which are more wearying and exhausting than elsewhere and for which, in the given condition of society as it is, the wages are not sufficient to recompensate and make up.

## REFERENCES


Ackerman, R. W. (1973), How Companies Respond to Social Demands, Harvard Business Review, 51 (5): 88-98.

Ackerman, R. W. and Bauer, R. A. (1976), Corporate Social Responsiveness, Reston, VA: Reston.

Agliette, Michel (2000) (1979), A Theory of Capitalist Regulation: The US Experience, London: Verso Classics.

Altman, B. W. and Cohen, Vaider, D. (2000), Corporate Citizenship in the New Millennium: Foundation for an Architecture of Excellence, Business and Society Review, 105 (1): 145-169.

Asongu, J. J. (2007), 'The Legitimacy of Strategic Corporate Social Responsibility', Journal of Business and Public Policy, 1: 1-12.

Bernstein, Edward (1898), 'The Struggle of Social Democracy and the Social Revolution', Nene Zeit, January 19.

Bowen, R. Howard (1953), Social Responsibilities of the Businessman, New York: Harper and Row.

Branco, Castelo Manual and Rodriques, Lima Lucia (2007), 'Positioning Stakeholder Theory within the Debate on Corporate Social Responsibility', Electronic Journal of Business Ethics and Organization Studies, 12(1).

Carr, A.Z. (1968), Is Business Bluffing Ethical, Business Ethics, 46(1): 143-146.

Carroll, Archie B. (1979), A Three Dimensional Conceptual Model of Corporate Performance, Academy of Management Review, 4 (4): 497-505.

Carroll, Archie B. (1999), Corporate Social Responsibility: Evolution of a Definitional Construct, Business & Society, 39(3): 268-295.

Committee for Economic Development (CED) (1971), Social Responsibilities of Business Corporations, New York: CED.

Crozier, Michel, Huntington, Samuel P., and Watanuki, Joji (1975), The Crisis of Democracy: Report on the Governability of Democracies to the Trilateral Commission, New York: New York University Press.

Dahl, Robert (1989), Democracy and Its Critics, New Haven: Yale University Press.

Davis, Keith (1960), Can Business Afford to Ignore Social Responsibilities? California Management Review, 2: 70-76.

Davies, Keith (1973), 'The Case for and against Business Assumption of Social Responsibilities,' Academy of Management Journal, 16: 312-322.

Deetz, Stanley, A. (1992), Democracy in the Age of Corporate Colonization: Developments in Communication and the Politics of Everyday Life, New York: State University of New York Press.

Donaldson, T. (1982), Corporations and Morality, New Jersey: Prentice Hall.

Donaldson, T. and Dunfee, T.W. (1999), Ties That Bind: A Social Contract Approach to Business Ethics, Boston: Harvard Business School Press.

Drucker, F. Peter (1954), The Practice of Management, New York: Harper & Brothers.

Drucker, F. Peter (2001), The Essential Drucker, New York: Harper Business.

Drucker, F. Peter (2004), People and Performance, The Best of Peter Drucker on Management, New Delhi: Butterworth.

Elkington, J. (1998), Cannibals with Forks: The Triple Bottom Line of the 21st Century Business, London: New Society.

Emshoff, J. R. and Freeman, R.E. (1978), Stakeholder Management, Working Paper from the Wharton Applied Research Centre (July).

Fitch, H. G. (1976), Achieving Corporate Social Responsibility, Academy of Management Review, 1: 38-46.

Frederick, W. C. (1960), The Growing Concern Over Business Responsibility, California Management Review, 2: 54-61.

Freeman, Richard E. (2006), 'Labor Market Institutions without Blunders: The Debate Over Flexibility and Labor Market Performance,' International Economic Journal, 19: 129.

Freeman, Richard E. (2010), Strategic Management: A Stakeholder Approach, London: Cambridge University Press.

Friedman, Milton (1970), The Social Responsibility of Business is to Increase its Profits, New York Times Magazine, 33: 122-126.

Garriga, Elisabeth and Mele, Domence (2004), 'Corporate Responsibility Theories: Mapping the Territory,' Journal of Business Ethics, 53: 51-71.

Gladwin, T. N. and Kennelly, J. J. (1995), Shifting Paradigms for Sustainable Development: Implications for Management Theory and Research, Academy of Management Review, 20 (4): 874-904.

Gramsci, Antonio (1971), Selections from the Prison Notebooks, New York: International Publishers.

Graves, W. M., Waddock, S. and Kelly, H. (2001), How Do You Measure Corporate Citizenship?, Business Ethics, 15(2): 17.

Gupta, Dipankar (2006), Ethics Incorporated, New Delhi: Sage.

Hart, Stuart L. (1997), Beyond Greening: Strategies for a Sustainable World, Harvard Business Review, Jan-Feb.

Hayek, Frederick (1944), The Road to Serfdom. Chicago: University of Chicago Press.

Hendersen, D. (2005), 'The Role of Business in the World Today,' Journal of Corporate Citizenship, 44(2): 110-125.

Heald, Morrell (1970), The Social Responsibilities of Business: Company and Community, 1900-1960, US and UK: Transaction Publishers.

Hirschman, Albert (1986), Rival Views of Market Society, New York: Viking.

https: //dogangocmen.files.wordpress.com/2013/02/theories-of-democracy3.pdf.

Jensen, M. C. (2001a). 'Value Maximization, Stakeholder Theory, and the Corporate Objective Function,' Journal of Applied Corporate Finance, 14(3), 8-21.

Jensen, M. C. (2001b). Value Maximization, Stakeholder Theory, and the Corporate Objective Function in J. Andriof et al. (eds.), Unfolding Stakeholder Thinking, Shefeld: Greenleaf Publishing, pp. 65-84.

Jones, T. M. (1980), Corporate Social Responsibility Revisited, Redefined, California Management Review, Spring: 59-67.

Jawahar, I. M. and McLaughlin, G. L. (2001), Toward a Descriptive Stakeholder Theory: An Organizational Life Cycle Approach, Academy of Management Review, 26(3): 397-414.

Judy, Fudge (2012), 'Blurring Legal Boundaries, Regulating for Decent Work', in Judy Fudge, Shae

Me Crystal and Kamala Sankaran (eds)., Challenging the Legal Boundaries of Work Regulation. Oxford: Hart Publishing, 1-26.

Johnson, L. Harold (1979), Disclosure of Corporate Social Performance Survey, Evaluation and Prospects, New York and London: Praeger Publishers.

Kaptein, M. and Tulder, Rob Van (2003), Towards Effective Stakeholder Dialogue, Business and Society Review, 108(2): 203-224.

Lantos, G. P. (2001), 'The Boundaries of Corporate Social Responsibility,' Journal of Consumer Marketing, 18(7): 595-630.

Lipietz, Alain (1997), The Post-Fordist World: Labor Relations, International Hierarchy and Global Ecology, Review of International Political Economy, 4(1): 1-41.

Levitt, T. (1958), The Dangers of Social Responsibility, Harvard Business Review, 36, September-October: 41-50.

Lukes, Steven (2005 [1974]), Power: A Radical View, Basingstoke, England: Palgrave Macmillan.

Maslow, A. H. (1954), Motivation and Personality, New York: Harper and Row.

Matten, D., Grave A. and Chapple, W. (2003), 'Behind the Mask: Revealing the True Face of Corporate Citizenship,' Journal of Business Ethics, 45(1): 117-127.

McElhaney, Kellie A. (2009), A Strategic Approach to Corporate Social Responsibility, Leader to Leader, Spring (52): 30-36.

McGuire, J. W. (1963), Business & Society, New York: Harper and Row.

Mundlak, Guy (2014), 'Workplace Democracy: Reclaiming the Effort to Foster Public-Private Isomorphism', Theoretical Inquiries in Law, 15 (1).

Parks, Susan. (1995). Improving Workplace Performance: Historical and Theoretical Contexts, Monthly Labor Review, May.

Porter, M. E. and Kramer, M. R. (2002), The Link Between Competitive Advantage and Corporate Social Responsibility, Harvard Business Review, 80(12): 56-68.

Prahalad, C. K. and Hart, Stuart, L. Hart (2002), The Fortune at the Bottom of the Pyramid, Strategy and Business, Issue 26, First Quarter.

Pollert, Anna (2012), 'How Britain's Low Paid Non-unionized Employee Deal With Workplace Problem' in Judy Fudge, Shae Me Crystal and Kamala Sankaran (eds.), Challenging the Legal Boundaries of Work Regulation, Oxford: Hart Publishing, p. 285.

Polyani, Karl (1944) The Great Transformation, Boston: Beacon Press.

Preston, L. E. and Post, J. E. (1975), Private Management and Public Policy, the Principle of Public Responsibility, New Jersey: Prentice Hall.

Ramani, Shyama V. and Mukherjee, Vivekananda (2010), CSR and Market Changing Product Innovations: Indian Case Studies, Working Paper Series, No. 026, United Nations University-Maastricht Economic and Social Research and Training Centre on Innovation and Technology.

Sabel, Charles (1997), 'Constitutional Ordering in Historical Contexts', in Robert Boyer and Rogers Hollingsworth (eds.), Contemporary Capitalism: The Embeddedness of Institutions, Cambridge: Cambridge University Press.

Savitz, W. Andrew (2006), Triple Bottom Line, USA: Wiley.

Schuller, Tom (1980), Common Discourse? The Language of Industrial Democracy, Economic and Industrial Democracy, 2 (2): 261-291.

Sethi, S. P. (1975), Dimensions of Corporate Social Performance: An Analytic Framework, California Management Review, 17: 58-64.

Solomon, R. C. (1994), The Bottom Line: An Introduction to Business Ethics, Forth Worth, TX:

Harcourt Brace College Publishers.

Steiner, G. A. (1971), Business & Society, New York: Random House.

Strand, Rich (1983), A Systems Paradigm of Organizational Adaptations to the Social Environment, Academy of Management Review, 8: 90-96.

Sternberg, E. (1997), The Defects of Stakeholder Theory, Corporate Governance, 5(1): 3-10.

Sundaram, A. K., & Inkpen, A. C. (2004), The Corporate Objective Revisited, Organization Science, 15(3): 353–363.

Sunder, Pushpa (2000), Beyond Business: From Merchant Charity to Corporate Citizenship, New Delhi: Tata-McGraw Hill.

Turner, R. J. (2006), Corporate Social Responsibility: Should Disclosure of Social Considerations be Mandatory? Submission to the Parliamentary Joint Committee on Corporation and Financial Services Enquiry, http: //www.aph.gov.au/senate/committee/corporationscttee/corporateresponsibility/submissions/sub05-pdf.

Tuzzolino, Frank and Armandi, Barry (1981), A Need Hierarchy Framework for Assessing Corporate Social Responsibility, Academy of Management Review, 6(1).

Vidal, Matt (2011), Reworking Post-Fordism: Labor Process vs Employment Relations, Sociology Compass 5 (4): 273-286.

Walton, C. C. (1967), Corporate Social Responsibilities, Belmont, CA: Wadsworth.

Werhane, P. H. and Freeman, R.E. (1999), 'Business Ethics: The State of the Art,' International Journal of Management Review, 1(1).

Wartick, S. L. and Cochran, P. G. (1985), The Evolution of Corporate Social Performance Model, Academy of Management Review, 10(4): 758-769.

Wartick, S. L. and Rude, R. E. (1986), Issues of Management: Corporate Fad or Corporate Function, California management Review, 29 (1): 124-132.

Wheeler, D., Colbert, B. and Freeman, R. E. (2003), 'Focusing On Value: Reconciling Corporate Social Responsibility, Sustainability and a Stakeholder Approach in a Networked World,' Journal of General Management, 28 (3): 1-29.

World Commission on Environment and Development (1987), Our Common Future, Oxford: Oxford University Press.

Wood, D. J. (1991), Corporate Social Performance Revisited, Academy of Management Review, 16 (4): 698-718.

Wood, D. J. and Jones, R. E. (1991), 'Stakeholder Matchmaking: A Theoretical Problem in Empirical Research on Corporate Social Performance,' The International Journal of Organizational Analysis, 3(3): 229-267.

Wood, D. J. and Logsdon, J. M. (2002), Business Citizenship: From Individuals to Organizations, Business Ethics Quarterly, Ruffin Series No. 3: 59-94.

Wren, Daniel A. (2005), The History of Management Thought, 5th Edition, Hoboken, New Jersey: John Wiley & Sons, Inc.

# 2

# Workplace Practices and Corporate Social Responsibility (CSR): A Democratic Discourse

## Introduction

All workplaces are organized on the basis of employment relations. The older version of the relation was that of master–servant relation slowly replaced in the late 19th century and early 20th century with the modern times' employer and employee relation (Ellerman, 2009).

David asserts that in an organization, the employment relation is inherently non-democratic. Neither the employer is the representative of the employee nor does the employer manage the organization in the interest of those who are managed. It is also true that the employees are not directly or indirectly part of the decision-making group or the employees have transferred to the employer the discretionary decision-making rights over their activities with the scope of the contract.

In the historical development of democracy, economic and social subordinate and its effects on the development of the capabilities for democratic self-governance were among the principal reasons for limiting the franchise.

Immanuel Kant (quoted in David Ellerman, 2009, 'The Workplace in Deliberative Democratic Theory: A Note on Kant, Mill and Dewey': 2) argued that, in order to be fit to vote, a person must have an independent position among the people. He should have a free will to participate in the community. According to Kant, from apprentices to merchants, servants who are not employed by the state, women, and minors have no civil personality. For women, it is different, for it is not based on master–servant relations but the domestic law that preaches women pass from the shelter of the father to the shelter of the husband, after marriage. It is a marriage contract. By the late

19th century and early 20th century, it was abolished, especially in those countries with a democratic order. But vestiges of such a system still persist, like the practices of the wife changing her family name, from that of her father to that of her husband.

Ironically, the master–servant relation has not been abolished. It has persisted in every society. But there are lots of literatures that do not pay much attention to economic relations of subordination. There are same theorists of deliberative democracy who were aware about the connections between the two.

Deliberative democracy, as a concept, was treated as "government by discussion" by some scholars. Philosophers like Socrates, Aristotle, Tocqueville, John Stuart Mill, John Dewey, Ernest Barker, and Jurgen Habermas earnestly worked on economic-political connection. J.S. Mill states that political institutions should be judged largely by the degree to which it promotes the mental advancement of the community. But one of the prime defects of representative government is it does not give importance to individual faculties, moral, intellectual, and actions of the people.

Mill has compared representative democracy as an agency of education of the nation. Discussions, debates, collision of opposite ideas, opinions lead to the well-being of the people. In his book, *Principle of Political Economy* (1848), Mill stated that workplace association could become a centre for civic virtues if it progressed beyond the employment relation. Public association, not isolation, will enable human beings to work with or for one another, and not just dependence on one another.

In early days, people who were not self-employed had to work under a master. Then with the advancement of modern associations, it is not that the capitalist maintained its dominance, and the workers existed without any hold in the management. This is not always the case; there were associations of laborers, in terms of equality, who collectively owned the capital, and working under managers, elected or sometimes removed by them.

Mill mentioned about "co-operatives of the Basque county of the Northern Spain or the LEGA co-operatives in northern Italy. Under this form of co-operation, Mill saw an increase in the productivity of work since the workers have their own enterprise". Though it is very difficult to rate it highly, but it acted as the beginning of a moral revolution. Through this revolution many healed the feud between capital and labor, transformed the conflict of classes between the haves and have not, with a new sense of security and independence in the laboring class.

Dewey (1985), proponent of deliberative democratic theory, rejects the use of public–private territories to demoralize the norms of democracy, but would rather apply the theory to all associations, spheres, activities etc. Dewey in his treatise "Economic Basis of New Society" primarily argued that, after the war, it is usually found that conducting a war for political democracy leaves industrial and economic autocracy untouched. Either a period of great unrest, depression, follows after the war. That is why, the socio-economic arrangement has to help the development of human capacities. It is also true that political democracy does not lead to the human beings associating with one another in terms of equality.

He observed that even though democratic political institutions were established, still men and women were not free, for they were controlled by the family, the church, business etc. So as long as this external arbitrary power persists, the political democracy is not secure. While discussing on direct participation, Dewey argues that in a democratic social organization, there is high scope for direct participation. But economically, still the control is external. He also attempted to understand the controlling mechanism from an ethical point of view, where the control in an industry is from the top downwards, not from the bottom upwards. A great number of people are subordinates and are used to receiving orders from the superiors. They have no active part in making plans or forming policies (Gregory, 2008).

Though legislations in industrial and labor relations had led to some changes, but still the governance in the employment relations is very non-democratic.

## Workplace Practices and Performance

A spectrum of issues comes to the forefront when we talk about workplace practices especially, the role of employee participation and decision making in an organization. These are somewhat related to high-performance workplace. Now, it is a norm that the high-performance workplace also demands a high-remuneration system, less hierarchical decision making (more worker participation in decisions), increased training for the employees and increased employment security.

Employee's assistance in making decisions is essential for innovation, quality improvement, and rapid response to change (Parks, 1995). In such situations, the firm provides worker incentives like information, skills to make the decisions etc.

A high-performance work system is regarded as a progressive strategy to improve productivity. But there are diverse opinions regarding this strategy. According to some, employee involvement may lead to transformation of the workplace, provided hierarchical work relations are minimized, and an ideal industrial democracy can exist in which both the employee and the owners benefit from the new work structures. In another view, employers may remain as the major beneficiaries, as the employees are more involved in voluntary contributions of their knowledge and intensive monitoring by the peers. Besides, there are other probable advantages, if there is a possible plant closure or increased competition, and then there will be a significant change in workplace practices. And, such practices may destabilize or eliminate competing unions (Brown and Reich, 1989).

Various ethical issues emerge, when high-performance work practices and improved productivity is discussed. Like any social phenomena, work practices too have a history. It is found that textile mills were the first organizational establishment to replace the home-based production processes (in the late 1700 to mid-1800). By 1880s, it became a dominant mode of economic organization. This change from home-based system to an organized factory system led to a huge change in the organization of work.

Hence, the centralized factory system began to dominate, and therefore, the traditional craftsman aspired for independence, to access capital to compete with the large manufacturing system. Labor was in a complex situation from independence to dependence on rules determined by others. To increase the productivity, that too from employees, whose interests were different from those of employers, was a huge struggle.

It is very immature to assume that the development of working environments, since the Industrial Revolution, has been a straightforward process. Workplace strategies provided alternative premises, flexibility in job assignment, performance incentives, external contracting, high concern for the company, and commitment of employees. This was evident in the early years of industrialization.

In the late 1890s, in America, National Cash Register Co.'s Welfare Department constructed avenues for interactions—libraries, recreation facilities and social clubs. Utopians like Robert Owen started the dialogue of social experimentation in 1800 by building communities for cooperative ventures. Again industrialists like George Pullman and N. Nelson built an entire community system for the employees (Pullman, 1967).

Even to attract labor and provide social control in geographically isolated locations, factories also were built around communities primarily designed for the workers (Parks, 1995: 20). Workplace practices and suitably designed workplace cannot be dissociated from workers' performances.

## Debating Issues and Workplace Practices

Debates and discussions on the nature of the workplace practices continue, but there is an urgent necessity to examine the conditions behind the high-performance work practices. One way to understand this relationship is to turn our attention to collaborative type of workplace structures. It primarily emphasizes on the new trends in technology and characteristics of workers so that companies can survive in the intensely competitive economy.

Labor cost is an important factor that has changed the workplace. Due to increased global competition and the deregulation of many sectors in the 1980s, the scope of domestic competition has increased. As the labor costs comprise 70 percent of the production costs, firms increase labor productivity. There are ways to deal with the situation. Few uses mass production to cut the labor costs, while others use highly skilled employees who can adapt to the flexible and rapidly changing markets and technologies. New technology has changed the workplace terrain. For instance, "microprocessor based technologies have cut the cost of advantage of mass production and increased the capacity for customization and diversity" (ibid: 21).

The new technologies usually require different types of work structures. Work becomes automatic, leading to a decline in the number of jobs and skills they require. And, it also leads to change in the worker–management cooperation. Then, the new technology may expect a different type of work practices. It is also observed that corporations that accept the new technology, creating a new learning environment with the help of management–labor cooperation and integration, are successful in using the new technologies.

There has been a shift in labor market characteristics. One very important change is the decline in labor union membership and bargaining agreements. Ironically, unionization has been declining since the mid-1950s, and it reached its low point in 1993. But, this played a major role in changing the structures and methods of decision making in the firm. It was also found that there was a rise in white-collar works, and raised expectations about job satisfaction. And, this has prompted them for higher expectations from their job and also broadened job categories and bigger role in decision making.

The relationship between labor and capital in the production system is very significant. According to classical economists Adam Smith, David Ricardo, Thomas Malthus and John Stuart Mill, labor should be treated in the same manner as land and capital. But the traditional economists also force the changing relationship between labor and management, especially in the context of competition in the market and also the market structure.

There is another view that traces the evolution of workplace as a search by employers to reduce labor costs and control workers. Even management adopted new technology to exhume some job skills and give management greater control over workplace.

Contrary to the classical economic view of labor and management, institutionalists like Richard T. Ely and Thorsten Veblen recognized the conflict of interest between the employers and employees. But compromise, negotiations and accommodations of democratic society can work wonder in a free economic enterprise. Environmental factors are also very important. The advocates of scientific management thought that by providing incentives to employee productivity, they could eliminate the differences between the workers and their employers.

The employer–employee relationship has drawn attention from not a particular period of history. Rather, it has been of interest from different quarters, for it affected the cause of economy and eventually the society. Say from World War I till 1920s, there was a shift in the emphasis towards co-opted unions by developing internal company-operated programs to improve commitment, loyalty, and performance through increasing employee participation and satisfaction of social needs. And then from 1950s, the concern was towards addressing conflicts of interest through collective bargaining and contract solutions.

The quest to find out an appropriate approach to employer–employee relations is still in vogue. David Levine and Laura D'Andrea Tyson (1990), two scholars tried to bridge the economic and environmental factors behind the employer–employee relations. They try to find out a solution to low incidence of high performance in workplaces in terms of environmental factors that create high economic costs. In order to sustain high performance in the workplace, they suggested certain measures: group incentive pay; measures to increase group cohesiveness, such as employee participation, and narrow the wage differentials; guaranteed individual rights; security and trust/group incentive pay; increase in group cohesiveness, like more employee participation, measure to narrow the wage differentials, guaranteed individual rights; security and trust.

Well, organizational flexibility could increase work participation. And, the contingent workforce could be given some serious thinking by the organizations. The contingent workforce may provide many employees a chance to balance work with other obligations or interests and perhaps increase the ability of jobless workers to find a job. But, it may so happen that, the remaining core workers will be benefitted at the expense of those in lower paid positions (Belons, 1989: 7-12). A malady may arise here: the employers will not be willing to invest in training or skill development, and education, as they would do for the core workers.

Workplace is a highly contested terrain. It is a terrain with high-level struggle especially over the control of the labor. Richard Edwards (1979) in his book, *Contested Terrain* argues that the workers are treated fairly, but they have no role in establishing the rules. He argues that the struggle over the material conditions of employment continues and the boundaries of this so-called contested terrain continue. Workplace still struggle over wages, working laws, working conditions, and terms of employment taken over by concepts like employment, employee involvement, and partnership. He feels the outcomes of such struggles and involvement of trade unions, worker organizations, corporate boards of directors, pension fund managers, shareholders and other interested parties will support democratic workplaces.

## Theoretical Perspectives to Workplace Democracy

Dahl (1985), an advocate of economic democracy, argues that if democracy is the norm of the state, then why authoritarianism prevails in the economy. From a very early time, he has tried to popularize the symmetry between polity and economy through his writings on democratic transformation of work. Through his theory of economic democracy, he tried to justify democratic reorganization of work.

In his treatise, "A Preface to Economic Democracy", he makes both a moral rights and a consequentialist argument for workplace democracy. According to Dahl, self-managed firm is not the only condition for the moral right of the employees. Rather, he felt that labor is entitled to not only democratic voice in the firm, but also a moral right of employees and also as a kind of compensation for subjection to the rules. Dahl in a way shifted from consequences to what justice demands. He asserted that "if power at work is a moral right of employees, then it is the entitlements of the individual that matter and not merely the relative desirability of this set of arrangements" (Dahl, 1985: 222). According to Mayer, the moral right for workplace democracy consists of three steps. The first, there should be specific conditions in an association to validate the claim to an equal share of power. The second step shows that such conditions only apply to economic associations, the third step tries to address the objection that the moral right to workplace democracy violates another alleged moral right i.e. the rights of owners to manage their property as they see fit.

There are certain assumptions on the basis of which Dahl has claimed the validity of the moral right of the employees. The assumptions are that (1) the association's rules are "binding on all members of the collectivity"; (2) there is a deliberative process before rules are adopted; (3) "binding collective decisions ought to be made only by persons who are subject to decisions"; (4) "good of each person is entitled to equal consideration"; (5) "each adult person in the association is entitled to be final judge of his or her own interests"; (6) "all the adult members of the association . . . are roughly equally well qualified to decide which matter do or do not require binding collective decisions" and (7) "when the claims of different persons to a scarce and valued thing are equally valid, and no persons claim is better or worse than any others, then if the thing is appropriately divisible into equal shares (as for example, vote can be divided, each equally 'qualified' claimant is entitled to an equal share)" (ibid: 57-58).

In order to understand the democratic right of labor, there are different strategies. Some argue for autonomy in moral right, while others persuade for a principle of distributive justice. Those who argue for autonomy, the democratic right in the firm is also the moral right to autonomy. The distributive justice arguments attempt to focus on an equal share of power in the firm.

The distributive justice argument can be traced back to Carl Cohen's (1971) analysis of the concept some thirty years back. Cohen admitted that an equal share of power within a firm can be possible on two counts: "first, that equals should be treated equally; and second, all members of that community are equal in the respect(s) properly relevant to the allocation of the right to participate in government". The first is somewhat widely accepted, but the second requires that members must be equal to claim their standing in the firm, in order to deserve equal voice in its governance system.

Dahl drew an analogy between democracy in politics and democracy in economics. Hence, he argues that "If democracy is justified in governing the state, then it must also be justified in governing economic enterprises" (Dahl, 1985: 111). Democratic governance system of a state can hold an inspiration for democratic governance of a business firm. Of the seven assumptions mentioned above, he points out that conditions 1 and 6 have some serious challenges and cannot be applied in the firm. If every member of an association claims their right for democracy, then they must be subjected to binding decisions by the associations. But, in some situations here, the analogy case for a firm's rules is not binding in the same way as the laws of a state. The state has a monopoly over using legitimate means of control within a territory, i.e. to use coercive power to enforce its laws, but the associations do not. This suggests that the decisions of an economic association are not binding enough to claim a democratic manner of its formulation.

But, Dahl counters such an analysis and argues that decisions of an association are binding as long as they are accompanied by severe sanctions on non-compliance. He points out that if termination of membership on non-compliance is enforced and as the members are equals, then each member has an equal right to know how the power is exercised. Then, the sixth assumption holds that members of an association must be equally qualified to make judgments about how the association should be run. Some are better able to understand the common good than others, probably because of their knowledge. But Dahl argues that it is not only the owner or the manager but also the laborers who care for the long-term good of the firm, because their exit options are very less. Dahl confirmed this through the actual behavior of worker-managed cooperatives. Thus, the principle of equality seems to be a plausible assumption. Dahl maintains that the principle of equality does not require that citizens should be equally competent in every respect. It is sufficient to believe that citizens are qualified enough to decide which matters do or do not require binding collective decisions and on matters they do not feel competent to decide themselves, they are qualified to set the terms on which they will delegate these decisions to others (Schweickart, 1993).

Dahl argues that the right to property is not a moral right. Individuals do have a moral right for economic liberty, but he rejects the claim that the right to property is a direct instantiation of moral right (Dahl in Mayer, 2001: 230). When there is a clash between property rights and the right to workplace democracy, then it must give way to preserve the uniqueness of the moral right. The denial of democratic rights to employees in the workplace is an injustice, a violation of the moral rights of the individuals as workers. He also refuted Tocqueville's claim that democracies are given to majority tyranny. He also accepts that citizens in a democracy are mostly employees of authoritarian firms and for same reasons they do not enforce the moral right to equality at work. Besides, his view on intensity of property rights has been refuted by Jan Narvesa, a noted libertarian scholar. He believes that moral right to private property triumphs over democratic voice at work.

But, this does not imply ownership is not a sufficient ground to confer authority on managers. Hence, employee's ownership of the physical assets of a business does not give him the license to boss around. Similarly, a democratic reorganization of the enterprise would not allow the labor to use another's property without the owner's consent.

In an economic democracy, owners could keep their property and workers would retain their voice and their interactions in the marketplace would be governed by contract. Instead of capital hiring labor, in a democratic economy, labor will hire capital, leasing it at interest from owners, but owners might remain free to keep their property if they do not wish to put it to productive use (Ellerman, 1990).

Mayer (2001: 232) argues that Dahl is not an expropriator, for he does not want to take from capital, the right to control property, but the power to control labor. Then, when democracy is at work, the labor loses the right to sell voice in exchange for a job. Capital also loses the right to buy voice, from the labor that this asset is taken. From a libertarian point of view, everything is property, but inalienable rights are illegitimate restrains on free trade. But Dahl's assertion that moral status should be denied to property less, sounds less convincing, as we perceive property is not just physical assets.

Dahl's analogy of political and economic democracy is questioned by Richard Arneston. If we go back to the first condition set by Dahl, the parallel or the analogy fails. This condition is not met by economic associations because the condition is the existence of binding decisions.

Arneston (1993) pointed out the differential voluntariness of the individual's relationship to politics and to work, which he insists "strongly conditions the force of the individual's claim to a democratic say in each area".

He argues that if an employee's subjection is voluntary and the existence of exit options are many, then one can claim that such exit options may weaken the analogy case (between political and economic democracy). Even in a market economy there are multiple opportunities for labor. Even, it is true for other professions. For instance in academics, if one are a faculty in a college, and then, he may quit the job, and be a visiting faculty for two to three colleges or be a freelance writer. Therefore, one has to admit the existence of many alternatives.

Dahl had high objections against the exit options. Because exit is so costly, membership in a firm is not significantly more voluntary or less compulsory than citizenship in a municipality or perhaps in a county (Dahl, 1985). If one analyzes it from another angle, then it can be argued that "case of exit" is one dimension and the other is "entrance into the association", for rules are binding, not only if one lacks an exit option, but also if one lacks the option not to be subject to the association (Mayer, 2001: 235).

If subjection is imposed regardless of choice, then the members of the association are not mere subject, but are also subjected. Now, Mayer argues that the presence of an exit option does not justify one's right to voice in an association, but the presence of a subjection option does. For, if we perceive in the following manner that an association imposes rules on its workers, regardless of one's choice, then the workers are equal in relevant aspects. Then, they have a moral right to an equal share of power in the association.

Another way to analyze the relevance of imposed subjection to the entitlement to democratic voice is unionization. In such a situation, one has to become a member of the union as a pre-condition of employment in a firm; then a subjection option is lacking and the members are entitled to self-government. Here, subjection to the rules includes payment of dues and in return, the member is entitled to the democratic voice for the imposition. Thus, one can say that the member has earned the democratic right within the firm as a result of the subjection. This type of firm does not have the discretion to withhold democratic right from the member.

In private clubs, competence is based on equality. Clubs do not have to be democratic, even in a democratic society. Here, founders have the right to design the governance structure, which they deem the best, and the new entries do not have the moral right to political equality. Once the entries are admitted, no fundamental injustice is done to them, even if equal voice is not granted. In "such organizations, distributive justice does not dictate how power should be divided because subjection to the rules is not required" (ibid: 240).

On another count, the parallel assumption is criticized. For instance, the laborers are not owners of private property and hence, are dependent on capital for employment. Though the labor market appears to have many choices, in the sense that one may apply to different employers, in reality, a few have an option of avoiding subjection to some capitalist firms. As the advantages enjoyed by the capitalist firms are immense, opportunities for self-employment are constrained. Thus, from this viewpoint, wage labor is conscripted by capital, not individually, but as a class.

If subjection to capitalist management on the part of the wage labor is required, a moment's reflection suggests that the appropriate readiness of this imposition is not in fact an equal share of voice in the firm, but rather the restoration of choice that has been unjustly constrained (ibid: 243). John Roemer (1988) pointed out that a right to workplace democracy in such a situation will not end exploitation.

From a Marxian perspective, even if the capital is not permitted to hire labor, exploitation will still occur, if labor is without property because capital can exploit its positive or advantageous position in the credit market, by extracting exorbitant interest, when it gives loans to labor. Thus, credit market capitalism can be as exploitative as labor market capitalism. This shows that democracy is not the cure for exploitation.

Mayer argues that if the circumstances are such that prospective employees lack effective choice and are forced to consent to powerlessness in the firm, then the best way to undo this injustice is to offer choices and also control the circumstances that try to constrain it. Again, if labor accepts voicelessness at work, due to exploitation, the community might try for a minimum degree of voice in the firm that cannot be bargained by establishing or forming unions or co-determination. Therefore, it is apparent that the right to workplace democracy is not equivalent to minimum wage, because democratic voice within the firm is not even minimum compensation of voluntary labor, but it is the maximum. Society needs to pressurize on a minimum degree of voice below which no employee may agree.

### Justification for the Existence of Workplace Democracies

The workplace democracy in some period was associated with worker-owned economy, workers' cooperatives, the Swedish model of broad tripartite representation of interests, and also Employee Stock Ownership Plans (ESOPs). But the term generally implies a normative system which requires applying democratic practices, both in public and private work situations.

The engagement with the idea of workplace democracy was at the peak in the post-war period, with the consolidation of the welfare state and the stability of the Fordist labor market. But in the later years, the very idea of workplace democracy decreased. There are few reasons: firstly, there was an increasing disenchantment with the cooperation forms. The Cold War and abolishment of Yugoslav Model did not provide an alternative to the capitalist system. Similarly, other institutional forms of democracy, such as trade unions, and collective bargaining encountered challenges, that too in developed countries. Stable enterprises can serve as communities in which democracy was practiced. Workers' cooperatives, trade unions negotiated collective agreements that stood for the lifelong tenure of the workers.

Corporatist state-wide bargaining, coupled with universal and a strong sector-based social security system, aims to advance equal distribution of wages and opportunities. Also, the states were considered to be the source of regulatory provisions that advance democratic alternatives within economic enterprises, overstepping the public–private divide.

The stability that resulted from democratic practices at the institutional level, at the state level, was substituted by marketization (phenomena related to globalization). It is also observed that the process of globalization has undermined the state's regulatory power to cover appropriate marketplace. The Fordist regime or the regime of accumulation was replaced by the post-Fordist regime, which is characterized by frequent transitions in the employment system, increase in the disparity between primary and secondary labor markets, disintegration of organizational hierarchies and a diversified workforce (Boyer, 1990).

There are several justifications for democratic workforce practices in an institutional set-up, both for public and private sectors. Workplace practices should be organized in a democratic manner because participation should be enjoyed by all employees and become self-fulfilling. Work is the centre of one's life. It is time consuming, but social institutions, formal and informal systems are evolved here. Formal includes health care, pension funds, non-firm–specific training and education; informal can be socialization with co-workers, and occupational identity. Now, the argument here is if democracy is intended to enhance self-development, then a democratic process must be implemented in small communities, where personal development actually takes place, predominantly in the workplace. Through participation, the worker is able to influence the community on which he/she depends for his/her self-development. For an effective voice to be granted for all those operating within the workplace environment, equal influence should be granted to all who are affected by it.

The democratic practices in a workplace can be also justified on the ground of economic well- being. For most individuals, work is the main source of income, compared with those who are minority, whose main source of income is welfare. That is why the socio-economic stratification should be eliminated by empowering workers at their workplace. It is also believed that economic status is a major determinant of political status, and workers, both individually and as a group, do not usually match the economic power of capital. Some argue that economic empowerment is tightly linked to the political quality of the national level democratic regime (Elster, 1986).

Now, the question here is without a distributive process, workers still remain dependent on the organization and at the same time owners of capital resist attempts at economic mobilization, redistribution of economic and political power.

The most important argument is economic argument, because it directly deals with the distribution of income. But equitable distribution of income may not necessarily lead to democratization of the workplace. Focus should be on the broader society, rather than on any organizational structure of a particular workplace. Then institutions associated with workplace democracy have a distinct link to work. In Mundlak's (2013) opinion, democratic workplace with its focus on sharing control among the owners of the various production factors allows a more egalitarian distribution of power that includes the property rights over financial resources as well as over the political institutions of power that generate future distribution of power.

Another viewpoint is that active political participation at work may have a positive spillover effect outside the workplace. Among participatory democratic theorists, the workplace represents the most important setting for the education of democratic citizens.

Participatory democratic discourses widely believed that democracy leads to more democracy. It insists that workplace represents one of the most important platforms for educating the people as democratic citizens.

The idea here is that if workplace arrangements encourage democratic participation within the walls of the firm, workers in such setting are more likely to be participatory and civic-minded citizens outside; workplace arrangements that discourage participation or fail to teach democratic skills or nurture democratic aspiration are likely to depress participation in other social institutions, especially in the world of conventional politics (Pateman, 1970). There are other scholars who suggest that if democracy is practiced in a workplace, it increases employees' sense of personal efficiency which helps them nurture feelings of political efficiency (Elden, 1981; Lafferty, 1985; Greenberg and Greenberg, 1999).

Verva (1995) argues that practicing and learning civic activities orient towards a set of skills such as organizing meetings, especially in public, debating and so on.

The most important of the spillover thesis is the democratic discourse that encourages people to understand the views, interests of others and to see beyond one's own self-interest and become more public spirited (Cole, 1919; Pateman, 1970; Greenberg, 1986).

In order to understand workplace participation, let's look into Pateman's classification of different types of workplace participation. He has identified three types of workplace participation: pseudo, partial and full participation. Pseudo participation refers to a number of management-initiated offers that persuade workers to accept decisions that have already been made. Partial participation involves lower level decisions and full participation takes place at different levels. In order to develop a clear understanding of democratic workplace participation, Pateman distinguished between democracy and participation, and argued that partial participation in a workplace does not require any democratization of the authority. She also stressed that participatory theory of democracy assumes genuine democratization of the entire organization to produce political efficacy.

Democratic participation can be found in cooperatives, whether it is direct or participatory, or indirect or representative democracy. It was very common for representative structure to exist in large cooperatives in France (Batstone, 1983), Italy (Earle, 1986) and in some parts of Great Britain (Mallore, 1988).

"Mondragon, the well-known thriving federation of over one hundred co-operatives in the Basque region of Spain has a dual structure in which a representative democratic structure operates alongside a management system" (Whyte and Whyte, 1988). Carter (2003) observed that in a single Mondragon cooperative, the General Assembly elects from its members a small Governing Council or Junta, which appoints a Management Council responsible for the day-to-day management of the cooperative.

Well, even in small cooperatives, there is no assurance that the direct participation results in active participation by all workers. But, there are existing issues within a cooperative. It is usually found that managers and committee members refrain from active involvement in the cooperative organization. It is also found that there are lots of people who won't voice their opinions.

The cooperative system attempts to shape both the choice of participatory structure and the degree of participation by members. Pateman (1970) attempted to construct a typology of cooperatives: four main types are endowed, defensive, alternative and job creation cooperatives. Endowed cooperatives occur when the ownership of an existing company is transferred to the employees, like British cooperatives. Due to closure of a business, employees form defensive, or rescue, cooperatives to preserve their jobs, for instance workers, especially shop floor workers are used to undemocratic management structures—have no wish to participate actively in decision making. They prefer to appoint or elect managers to make decisions. Participation in decision making is not welcomed by workers.

Carter argues that workers may seize on the cooperative idea, not because they have always wanted to run their own business, but because it turns out to be the best chance of salvaging at least some of the jobs from a factory closure. Hence, cooperatives may at times act as a safety net to keep the jobs.

The collective energy emerging from the social movements of 1960s and 1970s, primarily for social or political (not for economic) reasons, is termed as an alternative cooperative. Here, "the members joined the cooperatives because they had rejected the conventional bureaucratic organizational structures of the capitalist forms and were attracted by the democratic structures" (Rothschild and Whitt, 1986). A job creation cooperative is a small cooperative set by unemployed workers with support from a development agency to a group of professional lawyers or architects to start a business. It can be argued that cooperatives are formed by workers whose needs, demands are fulfilled or addressed by the management.

Carter also believed that the origins of cooperatives play an important role in the participatory structure, i.e. between direct and indirect participation. Origins of cooperatives may also explain the attitudes of workforce towards participation. For instance in an endowed cooperative, the workers are "conscripts", where participation has been imposed on them from the top; typically the workforce will be divided between those who relish the opportunity to get involved, and those who are completely uninterested. By contrast, in an alternative cooperative, most members are likely to regard democratic structures as intrinsically good and wish to utilize them.

Controlling mechanism of the cooperatives is very significant for workers' involvement. Organizational degeneration, a phenomenon greatly related to the controlling mechanisms of the cooperatives, emphasizes on how informal control is opposed to formal control.

Degeneration thesis rests on the argument that it can result from both internal and external pressures. The most significant "internal pressure" argument is the "Michel's Iron Law of Oligarchy". This argument stresses that direct democracy is not efficient, and in the long run, the elected leaders in democratic organizations will try becoming a ruling elite. There is some sort of tension running within a democratic organization operating a capitalist market. And, this makes it difficult for cooperatives to break away from principles associated with capitalist organization practices such as the quintessential management hierarchy, differentials, wage benefit and minimization of wage costs. There have been plenty of historical studies supporting the organizational degeneration thesis like the British (Webbs, 1914) and American analysis (Shirom, 1972; Russel, 1985). There are evidences that although there are strong external and internal pressures encouraging organizational degeneration, it is not inevitable. Nevertheless, where degeneration does occur, it is likely to have a significant impact on political efficacy. Indeed, one conclusion worth testing is that political efficacy and participation is likely to be higher amongst those active members who secure informal control within a cooperative than amongst non-active members.

Worker cooperatives are not a classical idea. If seen historically, they emerged as a counter action against economic mobilization by the capital control firms. Due to intense marketization of the economy, economic restructuring of industry, high unemployment, an interest in cooperatives spawned up, as a means of prevailing plant closings or even creating new opportunities (especially jobs).

Many theorists are of the opinion that cooperatives represent an alternative institutional structure which changes basic property relations and provides a conducive atmosphere for worker empowerment and social change. Some feel that for raising workers' consciousness of alternative means of economic organizations, cooperatives have been considered a first step for changing the wider economic and political system (Coater and Topham, 1968: 361). Cooperatives and workplace democracy can be also based on democratic theory. Dahl (1985) justified workplace democracy like political democracy.

However, the public support for worker cooperatives, as opposed to other small businesses, has been based on their economic and social advantages (Dickstein, 1988).

It has been argued by some scholars that cooperatives perform better than conventional private sector firms with respect to productivity, quality of jobs, job security, and job creation. If there is greater worker participation in decision making, then it may contribute to increased worker motivation, job satisfaction, increased personal dignity and elimination of conflict between labor and management. Besides, if the cooperatives are worker-controlled, they are more inclined to stay where the workers live, for example, the community employee-owned firms (Stern, Wood and Hamner, 1979). Worker cooperatives can also increase community control of the local economy, and eventually avoid the high social cost of unnecessary plant closings.

How do we define a worker cooperative? Well, it is a firm controlled by its workers, who are the members of the firm itself. It is open and cooperatives differ from private firms. Here, the control of the firm is based on personal rights which is derived from workers' labor, rather than on property rights derived from a capital contribution (Ellerman, 1984). According to Ellerman, a cooperative differs from an employee-owned firm, where employees have membership rights, because they directly or indirectly own the shares of the firm, keeping apart the functional role of working in a company. In order to operate as a viable enterprise, a cooperative must function as a democratically controlled and self-managed enterprise.

Some cooperatives stress on social and political goals which may include equitable pay structure, providing socially useful products at reasonable costs to the community, sometimes even supporting other cooperatives. Well, it is also observed that orientation of the cooperatives, and the way the cooperatives pursue their goals result from the context in which they are created.

The American study of the cooperative movement was different. ESOP, for the larger players' purchase, tax advantages prompt the workers to raise the necessary capital. It is also found that more than 150 ESOPs, in the 1980s, were results of workers' buyouts of failing companies or successful subsidiaries of large companies (Blasi, 1988). How does the ESOP operate/function? The company contributes stocks, cash, or real estate to the ESOP trust and these are deductible from corporate income tax. The trustees of the ESOP invest these contributions back in the company to purchase capital until the worker leaves or retires. Therefore, the company raises capital at a discount equal to its tax savings. Commercial lenders which make loans to ESOPs are permitted to deduct half the interest from their earnings. But the commercial lenders have an incentive. What is it? It is to pass the savings to the ESOP in reduced interest rates; ESOPs are also enthusiastic about making ownership accessible to workers who do not have the money to purchase stock. ESOPs were primarily established to expand worker ownership, broadening and distribution of wealth and also at the same time, improving the economic performance of American industry. But there are lots of accusations against the ESOPs. It is found that ESOP is primarily used for tax advantage without actually creating ownership of the workers.

It has also strategically excluded lower and middle paid workers, and passed the favor to high-ranking employees. Even democratic practices and ESOPs' actual manner of operation are at loggerheads.

If we go by the history of the cooperatives, Europe had a dramatic growth, but in the US the momentum could not sustain. It didn't have a supportive institutional structure. Europe, especially Western Europe, had a phenomenal growth of worker cooperative and employment rate (mid-1970s), even surpassing the growth of capitalist firms. These cooperatives are concentrated in the construction and manufacturing sectors, and then their growth was also observable in the service sector. These firms avoid capital-intensive industries because they cannot accumulate large amounts of capital. And buyouts of capital-intensive firms have occurred through ESOPs. There has been a debate regarding cooperatives' performance.

Some argue that cooperative performance is uneven. It is observed that profitability is a consistent measure of return on investment for private firms, but it is highly unpredictable for cooperative performance. Say, cooperatives often value non-market outputs and may trade profit maximization for increased democratic control and participation (Levin, 1982). Some find that cooperatives perform very well. But the performance of the cooperative sector as a whole is uneven. But in the US and Europe among same worker cooperatives, there are high levels of endurance and they have survived long periods and can make profits (Thomas and Logan, 1989).

It is also found that worker cooperatives survive when capitalist firms cannot make it. This success has been due to increased productivity, reductions of the workforce, as well as a willingness to accept a lower rate of return (Paton, 1987; Bradley and Gelb, 1983; Estrin, 1985). Even performance of the cooperatives varies within the same industrial sectors; variations were observed in profitability in 19th-century study on foundry, footwear, cigar-making and furniture-manufacturing cooperatives (Jones, 1979). But one thing was for sure that profitability of these cooperatives was not comparable to capitalist measures, and in fact, it was unadjusted for capitalist equivalent wages. Scholars like Berman (1967) and Bellas (1972) in their study of the plywood cooperatives in the Pacific Northwest found that some of them had higher performance levels.

Various studies were conducted on ESOPs. These studies pointed towards positive impacts of labor management cooperation. One noted example is of the Weirton Steel; it was the largest wholly employee-owned ESOP in the country, until it went public in 1989. This was primarily due to employee participation, problem solving measure, and effective communication channels initiated by the management (Quarrey, Blasi and Rosen, 1986).

The effect of participation and productivity is a very dicey phenomenon. Various studies were made to understand the link between participation and productivity. Conte (1982) pointed that worker participation is related to individual motivation, but it is still not clear as to what conditions provide an efficient co-relation between the two. But, subsequently, other studies were conducted to find out the relation, especially on ESOPs (Rosen, Klein and Young, 1986). These scholars found a strong positive relationship between worker participation and employee satisfaction based on certain grounds.

## Dilemmas in Workplace Democracy and Democratic Governance

There are diverse perspectives to worker cooperatives. One such perspective could be that cooperatives improve their quality by increasing job responsibility of their members.

Cornforth (1988), in his quest for a better quality working life, found that in British worker cooperatives, workers have control over their daily work life and have the opportunity to be with fellow workers with whom they are compatible. But some workers were against the long hours, monotonous jobs and poor working conditions. One very significant aspect was despite severe limitations imposed by the market, the British cooperatives had some flexibility in choosing technologies which improved the quality of working life. Sometimes, overall pay and benefit levels contribute to job quality and depend on the market conditions, but it is not totally determined by the industry (Dickstein, 1988: 7).

There is another perspective that argues that cooperatives made up a small sector of the most market economies in the western world. If the cooperatives are economically and socially advantageous, then why aren't they common? Well, probably very few worker cooperatives point to their inefficiency. Alchian and Demsetz (1972) attribute the small numbers to the lack of incentives to produce efficiently.

Other theorists argue that the formation of the worker cooperatives is highly dependent on the wider economic, social and political environment. Besides, there are others who feel that low cooperative formation is due to lack of institutional support. Here, institutional problems represent a type of market failure and may account for the absence of cooperatives rather than inherent technical or allocative inefficiencies.

Countries which have well-established cooperative support organizations have been able to reduce the uncertainties of cooperative formation by providing access to financing, information, and technical assistance, and lobbying for adoption of cooperatives legal structures (Dickstein, 1988). There was a remarkable growth in cooperative development agencies (CDAs; Ben-Ner, 1988; Taylor, 1983; Cornforth and Lewis, 1985, 1988), primarily to reduce the uncertainties of cooperative formation.

Worker cooperatives face lots of constraints in their growth, unlike the conventional firms; they face difficulty in obtaining basic inputs of capital, entrepreneurial support and managerial talent.

Raising internal finance is a big issue of the cooperatives. Members of the cooperatives cannot recoup the amount invested because of the non-availability of secondary market in cooperative shares. Members can only benefit from increased investment if it results in greater productivity and therefore, greater income for the workers. Workers have a greater incentive to take capital out of the cooperative by voting themselves higher wages and investing their personal income elsewhere. Vanek (1977) argues that to compensate for this, the capital of worker cooperatives should be socially owned and nanced externally through specialized nancial institutions that provide social criteria for the allocation of capital among rms to improve the allocation efficiency of capital.

As opposed to Vanek's argument, a system called "internal capital accounts" was first used in a cooperative, i.e. Mondragon cooperatives. It is a process by which accounts are set up for workers which credit or debit the share of a cooperative's profits to a capital reserve fund and to a special fund after the allocations are made. But this does not imply that the internal capital accounts are bereft of the problem. It may face a liquidity problem, if it must reinvest prots in expensive capital equipment or pay out members who leave or die.

External functionality can solve the financial problems of the cooperatives to a certain extent. Worker cooperatives are regarded as very risky, in terms of investment and conventional lenders not being keen to judge them. Sometimes, the internal structure of the cooperative prohibits it from external sources of capital.

Worker cooperative's another problem is the difficulty in attracting talented entrepreneurs and managers. From one point of view, the cooperative does not provide enough remuneration to attract reputed/established entrepreneurs. Even if the monetary return is provided (as in conventional firm), it entails high risk. The individual entrepreneurs may end up incurring higher information costs for establishing a cooperative. Even the traditional entrepreneurs are not easily attracted towards the cooperatives.

It is also noted that workers in cooperatives do not behave like entrepreneurs. There is a saying common in the market, i.e. workers know what is best in production, not markets. Even their limited training and expertise does not equip them to be sensitive to markets and entrepreneurial opportunities. It is also claimed that business opportunities are usually perceived by an individual and not by a group.

It is suggested that people drawn to such reform experiments out of self-interest may have no entrepreneurial skills. Even worse, those attracted maybe unstable or excessive risk takers (Putterman, 1982). Then there is the problem of cooperatives in a capitalist environment. Capitalist environment refers to hierarchically controlled organizations which mean absence of democratic governance. If there is a new cooperative, that would provide few benefits to managers, and unless they have some ideological commitment or significant sacrifices, they simply try to save their jobs as a result of plant closing.

Cooperative degeneration is a phenomenon where control becomes increasingly concentrated in the hands of a few, governed by a capitalistic mechanism. It is primarily based on two different premises, i.e. internal structure and the external structure. The internal structure argument states that the internal structure of worker cooperatives leads to their inevitable degeneration and turn them into capitalist organization. Marxist theories consider external pressures to conform to the values and structures of the capitalist order. It is also an irony that sometimes the success of cooperatives may lead to their degeneration into capitalist rms. If cooperatives are financed by internal shares and their assets appreciate, the purchase price becomes out of reach to new members (Ellerman, 1984)

Degenerative tendencies can also flourish, when a successful cooperative begins to hire labor. It may develop as a result of environmental pressures or loss of commitment to cooperative principles. There is a dilemma here: suppose a cooperative is successful and grows because of the hard work of original members, and new members join at the same cost. The new members didn't undergo the risks which the original members did to achieve prosperity. It may also happen that a "collective selfishness" is likely to overcome the original cooperative members (Hammer, Stern and Whyte, 1983). Incentives are there within the firms for the existing members to distribute the profits among fewer members, and bar new members. Rather, the existing members hire non-members at lower wages, creating two types/classes of workers, which undermined the collective purpose of the cooperative. Then, the legal mechanism can attempt to stop the practice of hired labor.

It is also believed that sometimes, democratic organizations become dominated by elites because of their technical expertise or leadership skills, or both. Even members of organizations feel the need for leaders, but once installed, those leaders have a natural inclination to assume power and centralize operations (Michels, 1949). Even the participatory process within a firm also gets easily influenced by the market situation, especially when the market remains highly competitive. To establish themselves in the complex situation, where there are technical, managerial expertise, secrecy of information concerning new products, and market decisions in response to the changing conditions, the cooperatives have same kind of pressure to establish a hierarchical system.

As against this perspective, some scholars give importance to values and orientation of members as more important to prevent such oligarchical system to grow. Kibbutzim system (Israel) is an example of social equality, social solidarity, and value commitment. It demonstrates a direct democratic system, with a strict model of regulation, despite growing specialization (Rosner and Cohen, 1982). On a similar note, R. Bernstein (1976) came up with "participatory consciousness" as a precondition for effective cooperative organization and democratic management. What is "participatory consciousness"? It is basically characterized by self-reliance, flexibility, openness to learning and a willingness to educate on the part of the workers.

It is also found that "participatory consciousness" is something very high. Workers are not that keen on going for it. And, it is also a norm that workers are attracted towards cooperatives out of desperation for jobs due to plant closings. Workers are guided by their instrumental orientation.

It is not always a degenerative orientation that guided the cooperatives. There were others that tried to cross the barriers, and establish a well-integrated system. The Mondragon cooperatives in the Basque region of Spain deviated from the common patterns of worker cooperatives. They are mostly capital-intensive and export-oriented. As they are manufacturing orientated, they are much larger than any average European cooperative.

It was started with the motive of cooperation, by few highly dedicated engineers, who were students of Mondragon's founder, Father Jose Arizmendi. Thanks to Arizmendi, for he tried to make his students socially driven (with his catholic background). Though it faced severe repression politically (Franco's regime), it was successful in developing a support system, which offered assistance in research and development, financing and technical assistance. The managers of the cooperative acted as a godfather to the new entrepreneurs by guiding them through the start-up period and providing hands-on training (Ellerman, 1982).

Another significant characteristics of the cooperatives, is "labor entrepreneurship", which is also one of the prime reasons behind its expansion. Here "a new group" of cooperatives is encouraged to spin off new ventures with support from their own cooperatives and the Mondragon support structure (Gutierrez-Johnson, 1984). There are other positive elements in these cooperatives. Wage flexibility and work sharing is very common to worker cooperatives, but Mondragon cooperatives have developed a system of relocating redundant workers to other growing cooperatives in the system.

During the recessionary period of the late 1970s and early 1980s, the Mondragon cooperatives had far lower unemployment rates than other Basque firms and provided displaced workers with far more employment and financial assistance than what was available in private Spanish enterprises (Whyte and Whyte, 1988).

Theorists and practitioners have developed a great deal of curiosity in the success of Mondragon, especially, the course behind its unique success mantra. The prime reason for the cohesiveness and success of the Mondragon system is the integration of the cooperative members into their local community through strong family and friendship networks, their isolation from other labor markets and lifestyles, and labor immobility (Bradly and Gelb, 1983).

Again, one can also attribute its dynamism to its unique culture within the organization. According to Whyte (1988), it is the guiding principle that provides direction for its leaders together with the institutions, policies, and decision processes which support those principles.

## Developing a Support System for Workplace Democracies

Organizations require a support system in providing guidance, assistance, and resources. Like any institute, worker cooperatives too require a cooperative support structure. It provides resources directly to cooperatives in the form of finance, education and training, and business assistance; it strengthens inter-cooperative linkages and it creates a supportive environment for cooperatives through lobbying activities and providing models of success (Dickstein, 1988; Cornforth et al., 1988; Cornforth, 1989).

CDAs have been formed "top down" by government or private sponsors that wish to stimulate cooperative development (Dickstein, 1988). CDAs began to develop in the 1970s, especially in Britain, but it took shape of a movement in the 1980s. In the US, CDAs focused on cooperative development rather than ESOPs. They were either nationally or regionally based.

As they are development oriented, they require aggressive strategy to be affective. It is observable that most of the opportunities for cooperative development in the US and in Britain have arisen from plant closings or high unemployment. There is a belief that cooperatives should emerge "bottom up" from those workers with the strongest stake in the business taking the initiative (Cornforth et al., 1988). CDAs then limit themselves to responding to demand for cooperative assistance, usually from people in crisis situations, with limited business skills and access to resources (Dickstein, 1988: 17). Besides, CDAs should make a pro-active development approach. They should target specific ventures, or sectors, where cooperatives have advantages and where systems of cooperative can develop. Against this backdrop, would CDAs be able to attract mainstream entrepreneurs? But yes, if there are financial movements, these entrepreneurs might join the cooperatives.

Then, the next important question is, if CDAs are successful in attracting exports and mainstream talent, then will these cooperatives be managed democratically or even remain as cooperatives?

Many scholars feel cooperation and democratic participation are learning experiences and if the cooperatives are truly democratic, then they will not evolve immediately in a capitalist environment.

Cooperatives are usually given a less privileged status than capitalist firms. Then, how to elevate the status of the cooperatives? One way could be through tax incentives or sheltering markets to incubate their development. Government could move on a step further and mandate cooperatives legislatively. But this is just not enough. Rather, Dickstein argues that "social and economic changes are needed, if people forming cooperatives are to come together with more equal interests and create the necessary common bonds and mutual respect for successful cooperation". Thus, cooperative development must go hand in hand with other grassroots planning processes that advocate a more equitable distribution of resources and encourage greater community participation and self-management.

In spite of their limitations, cooperative systems can be a viable way for job creation and retention. If structured properly, then they can provide a number of economic and social benefits to their members, and also increase local ownership and control of the economy.

## Industrial Democracy – Is It another Form of Workplace Democracy?

International awakening movement for participatory democracy was evident in the later part of 1960s. Whether it is the community action groups, or student power groups, anti-war demonstrators or women rights groups, or racial liberation groups, all have struggled against authoritative structures.

Karl Marx adopted the term industrial democracy from the Fabian Society after a long stay in London in 1912. He defined industrial democracy as the whole spectrum from workshop participation over collective bargaining to co-determination in the regional and national economy. Muller-Jeutsch (2008) referred the state of co-determination as "industrial constitutionalism" being a transitional stage on the road to socialism. Well, according to Hugh Cleeg (1960), industrial democracy can be understood as a mechanism for protecting the rights and safeguarding the interest of industrial workers.

Academicians and scholars favored worker committees in factories, before the trade unions adopted co-determination as their goal. There were some socially conscious businessmen who introduced workers' committee in their firms. These businessmen were motivated to mitigate the antagonism between workers and entrepreneurs. Some employers with a liberal mindset regarded their employees as equal and not as subordinates.

It was the Frankfurt Parliament (1848) which took the lead, to establish the worker committees though it was rolled back later. During the World War I, the state passed a law (1916) to establish trade unions, as legitimate representatives of workers. Thus, worker committees were prescribed for all war essential companies with 50 or more workers and co-determination at institutional level spread across all industries.

The mounting dissatisfaction with the structure of life, and with the heightened awareness about the rights of political and social participation, labor, management, national governments as well as academic researchers and political activists have all developed strategies for introducing workplace reforms.

In Western Europe and in North America, traditional forms of industrial democracy have been expanded and were complemented by new channels for participation, for instance, the Tripartite Bullock Commission in Great Britain, the Biedenkoph Commission in West Germany, and the Sudreau Commission of France (Jain, 1980). Such expansionist trend added a new dimension to workers' participation.

Even the International Labor Organization (ILO) has developed a great amount of energy to this area (ibid). Such consciousness was also growing in Europe; for instance, the European Economic Community (EEC) has urged for worker participation at all levels of the enterprise (EEC, 1977, 1980).

Participation and dynamics of power relation are at the core of industrial democracy. Industrial democracy stresses on participation within the enterprise, and it involves a change in the power relationship between labor and management. It is the restructuring of power relations of ways to organize different forms of industrial democracy: (1) collective bargaining; (2) workers' representation on boards, co-determination; (3) joint consultation and information, worker's councils; (4) humanization of work; (5) self-management; and (6) economic democracy.

Collective bargaining is the most common form of industrial democracy. This has been seen as a major tool for influencing workers in the US, Great Britain, Australia and Canada. The basic premise here is equal parties come together to negotiate the terms of employment. Based on such an idea, workers have rights directly planning from their contribution of labor, trade unions, arguing for workers' rights and negotiating on a whole range of issues. Albrecht (1981) opined that collective bargaining is more often associated with the economic conditions of employment rather than the non-economic issues of the workplace.

## Approaches to Democratic Workplace Practices

Economic issues were of great concern, but there has been a steady growth of attention devoted to non-economic issues of participation, like job security and length of the work cycle.

In different parts of Europe, the eagerness towards industrial democracy was not the same. For instance, Italy has lagged behind other European nations in industrial democracy, but it has gained some benefits that have come from collective bargaining, because it covered both economic and non-economic factors. Sweden manipulated the atmosphere in a different manner. It was successful in pushing industrial democracy, and supported collective bargaining and established a framework law on the Joint Regulation of Working Life/ The Joint Regulation of Factory Life Act.

This particular step (The Joint Regulation of Working Life Act, 1976) gave unions the right to negotiate collective agreements on all aspects of supervision and management that had formerly been the sole right of management (Albrecht, 1980, 1981; Martin, 1976, 1977). This act has broadened the base of collective bargaining to encompass more and more non-economic factors in the workplace. Collective bargaining became an instrument for increased industrial democracy, especially in the seventies and eighties.

Workers' Representation on Boards – Co-determination involves seating voting representatives of labor on the governing bodies of enterprises. It is one of the easiest forms of bargaining between labor and management at the level of the firm. It is somewhat viewed as one of the decentralized form of bargaining system where labor has an equal footing with the management. It is also conceived of as a form of "cooperative" participation between labor and management in pursuit of a common goal, the economic success of the enterprise (Poole 1979). Co-determination was mostly associated with the West German industrial relations, but it is also found in other countries as well. Norway, Sweden, Denmark with enactment supported co-determination and called for representatives from workers in corporate bodies. Co-determination has been introduced through legislative bodies. In Great Britain, a decision on co-determination was strongly opposed by managerial class, but Bullock Report came out in support of it, and action has not been taken yet.

Co-determination had its own fallouts. In many firms, having labor representatives on company boards has not resulted in any major changes in the decision-making policies of enterprise. Employee representatives, primarily in the minority, have not exerted over-riding influences on the boards. Because of this, trade unions have been less than enthusiastic to this form of participation, and, in fact have seen its potential to undermine their primary role of collective bargaining (Albrecht, 1983: 51). Under many instances, board representation has complemented collective bargaining and expanded the influence of workers on major decisions of the enterprise. For instance, labor was able to guarantee job security for its West German employees when Volkswagen Company wanted to invest in automobile plants in the United States.

Still, there were differences in approach to co-determination. For example, the West German and the Scandinavian approaches to board representation was very different. The West German legislation aimed at extending the balance of power within the supervisory boards, whereas Scandinavian laws have settled for minority representation on the board.

The Swedish Industrial Democracy has never emphasized on board representation as a way to influence of workers, but used it as an alternative, put forward by the Joint Regulation of Life Act (JRL). West Germany has moved for greater labor representation, but Sweden has opted for minority representation for the purpose of increasing information to the labor, about the measures taken by the corporation.

Work councils are another form of democratic practices with a firm to withhold harmonious relationships between labor and management. A typical work council consists of a joint labor management committee at the firm level.

The role of workers' representatives in these bodies has been one of consultation rather than influence, since management still retains the right to make the final decision after collaboration. For that reason, often they have been regarded as weak arrangements for true worker participation, sometimes referred to as "phony participation" (Strauss, 1979). But they didn't remain the same.

Towards the later part of the seventies, there was a change in their roles. There was a move from a harmonious role to a more adversarial position. Their rights of the councils have been expanded and they are playing a larger and larger role in protecting the interests of workers with the firm. The expanded role of the worker councils could be observed in the Netherlands, and Belgium. Even the law has mandated the expanded role of work councils in Denmark (1980), Austria (1974). The change in the role led to their acceptance in different countries of Europe and outside. In West Germany too, change was observed.

There was a change in the functioning of the work councils in West Germany. Here, these councils were made up of only employee representatives, but their role was expanded. They increased decision-making rights on issues like setting of wage rates above the minimum determined by collective bargaining. The work councils in Italy have directed their attention towards sole representation, from joint labor management.

To some scholars, the revamping of work councils in Western Europe with their new decision-making rights is seen as the dramatic change that has taken place in the area of participation (Cordova, 1982). But in the United States, the new developments in Work Councils were termed as "quality control circles" designed in the 1950s by American managers, for the Japanese firms to improve the quality and production of the firms. They again reemerged in America, because of their success. The idea behind these quality control circles is that the goals of quality and production are mutually beneficial to both workers and management, and therefore, both groups should come together in a cooperative atmosphere to seek ways to improving and increasing quality production (Albrecht, 1983: 53). These councils comprised voluntary group of workers who meet, discuss and exchange ideas, to improve efficiency, production, quality, working conditions, and solve workers problems.

There is a high probability that, unlike the Western European work councils, quality control circles may prove to be a system that can control the management.

These three forms of worker participation tried to integrate the workers and management. These systems have tried to deal with the issues of productivity, security of employment, and working conditions. But, there are others that tried to deal with the issues in a different manner. Humanization of work is such a form of participation in the workplace that is directly concerned with the improvement of working conditions at the shop floor level. This movement to reform the workplace at the shop floor began in the 1960s. It happened as a result of the concern, shown by the governments, the workers, and also the management, due to various reasons: increased absenteeism, low production, high turnover rates. Several reasons were cited for such abnormalities, such as problem in the structure of the work: "a division of labor that was so detailed that a worker felt alienated from the entire labor process, physiological as well as psychological hazards on the job, and the rapid introduction of new technology into the workplace" (ibid: 54).

A study made in 1972 ("Work in America") pointed out that a number of workers in American firms were dissatisfied with the quality of their lives as workers. It was causing high discontentment at all occupational levels.

That is why, workplace reforms were seen as one of the best solution to the growing problems in the workplace. How to carry forward the reforms in the workplace?

One possible manner would be replacing the assembly line with the semi-autonomous work group, job rotation, flexible work schedules. These measures aimed at fusing tasks that were separated and provided a meaningful situation in the workplace. Again, if the workers are provided discretionary powers to carry out the day-to-day activities, it may increase the autonomy and improve the overall job satisfaction.

In the late 1960s and early 1970s, humanization of work projects was introduced in many firms, in both America and Europe. These projects were invited by the managements of the firms. This was done with the prime motive to increase productivity, stop absenteeism and decrease labor turnover. Trade unions were skeptical about this form of workplace participation. They could anticipate the outcome of such measures, because it was designed to increase workers' satisfaction with their everyday surroundings without disturbing the authority structure of the enterprise.

In some situations, these measures were initiated to keep at bay political unionization. That is why trade unions in America and Europe were less enthusiastic about the reforms in the workplace. It was the joint labor management project that drew interest from the trade unions. It was also observed that in the absence of unionization, where management introduced reforms, their appraisal still remains negative. "Where unions" and employees are actively involved in deciding what these changes in the workplace will be, support for such experiments has steadily grown (Hanlon, 1982).

Another work environment reform is closely related to workplace reform. Work environmental reform is different in the sense that it has defined the role of safety and health at work. It also pressed for more democracy in the workplace. In support of the reform movement, several Acts were passed, in different countries across Europe and in America. The Swedish Work Environment Act (1978) stresses that work conditions shall be adapted to the physical and psychological abilities of human beings. Then, the Norwegian Work Environment Act stressed on inclusion of technology, production systems and related factors.

Even countries like the Netherlands have followed suit; the Netherlands Employment Conditions Act (1980) deals with worker isolation and the social aspects of the work environment building on the substantial body of research on psycho-social aspects of work life (Asplund, 1981). In the US, the Occupational Safety and Health Administration (OSHA) stipulates to improve health standards, initiated training and education progress, and sought worker unions' involvement in the process.

The expression of the work environment reform movement is primarily to recognize that workers should be able to participate in decisions related to health and safety, as well as introduction of new technology in the workplace. Thus, democratizing the workplace has become a concern to expand the worker's rights in the workplace.

Self-management is another way of looking at democratic workplace. Here the management of the enterprise is in the hands of workers or their representatives. Workers have the final say in decision making. The Yugoslav's model of workplace democracy follows the self-management system. Before going deep into it, we need to know few things about workers' self-management system. In this system, workers may participate in some form of stock ownership in their company, and still not get any voting power within the firm, for instance, the ESOPs in America.

In these plans, an Employee Stock Ownership Trust (ESOT) is set up which borrows money from the bank and transfers this money to the corporation. In return for the loan, the corporation transfers a certain amount of corporate stock to the trust. Part of the corporate profits each year goes to the trust for repayment of the loan. Shares are released to workers equal to the percentage of the loan paid off. These shares can be cashed in by the workers when they leave the firm. It is very much apparent that the goal of ESOPs has been to provide tax benefits to management rather than to increase worker influence through ownership or voting powers. Repayment of the loan is tax free because it is regarded as a pension contribution and deferred labor compensation.

The unreleased shares are not voting stock of the employees, and voting is entrusted on a trust committee set up by the bank, and not on the employees. Besides, the stock amount held within the trust varies according to the needs of management. It is very much apparent that though ESOP workers share the same amount of profits of the company, but it never increases the power of the workers (Dawson, 1978; Industrial Cooperative Association, 1978).

ESOPs are far removed from the democratic workplace practice that workplace should provide. Producer cooperatives, another symbol of workers' participation, are somewhat closest to workers' ownership. These cooperatives have been there in the US and Western Europe for a long time. Due to heightened economic crisis, there has been a revival of producer cooperatives in the US and also in Great Britain. In order to save their jobs, workers have collectively tried to buyout plants before they shut down (Strauss, 1979). That is why support for workers being owners has been increasingly generated. Since then, there has been an increasing amount of support for the concept of workers being owners (Russell, 1982). Less attention has been paid to the idea of workers being managers, and that is why workers' self-management, which stood for radical transformation, was met with resistance.

All the categories of industrial democracy have argued for workers' control over decision-making power within the firms. People were not just contended with democracy within the firm; rather they felt, that it should broaden its reach. Thus, economic democracy deals more with increasing the decision-making powers in the economy as a whole. It is the control the workers will have over capital.

The economic democracy does not imply participation in the distribution of capital. It is not just sharing the company profit with the individual workers, but instead implies actual participation in the decision-making process, which stems from the ownership of capital. Thus, we can see it as the third angle in the democratization of political, social, and economic democracy.

The well-known economic democracy, the Swedish Wage Earner Investment Funds, called for the transfer of a certain percentage of company profits into shares to be collectively owned and controlled by labor and its representatives (Asard, 1980; Hancock, 1981). This form, keeping apart its controversy, has set a new trend in worker participation. According to Albrecht, this movement in Sweden has undergone revisions, and the history of its development is a reflection of changes in the political as well as economic situation within Sweden.

In the United States, labor movement was interested in finding out how the vast amount of capital in the employee pension funds is being invested. Due to high growth in plant closings and run-away shops in the United States, there is pending legislation in a number of states to give workers and communities more control over the investment/disinvestment decisions of companies in their locality (Deutsch and Albrecht, 1983). The labor movement's quest to know about the utilization of the capital from the employee pension funds was a symptom of democratic behavior in workplace practices.

Economic democracy met lots of resistance, on the part of management, and it touches the most vital element of management system, i.e. the core of capital ownership. But we have to recognize that it is a movement that argued for greater representation of workers in the decision-making process. This definitely affects their lives, both at the work and in the larger social context. Such consciousness made a breakthrough, at the time of economic crisis that the western industrial countries were facing.

It is a real, conscious field of development to which most of the European countries, as well as United States, took unnecessary steps in a variable manner, towards expanded employee rights. It is an established fact that only real and potential forms of industrial and economic democracy result in an increased decision-making power on the part of labor with a corresponding decrease in managerial prerogatives and capital ownership (Albrecht, 1983: 59). Whatever change has occurred shouldn't merely be a face-lifting one, and rather can be considered as real, and incorporative.

The humanization of work projects in the United States can be seen as a way for the management of the firms, to introduce changes in the workplace for better work atmosphere, to increase labor productivity, but relatively keeping all decision-making power with the management.

### Economic and Industrial Democracy: An Analysis

Industrial and economic democracy has resulted in the restructuring of the workplace. Such restructuring narrowed down managerial prerogatives in decision making, and this led to expansion of workers' rights. Collective bargaining, another way of looking at workplace democracy, stipulated not only the economic conditions of employment, but the non-economic aspects of work as well.

Work councils in many countries in Europe were considered to be the best form of industrial democracy. Similarly, the humanization projects were welcomed across Western Europe and North America. Though self-management has occupied least important role in this movement, its multiple forms were very much visible. Economic democracy has broadened the field of democratic workplace practices, i.e. from the firm to the whole economy. These different perspectives try to shift the emphasis from the distribution of economic resources to distribution of power.

This movement though happened sometimes during the period of economic growth. Amidst its growth and dilemma, it was established that all these forms of democratic workplace practices have provided a way to solve the problems that exist in a workplace.

## Justification for Workplace Democracy

The best way is to identify the relationship between the organization of work, workplace, the labor market and democratic values on which the work principles are based. In the opinion of Mundlak (2013), democracy at workplace is characterized by three components: the existence of a community, the participatory processes that secure a roughly equal distribution of effective power among the community's constituents, and the acknowledgement of the need for substantive rights to protect individuals and groups from unwarranted use of power by others.

For a democratic institution to flourish, the existence of a community is a must. Some state that the workplace practices are instrumental to the democratic quality of the state, whereas, others feel that workplace is the primary unit, within which democratic practices must take place. Various forms of workers' ownership whether it is the Yugoslav model of workers-owned economy, workers' co-operatives or ESOPs, all aim to establish a community in which all the constituents are workers. There are other forms of community, like the multi-constituency forum, which is responsible for the interest of various stakeholders. The existence of the community makes the governance system democratic.

Is the workplace community different from the nation-state? In a broader perspective, it is different. Workplace community is embedded in a social, political and economic environment and the constituents have certain limitations. Here, the community has to compete according to the dictates of the market. This is just not enough; they have to be a part of the broader economic system, where rules of entry and exit are determined by one voice and loyalty.

A democratic constitutional order must prevail within the community in a firm. Mundlak opined that rules that guide the constitutional order of the firm may be found in the company's by-laws, in external regulation (such as laws that mandate co-determination on the board or work councils within the firm), or in collective agreement (basic agreements that set up employee participation). In a democratic order, every individual should have the same degree of power to affect the outcomes of the firm's decision-making process.

If we argue from a conventional point of view, a democratic order is always associated with voting, i.e. One person one vote 'OPOV'. Some of the workplace democratic practices, like self-management in workers' cooperatives, shareholders in ESOP firms, voting rules on board of directors in which workers are represented, or collective agreements, are linked to voting practices.

Voting rules in general, and OPOV in particular, cannot be an adequate measure to secure a democratic order. It is likely to work in small ideological cooperatives. Moreover, voting is such a power in which some succeed in overriding the power of others; it can be a feasible method for self-governance, but it cannot deal with the actual distribution of effective power in the community. Again, in a workplace where there are multiple communities, OPOV has to give up, in favor of collective power of a constituency which intertwines with the distribution of individual power with the community.

Voting may be one of the institutional forms that allow some to exert power over others. Even applying principles of subsidiary to democracy may encourage an active democratic environment. Again, the negative use of power can be overridden, with positive forms of power that encourage vibrant democratic environment.

The simplistic element in voting may turn it to be major drawback. Voting is in fact removed from host of market practices, like subcontracting, temporary, hourly work, off-shoring and informal patterns of work. Moreover, one single form of institutional practices cannot be the most essential form of democracy. Rather, it should be inclined in each and every level—from the design of production, the division of labor and work processor, organizational structure and political representation. If we reflect upon democratic commitment, it is the privilege of some, at the price of others.

In order to practice democracy at the workplace, then representative democracy must be complemented with or replaced with deliberative or participatory forms of democratic practices. These practices require a system that is measured by its success in forging trust and legitimacy (Fox, 1974).

Here trust is primarily concerned with the relationship between the individual constituents of the community (Offe, 1999).

To practice a democratic constitutional order within the workplace, the urgent requirement is to enable the constituents in a unitary or a plural workplace environment to engage in self-governance. To totally rely on process would be risky. It is found that democracy with its additional component of fundamental rights can protect individuals and collectivities from all forms of tyranny. But all fundamental rights cannot enter the constitutional order of the firm. That is why the concern should be those rights that can define the basic structure of the democratic community.

Rights are themselves a form of power and the distinction between the process-based components of the democratic order and the substantive protection of rights should not be overstated. Both have positive and negative implications; both span process and substance. Functionally, they are used in different situations and are part and parcel of the democratic order (Mundlak, 2013: 15).

The constituents' rights draw their origin from two sources, namely the exogenous, from the workplace itself, and from within. Exogenous are general legislations, industrial custom, and collective bargaining, applied at both the national and sectoral levels. The other one applies to company policy, localized collective bargaining and individual contracts. Again, both the rights may not be equal. A tradeoff between the degree of protection and the legitimacy of right can be mitigated to the extent that it needs to be enforced and protected. Therefore, if there are no elaborate mechanisms for the enforcement of rights, then these rights have to be protected by internal mechanisms.

Steven Lukes has put forwarded a radical view of power. Though he analyzed the three dimensions of power, his first dimension of power was positivist in outlook where the actors of the power game participated in decision making where influence over others could be easily understood. Dahl (1961) states that Lukes' concept of power draws an intuitive idea of power, and it is the exercise of power which is central to the three-dimensional view of power.

Dahl's goal was to determine for each decision which participants had initiated alternatives that were finally adopted, had vetoed alternatives initiated by others, or had proposed alternatives that were turned down. These actions were then tabulated as individual "successes" or "defeats". The participants with the greatest proposition of successes out of the total number of successes were then considered to be the most influential.

It is also observed that among the pluralists (Dahl, Polsby, Wolfinge and others), "power" and "influence" are used changeably. When the pluralists refer to observable behavior in identifying power, it points at the pluralists' stress on decision making as central to power. It can be argued that Dahl (1985) analyzed power after carefully examining a series of concrete decisions. Polsby (1974) argues that those decisions prevail out of which individuals or groups have more power in social life, because a direct conflict between actors leads to a situation, say an experimental test of their capacities to affect outcomes.

Decisions should involve both actual and observable conflicts. The pluralists speak of the decisions being taken about issues in selected key areas. According to Dahl, it is necessary but possibly not a sufficient condition that the key issue should involve actual disagreement in preferences among two or more groups. In his book *Who Governs?* (1961), Dahl is sensitive to the operation of power or influence in the absence of conflict. He even writes that a person's overt or covert influence is apparent when successfully initiated against the opposition by other or initiates a policy when no opposition appears. According to the one-dimensional view of power, conflict is assumed to take place between preferences, which are consciously, exhibited in a clear manner and discovered by observing people's behavior. Besides, the pluralists assume that interests are policy preferences, because conflict of interest is at par with conflict of preferences.

Lukes states that one-dimensional view of power involves focus on behavior in the making of decisions on issues over which there is an observable conflict of interests, seen as expressive policy preferences and revealed by political participants (Lukes, 1974: 19)

Bachrach and Baratz (1962) challenged Dahl's approach and argued for leaving out of consideration, "What does not happen", in decision-making settings, namely, those issues that are unwittingly neglected or consciously excluded from the agenda. Power can be exercised through non-issues and non–decision making as well. For Lukes, this is the second dimension of power: control of the agenda (David, 2005).

The two-dimensional power involves both decision making and non–decision making. Bachrach and Baratz argued that, for the pluralists, boundaries are set by the political system being observed, or rather by the elites. For the pluralists, those boundaries are set by the political system.

The pluralists argue that boundaries are set by the political system being observed, or set by elites within it. But for Bachrach and Baratz, it is important to identify the political issues, that non–decision making prevents from actually being done.

Though there are crucial differences between the two-dimensional view with the pluralists, there is a significant common feature between the two as the pluralists hold that power in decision making is very crucial. But two-dimensional views are inadequate on three counts.

In the first count, though it is a critic of behaviourism, it still follows behaviourism or studies actual overt behaviour and tries to exclude all potential issues from the political agenda to the paradigm of the decision, and it is quite misleading. In this sense, groups, institutions exclude potential issues from the political process.

On the second count, the two-dimensional view of power is inadequate, in its association of power with the actual observable conflict. Insistence on actual conflict as essential to power will not work, because, two types of power may not involve conflict, especially, manipulation and authority, which Bachrach and Baratz have conceived as agreement based upon reason. Again, the insistence on actual and observable conflict will not work, because it is not satisfactory to predict that power is only exercised in situations of conflict.

On the third count, it is the inadequacy which is closely linked to the insistence on non-decision-making power that exists where there are grievances, which are not addressed in the political process.

Lukes found the two-dimensional view as a major advance over the one-dimensional view. He was influenced by Gramsci's notion of hegemony. He argued that the third dimension notion of power consists of deeply rooted forms of political socialization, which unwittingly follow the dictates of power even against their best interests. Lukes made a conceptual shift in his analysis of power. He found few limitations in his previous conceptualization.

First, the broad understanding of power should not limit to the visible exercise of power, for one needs to regard power as a capacity or ability that may or may not be explicitly activated in given situations.

Second, power should not limit to asymmetric power relations, or "power area". It also needs to deal with "power to". Lukes admits that not all power is negative. Some forms of power can be positive, productive, and transformative, and thus domination is just one type of "power over".

In the third conceptualization, he includes several types of "power over". He argues that power over other can be "productive, transformative, authoritative and compatible with dignity, even for dependents under certain conditions" (Lukes, 1974: 3).

Fourth, Lukes assumed that actors in asymmetrical relations have unitary and opposing interests. Later, he argued that actors have multiple interests and some might be conflictual and there can be multiple actors, and with divergent interests.

### Workplace Democracy and Proceduralization

Workplace democracy and proceduralization of labor law is very much related. Adaptation of traditional means with workplace democracy is very complex, but it shows a new direction. For instance, the case of the port workers, or industrial action around the world, and solidarity with the plight of the Liverpool dock worker at the time of privatization, all pointed towards proceduralization of the laws (Castree, 2000).

New process-based labor law emerged at multiple levels. Various studies were conducted to study new labor law. Estlund (2003) emphasized developments in the United States, and Davial Dooring offered an account of the Canadian Law, and developments within European states were also observed. Change in the labor law has not only affected the organizational structure of the single firm, but also affected supply chains, trade arrangements and non-territorial developments.

Disempowerment in one firm was balanced with the positive power accumulated through collective action. Even the right to association in various countries made global alliances somewhat possible. And ILO took the responsibility to promote the right, and this indicated another institutional intervention. In this context, we can refer to the spheres of influences, ranging from individual action at the workplace to the agendas to promote core labor right by ILO including freedom of association.

There are many new procedures of labor law. Even with employment, there is a tendency to turn towards process-based laws. There are many issues in employment that the new law can set certain rational procedures. Like the level of minimum wage and the number of working hours, dismissal from the job with due process hearing, layoffs, and workers' privacy with clear guidelines and consultation with work councils. Company should also conduct regular self-audits to guarantee compliance with wage requirements as well as occupational health and safety measures. There are other important issues, anti-discrimination and equal opportunities, which require explicit well-documented diversity programmmes (Dobbin et al., 2011). Such developments may set a new trend in the proceduralization in the workplace. Sexual harassment is also a matter of internal monitoring and enforcement within the firm (Cohen, 2002). Thus, all the above-mentioned dimensions together with regulations in the national, international and transnational law indicate new processes at the workplace.

CSR gathers an edge over, when the local, national, transnational proceduralization of law takes place. When the codes of conduct developed by the companies are complemented with international standards, then the CSR of the firm tends to move towards a democratic outlook. Some of these standards set substantive norms (SA8000), while others require corporations to comply with their own self-imposed standards (such as ISO 26000; Gilbert et al., 2010).

Proceduralization does play an important role in establishing democracy at the workplace. New proceduralizations are coming to the foray, where formal institutions are absent. All organizations are to some extent regulated by substantive standards even though workers are situated in different territories of work. Even the informal sector has certain standards of regulatory coverage.

Process-based standards seek to introduce what result-oriented standards avoid—forging a deliberative encounter between individual and groups who hold different interests so that they can dispute the norms, listen, use force, reason, decide to litigate or even strike, sabotage, or cooperate.

It is found that new proceduralization that takes place at multiple levels automatically creates compliance in norms. It was assumed that workers in a democratic firm would replicate into democracy at the public sphere. But it was not made clear, as to how it was possible. And processes like marketization and globalization changed the structure of the organization of work, but the connection became very thin.

The emergence of process-based law draws upon norms of different kinds that attract similar ideal of visibility or compatibility; it may lead to congruence at different levels, i.e. the enterprise with its workers, the state with trade unions or work centres, the state and other states, international organizations and its member states, NGOs, trade unions, civil society organizations, MNCs and its customers, suppliers, and financial institutions.

Due to the emergence of multiple levels of process-based law, no one can take it that workers are constituents of a stable work community. Lacklau and Chantal (1985) argued that a new form has emerged; work and the workplace are part and parcel of a broader engagement in which agents of different types take an active part in the transformation practices. The broader engagement between different agents has created change in the proceduralization process.

Several studies have been conducted to examine issues related to labor within the firms. On such study was conducted to examine the self-monitoring system of Nike, a sportswear and apparel MNC. Locke and Romis (2010) have done an in-depth study of the working conditions of two plants located in the same country (Mexico); though both the plants scored perfect scores for compliance mechanisms, very different realities in terms of working conditions and rights existed in both the firms, especially with regard to wage systems, working hours, and employees' representation.

One factory is located in Estado de Mexico, owned by a Mexican family who has been running the factory since 1955. By then, the North American Free Trade Agreement (NAFTA) had been signed. The group started exporting since then. It developed a new strategy and invested on state of the art technology and trained its technical operation and administrative staff. The other factory was located in Western Mexican State, with a regional office in Mexico City, and run by a Taiwanese group. The Taiwanese group has been manufacturing fabrics for other companies, and it started producing for Nike in 1991.

Now, both the factories manufacture the same product for Nike, pay the same legal minimum wage, have the same informal skill promotion policies, and the labor forces in both the plants are unionized. A more detailed comparison was made between the plants, based on comparison of employee satisfaction, worker participation in production-related issues, work hours and over time. It was found that the plant run by the Mexican family offered higher wages to the workers, than the Taiwanese one. Employees are more satisfied, and they participated in decision making affecting the production. In terms of employee satisfaction too, workers in Mexican family–owned plant was satisfied than the Taiwanese-owned plant.

In the first one, employees work in team, operate more than one type of sewing machine, and are responsible for routine maintenance of the equipment. In the other one, work is fixed and workers perform the same operation over the course of work. The work is highly routinized and repetitive.

Workers in the Mexican-owned plant participate in decisions affecting the production targets, scheduling, but in the Taiwanese-owned plant, workers need to follow orders from above, and are not permitted to give their input in the production planning. The relationship between different levels of work is hierarchical. In terms of working hours, workers at the Mexican-owned plant had a better work schedule than the Taiwanese-owned plant.

In Locke and Romis' opinion, the level of worker satisfaction in the Mexican-owned plant was higher than in the hierarchical one.

Workplace practices and democracy have clear linkages. Be it governance, participatory regulator, or international labor standards, all try to enforce a system of equality among the workers and between the workers and the management of the firms.

A study on similar lines (Locke and Romis, 2010) was also conducted by Rodriguez-Garavito (2005) on textile plants in Mexico and Guatemala. After a detailed field research with different constituents of the firm (union leaders, factory owner, independent, commercial monitor, brand representations, and labor advocates), it was found that the state is not a reliable enforcer of labor laws. Even the National and International labor advocacy organizations hold a pessimistic view of the prospects for improving the state's regulatory capacity.

Countries like Guatemala face the fundamental infrastructure problems, but Mexico can rely on a state apparatus. If the state apparatus functions well, then labor rights can achieve a much higher level of compliance. But ironically, the situation was not so compliant.

Besides, state incapacity, corrupt practices, and the corporatist relations between the state, capital and co-opted organized labor have also provided an incentive for workers, unions, to experiment with the codes of conduct. In Mexico, corruption has taken such a toll, that it had involved extreme cases of bribing labor judges and also inspectors.

In the case of Guatemala, an extreme form of repression of unions, and a system of appointing former labor inspectors as heads of human resources in apparel factories gave an appalling picture of anomalies in the system. The reason for experimentation with codes of conduct could be a way of opposition to worker organizations (worker unions), by the factory owners and managers in the garment industry. In fact, in Guatemala, industrialists came together to fight against any form of unionization in the factory.

Well, the application of the code of conduct was a real issue. The effect of monitoring system on workers' capacity to organize, and also on the durable improvements in working conditions was very important. Garavito was interested in third-party monitoring, and it involves a code of conduct formulated by a multi-stakeholder organization, due to lack of credibility of first-party monitoring, where a single manufacturing monitors the compliance mechanism and second-party monitoring, where a business association formulates a code of conduct; but the third-party monitoring is independent, comprehensive transparent, and sanctions are non-compliant.

The code of conduct may sometimes lead to the rise of international communities of accountability. And, as such, it can act as a check to the growth of power of transnational companies. There was a growth of workers' power in the form of unions, global unions, NGOs, local pressure and local processes of deliberation and negotiation that involved Guatemalan and Mexican unions, labor support organization, and state authorities as well as the international actors sent as representatives to the factories to directly mediate in the negotiation process. Hence, external pressure, local dialogue, resulted in participation of mix of actors in the negotiation process.

This study pointed at the emergence of initiatives and mechanisms involving different actors, and also incorporation of system into the monitoring schemes that can facilitate workers' organization and gain in working conditions. With the independent monitoring organization, the locations of the supplier factories were disclosed. Even publishing the audit reports proved to be conducive to international and local engagement into monitoring system. To gather reliable data, it is necessary for systematically incorporating process of informed international and local engagement into monitoring system.

Garavito argued that to enforce more accountability in the textile plants in Mexico and Guatemala, the role of external agents—like trade unions, social movements—is very important. He was also concerned about the rights of the workers, so that they can voice their opinions and make their demands. He also observed that mere deliberation is not enough, for high levels of inequalities persisted within the firm. That's why, he proposed that support from different communities and representation, as well as maintaining minimum international and national labor standards is necessary.

Garavito also pointed out that without involving the external agents (NGOs, social movement), a complete responsibility on the part of the firms toward their workers cannot be ascertained.

In order to make democracy a workplace norm, it has to be endorsed at all levels, be it at the regional, national or transnational level. Several studies have been carried out to understand the enforcement mechanisms at the transnational level. One such study was made by Barenberg (2009) to examine transnational enforcement mechanisms based on trade laws, international labor standards, measurements of private–self enforcement measures.

Though he observed the advantage of the multiple enforcement systems, he was also aware about their weaknesses. After thorough analysis, he found that the urgent requirement has to be integrating regulatory techniques with components of democracy.

Barenberg has suggested few measures for the integrating regulatory techniques: (a) the bodies that formulate the criteria and performance measures and that oversee the investigation staff should comprise worker representatives and jurists and (b) prior to worker representatives' and jurists' promulgation of the criteria and measures, other interested and knowledgeable actors, such as domestic enforcement officials, specialists in production systems, specialists in occupational health, managerial representatives, representatives of the informal sector, women's organizations and village associations, should participate in the deliberation process. In fact, workers should actively participate in the enforcement process, and hence, enhance the administrative, and the workers' capacities.

These analyses has emphasized on democratic practices in the workplace. But, it has not relegated these practices to any form of regulations. They have identified such interactions of different actors within and between workplaces, and such interactions differ from the traditional concept of workplace as an ambiguous terrain. It didn't have a clear picture of engagements between different actors of work.

The above-mentioned studies emphasized on workplace practices–democracy nexus, in a transnational setting, but Mundlak argued that they are not just limited to such terrain and can be also placed in a local setting. The state, the firm, the community and the civil society are not same, but all are in a way moving towards a similar set of values.

When we think about democratic institutions at work, it is clearly found that the community at work is normally disassociated from the place of work. Democratic process is always the central focus of the democratic order, drawing mostly upon legal concepts that govern the public sphere. Rights are essential components of democracy. These include right to work, right to participate, right to prelists, right to demonstrate, right to speak and protest within and outside the work communities and substantive rights that de-commodify the workers' achievements.

While trying to work out an applicable model of workplace democracy, certain cautious notes have to be adopted. We have to keep in mind that process-based law cannot substitute and replace substantive standards. It can aid institutions, or individuals, or groups, who can take part in these struggles, which in fact makes power effective eventually. The rights component of workplace democracy is very significant, and relevant, as it was from the beginning.

Workplace democracy is not denying the significance of free market or regulation or distribution mechanism; rather, it should be seen as an added value to the positive effect of deliberation, and economic inclusion. These elements are translated into institutions that seek to expand capacities for impacting further change, for empowerment of individuals and groups and for creating bases of power that are sustained over time. Some fail while others succeed.

Therefore, it is an established fact that the alternative to process-based law is not consistently effective in changing the power structures. The command and control regulation, pulling of property rights sharply when the notion of community is ambiguous, cannot be empirically tested. The labor market inequalities, positive benefits of demand and the externalities are as significant today, as they were before. All this analysis does not render the normative path of workplace democracy, or even the process-based law to be an archaic institution. Rather, there is an ongoing strong adaptation to the changing trend of the state and enterprises.

Workplace democracy and the current debates on regulation, governance of the labor market and the organization of human resources management should not be perceived as a matter of baggage.

## Fordism and Post-Fordism

Whether it is Fordism or post-Fordism, workplace practice is an integral part of it. It is a known fact that for different sectors, especially, the manufacturing sector across all the advanced economies, the lean production has emerged as a technical success to the just-in-case labor process of Fordism. Well, one can ask as to what will happen to the service sector, which comprises the majority of employment in post-Fordist economies? Then, a complex labor process along with simpler forms has evolved.

Vidal (2011) argued that valid permutations and combinations of post-Fordist employment relations, the erosion of the Fordist institutional framework, and forces of international financialization and deindustrialization and several other forces have led to the decadence of the Fordist system.

Indeed, Gramsci's broadening of the hegemony theory led to the emergence of Fordism. Hegemonistic perspective of Gramsci focused on political and moral leadership that incorporates the working class by the capitalist class. Gramsci found Taylorism and mechanization as too divisive.

Like Gramsci, political economist scholars, like Michel Aglietta (2000), refer to Fordism as a form of society that is based on a system of mass production, with extreme form of task fragmentation with a hierarchical authoritative system. In Aglietta's opinion, Fordism was not just a system of production, but a new form of capitalist mode of consumption. But Fordism came into crisis in the late 1960s and early 1970s, due to decreasing productivity and profit rates.

The concept of post-Fordism did not appeal to scholars, who were studying the changes in the production system. Why the concept of post-Fordism did not pick up? Probably, the period after Fordism is characterized by an increasing disconnectedness—between traditional welfare industry and labor market policies and between labor process and employment relations (Thomson, 2003). Thomson, also identified that, there was zero commitment of the employers towards the workers, probably because of the pressures from the competitive environment, credit markets, and too much of emphasis on shareholders' value.

Alternatives to post-Fordism developed immediately after Fordism failed. One of the earliest alternatives was the socio-technical system approach.

It developed from the studies carried out in the 1950s at the Tavistock Institute in Britain, which focused on how to humanize factory work (Trist, 1981). There are other models of post-Fordism, like flexible specification which is based on the Italian industrial system. Flexible specialization is a system where highly skilled workers and flexible machinery create a diverse range of high-quality products. This happens within a decentralized production community that encourages workers to be cooperative and innovative.

In Germany, due to strong labor unions and workplace co-determination laws, the German industry was forced to develop a system based on maintaining craft skills and increasing organization flexibility. Thus, it encouraged on customization and quality, rather than on standardization and price. According to Herrigel and Sabel (1999), in the 1990s firms began to experiment with new types of teamwork, but still in the late 1990s lean production made a strong entry in the German industry.

But in Germany, socio-technical systems have been adopted in a piecemeal way which focused on productivity and without any humanist agenda (Schumann, 1998). It was an all in all rejection of Fordism. Such a new system was applied in the system of production at Volvo. As a result of the high employment rate in Sweden in the 1980s, the Volvo company had trouble in appointing and retaining workers in the Taylorized assembly line. Volvo transformed the Fordist labor process into an entirely new system, known as the Swedish model. This model was characterized by long cycle of work lasting for several hours, as against Taylorized short job cycles. It was argued that the plants of Volvo far exceeded the productivity and quality levels, than the larger production factory. Due to adoption of lean production system, in the same plant, it has accelerated the productivity of the factory.

Lean production is a post-Fordist system and also known as Toyota Production System, or Just in Time (JIT) production, or the Japanese model of Toyotaism. Lean production system is a demand-driven production and it is based on continuous flow. Though most of the scholars continued to vouch for one or two post-Fordist alternatives, but by the end of the 1990s, it was established that lean production has an edge over others.

In the context of Fordist or post-Fordist system, it was observed that there is a clear distinction between the labor process and the employment relations (Wood, 1991; Thompson, 2003). Labor process refers to the concrete organization of tasks, processes and relations in the workplace. But employment relation is wage related, i.e. there are norms related to wage, and the structure and governance system of the firm. The distinction seems to be analytical, but they are closely related.

The post-Fordist labor process is less restricted with a total emphasis on standardization. But in particular situations, if a certain degree of autonomy is allowed, then there will be conflict with standardization. With the application of lean production system, there are changes in the employment relation. Due to internationalization of production, wage becomes a source of competition. Other elements of change in employment relation are the vertical disintegration of large companies through outsourcing, sub-contracting and down-signing. Even there can be decline of internal labor markets and a growth of market-mediated employment.

Herrigel and Wittke (2004) stated that vertical disintegration and labor recommendation, through market-mediated employment relation, have been witnessed in the advance economies of the world. These changes are pushing towards a new form of financialization. Lazonick and O'Sullivan (2000) opined that these changes led to the growth of shareholders value of corporate governance.

The just-in-case labor process of Fordism was disintegrated due to several reasons. First, it could be the diversity among employer practices, and its resultant disconnection between the labor process and broader approach to employment relations. In fact, there is also less coherence between core elements of employment relations. A very significant development was different aspects of the Fordist model of employment relation were disintegrated in different degrees in different places. The lean model of production has succeeded Fordism, due to technical superiority. But variability in the post-Fordist system can be observed across individual firms, which must have changed various aspects of employment relations.

Though such transformations are part of post-Fordism, but diversities do exist in the advanced capitalist economies. The process of internationalization and financialization has affected all the economies of the world. Therefore, it has to be noted that internationalization, a structural source of wage, has become a full-fledged source of competition. The renewal wage competition may act as a general pressure on firms, and as such, this may prompt firm-level employment relations.

It is not only the manufacturing sector, but service sector too was affected by the Post-Fordist trend. Post-industrialization did to the service sector, as Post-Fordism did in the manufacturing sector. It focuses on the growth of the knowledge economy, i.e. the information and communication technologies. There is a growth of externalization model of employment relations across sectors, primarily driven by the shareholder value model of corporate governance. Externalization has set in changes in manufacturing especially in the liberal economies of the world. Ironically, externalization of employment is distinct and separate from lean system. Another significant point is that post-Fordist employment relation has led to the collapse of internal labor markets and growth of dead-end jobs.

The effect of externalization and anti-unionism, market-mediated employment, off-shoring was common to both the services, and the manufacturing sector. The effect may vary in intensity across different countries, depending upon the nature of resilience of national institutions.

Regarding, work organization, the lean system is common across manufacturing and service sector: "Lean practice such as team work, continuous flow models, value stream mapping, waste elimination practices and various tools for work rationalization and standardization increasingly being applied in the service sector" (Womack, 2005; Allway and Corbett, 2002; Staats and Upton, 2009). Lean principles are also applied in services like fast food. With regard to the service sector, wherever the labor process consists of multiple steps, lean tools can be applied. For instance, in simple service-sector labor processes, such as retail sales, with extreme competitive pressure, there can be an ascendancy of the shareholder's value model of corporate governance.

The diversity of work arrangement under post-Fordism should be analyzed in the context of broad pressures, and dominant tendencies, for instance, the call centre work. It is generally found that call centre work tends to have highly standardized work routines. It is usually subject to pressure for intensification of the work (Taylor and Ban, 1999)

In Germany, when managers are interested to pursue very individualized and Taylorized strategies, and if there are unions with effective participation rights (work councils), then work organizations are managed with post-Fordist strategies, with high-level team monitoring, and worker discretion over law .

Doellgast (2010) argues that even with high levels of worker discretion, and minimal individualized practices, the labor process was subject to acute pressures. Even if the service sector employment relations were organized in post-Taylorist line, employment relations were going to be reshaped by the externalized employment model characterized by vertical disintegration, market-mediated employment, anti-unionism, and individualized employment relations.

## Fordist and Post-Fordist System and Democratic Practices in Workplace

Fordism was somewhat nearer to Taylorism, plus mechanization. Taylorism signified separation between the organization of the production process, which was the domain of technical officer, and "the execution of standardized and formally prescribed tasks" (Lipietz, 1997: 2).

It is to be noted that in such system of production process, the involvement of direct labor was not necessary in carrying out the task of the technical office. Besides, gains in productivity in this system would be having its counterpart in financial investment from profits, and also from the increased purchasing power of wage laborers. A vast socialization of revenues through the welfare state assured a permanent financial income of wage laborer.

Democratic workplace is supposed to characterize, by existence of a community, a participatory atmosphere, equal distribution of effective power, some substantive rights to protect individuals and preventing groups from unwarranted use of power.

The workplace community is different from the nation-state, its social, economic, and political milieu is also different from the nation-state. It takes part in a broader competitive market, and its ability to compete is judged according to the dictates of the market. Such arguments try to identify the differences between democracy in the context of nation-state, and democracy in the workplace. But these arguments cannot understate the view that democracy cannot be practiced in the workplace. Issues are there within this domain. It is the indistinct boundaries of the workplace that might become a crucial factor in the gradual disappearance of the democratic workplace. Then, such situations need not be apprehended as a universal phenomenon.

Braverman (1979) condemned capitalism, for de-skilling work and increasing managerial control over workers, especially when there is a high level Taylorization of work. But with post-Fordism, a new force developed with high-level business growth, with higher skill, but more fulfilling work (for the workers).

Fordist production can be referred to the labor process prevalent in the Henry Ford's car factories. It is characterized by unskilled or semi-skilled work in large mass-production firms. The post-Fordist work organization, to some scholars, is more efficient and fulfilling alternative to Fordist Production. Japanese Management Technology, a post-Fordist system of organization, associated with team work, multi-skilling or multi-tasking, worker involvement schemes, departed from the Fordist production system.

Due to growing synergy between interests of labor and capital, Fordism declined. Towards mid-80s, it was sheer conviction that stressed on greater flexibility within production, more devolution of responsibility, and more cooperative management and labor relations.

The Japanese system of work organization, with high level of team working, multi-skilling had a team hierarchical structure. In fact, Womack et al. (1990) claimed that this new system of work was more challenging and fulfilling.

Authors like Womack, Jones and Roo gave a very optimistic account of Japanese management. But, there were Fordist scholars who did not appear to be that optimistic about the Japanese system, but of course, they too admitted that it is an opportunity to come out of the drudgery of Fordist labor practices.

J. Mathews commented that "work should no longer be performed in condition of anger, frustration and alienations" (1989: 1). There should be some amount of freedom and involvement in the workplace.

Japanese Management Technique or Lean Production with JIT flexibility and team working may extend the social organization of work in Japan, and the implication on labor. Sometimes, lean plants typified by large and flexible hours may end up with large amounts of overtime. Garrahan and Stewart (1992) opine that Japanese plants prefer a unitary environment. They argued that in a unitary system, workplaces are supposed to be integrated and the workers work for a common goal. There is no conflict between management and workers, and they have a disdain for trade unions. Trade unions are viewed as illegitimate to the co-operative structure of the work force. Some Japanese firms have accepted unions, but they have avoided it in the US.

It is an established fact that Lean Production gave a fundamental break from Taylorist work organizations. Various studies have been conducted to examine the effect of Lean Production. One study pointed out that workers in lean plants are less able to influence the work process (Lew Chuck and Robertson, 1996). In another study, it was found out that teamwork hardly gave little control to the workers (Dassbach, 1996). Advantages were also there in lean production, like greater job security in lean plants has been reported in the case of American transplants (Berggren, 1993: 172-3).

In Brazil, adoption of Japanese techniques led to a new change in the attitudes towards workers. It led to stable employment and, softening of attitude towards the workers (Fluey and Humphrey, 1993).

However, it has to be noted that Lean Production has been associated with "Greenfield" location, and against any independent trade union, establishing a unitary "company culture". But Lean Production is not just flexibility, greater job security, or stable employment, but has its own form of "coercion" and "consent" (Yanarella and Green, 1996).

Humanism in workplace is not restrictive. Europe had devised various methods to humanize the workplace. Such a model is the Swedish socio-technical model. It functions through a qualitatively different system of work organization, than Lean Production. It involves a considerable amount of worker autonomy and upskilling. This is not same for all the plants. For instance, in Volvo's Uddervalla plant (Cressey, 1993), workers built car with a cycle time of 2 months and 16 days, whereas it is 1 month in lean production plants (Adler and Cole, 1992). It was found that Volvo model also involves co-determination and worker participation, as against any functional forms of worker participation associated with Lean Production.

In many instances, lean production was found to be not that friendly to labor relation. An attempt was made to construct an alternative to Lean Production in Germany. Here, few powerful unions came together and forged a strategy known as "Going our own way". It stressed on team working, reasonable production goals, and workplace solidarity (Roth, 1992). This led to the "humanization of work" campaigns in the 1970s. Turner and Aver (1996) opined that co-determinist structures such as work councils played a leading role in designing group work system.

In another instance, Turner and Aver (1996) made a comparative study of the Swedish, German models with the Lean Production system (popular in the US). The study found that the first two systems offer much greater skill enhancement and control by workers than lean production.

The studies on employee relation were not just restricted to European countries. They were also popular in Latin America. Humphrey's (1993) work on Brazil inspired others to examine worker relation in other countries. Brazil has a history of low levels of mutual commitment between management and labor, and firms also had a long history of authorization management. Similar situations prevailed in South Africa. To improve the systems, both the countries offered their keenness in exporting and improving competitiveness. And both the countries looked up to the Japanese production system. In Brazil, the workers were very apprehensive, when JMT was introduced. Then, there was implicit bargain, where workers accepted change, and the management provided more stable employment, linking productivity with gain, and softening the management style by placing greater value on workers.

It was found that the Brazilian employers, despite weak unions, were unable to impose condition on labor, as severe as the Western cases probably because of the poor historic conditions in Brazil. These conditions were not permanent; management was learning to develop the evaluation and control system needed to increase pressures on workers.

South Africa too was facing a considerable economic problem in the late 1980s. That is why post-Fordist production was promoted in the manufacturing sector. Though post-Fordism did not have a universal positive assessment, but in the early 1990s it remained very influential in South Africa. The industrial strategy project proposed to improve the competitiveness of industry as protection was reduced and exports were encouraged.

The focus on post-Fordist firm-level prescription was consistent with the shift in economic policy within the democratic movement in the early 1990s. And, it was somewhat distant from a national demand-side interventionist approach, towards a more global supply-side strategy for economic reconstruction (Padayachee, 1997: 4). Timely, the report of the Industrial Strategy Project (ISP; Joffe, Kaplan, Kaplinsky and Lewis, 1995) was prepared and it aimed at increasing supply-side measures that would benefit competiveness, but it would reduce hierarchies, de-Taylorization of work, and democratize work through team building. These polices have to be supported, institutionally with a new training system, a legislative framework promoting co-operation labor–management relation. In the hindsight, the workers would benefit through high skilled, more democratic work practice, better remuneration, while the management would achieve greater productivity, flexibility, and skills, incentivizing them to move into higher value-added production. These lead to high optimism of post-Fordist work.

## Workplace Practices and Democracy: An Analysis

J.S. Mill, a pioneer in representative democracy, perceived workplace as centre for people's association that moved beyond first employment relation. It is the public association that will make people to work together, not first dependence. Dewey, a proponent of deliberative democracy, declined to accept the public–private terrain of democracy and rather argued for its application to all spheres of life.

Workplace practice, where employee participation and decision making should be a democratic norm, somewhat related to high-performance work system is a strategy primarily driven towards high productivity. But to achieve this, it should be less hierarchical, especially on crucial matters between the employers and the employees. This may also be cost intensive shifting the rights to the employees. But, in return, the firm has to take the responsibility of the future of the employees.

If we see from a historical perspective, unorganized to an organized system, organizational establishment replaced the home-based production process. But the centralized factory system curtailed the liberty of the labors. That is why, to push the production, employers faced a huge resistance from the employees. So the working environment has never been a smooth process.

Industrial revolution was not a straightforward process, but the workplace was not always a divided practice. Along with flexibility in job assignment and performance incentives, there was high commitment on the part of the employees.

Workplace was assumed to be a mechanized terrain, but there were evidence of concern by the employers towards the employees. Whether it is the National Cash Register (1890 in America) or Owen's building communities for cooperative venture, or Pullman's community concern, employees remained as centre of attention for the employers, though it was not a universal acceptance. Even in isolated location, community concern was evident for the workers.

Increase in technology due to competitive market automatically raised the labor costs. It was a complex situation for the management. Few opted for mass production (Taylorist production) to cut the labor costs, while others opted for highly skilled employees to adapt to the changing environment. The changing environment cannot first run on the Taylorian mass production system. A new system of workers–management cooperation evolved. An integrative technology-driven cooperative system was welcomed.

There was a shift in the labor market, with a decline in union membership (in mid-1950s till 1993), and also in the method of decision making in the firm. Though there has been rise in the white-collar workers, but the relationship between labor and capital was considered significant to the production system.

The classical economist treated labor the way land and capital was viewed. The employer–employee relation has not been same though, but it has affected the cause of economy, and also the society. From World War I till 1920s, an emphasis on co-opted union was visible. Internal company operated programs, to employee commitment, employee participation and satisfaction of social needs, were sought by the firms.

The workplace being a highly contested terrain, there are high levels of struggle, over the control of the labor. Edwards (1979) pointed out that the workers were treated fairly, but they have no roles in establishing the rules; still it remained a contested terrain, and workers still struggle over wages, working hours, working conditions, terms of employment. But empowerment, employee involvement, and partnership are making leeway into this contested terrain. More and more incentives are offered to the employees to improve quality and productivity, and then one can anticipate strength of democratic practice in the workplace.

Dahl looked at workplace democracy from an economic democracy perspective. According to him, it is the moral right of the employees to be part of the democratic practices inside the firm. Democratic right to labor can be also understood as autonomy in moral rights. There are others who persuade for a principle of distributive justice. The distributive justice argument focuses on the equal share of power in the firm.

Democratic workplace practices have been justified on certain significant grounds. Participation in an institutional setup should be enjoyed by all employees; it should be self-fulfilling. Work is the centre for most individuals, for both formal and informal systems have evolved within the workplace. Participation is an integral part of democratic practices in the workplace. Through participation, the worker is able to influence the community on which she or he depends for self-development; besides, democratic practice also ensures economic well-being. But without a distributive justice process, it is evident that workers still remain dependent on the organization. And, the management resists economic mobilization, distribution of economic and political powers. But distribution of income may not necessarily lead to democratization of the workplace. Workplace is an extension of the broader society, rather than being a mere institutional structure. Active participation at work may also have an effect outside the workplace, which is popularly known as spillover effect.

Workplace is the terrain for educating the workers as democratic citizens. Pateman's spillover thesis strongly asserts that if workplace structure discourages participation or fails to teach democratic skills, then there is a high probability that these workers may abstain from conventional politics. Some other argue in the same vein that learning civic activities can orient the workers towards inculcating certain skills like organizing meetings debating and speaking in public. But the most popular view of the spillover thesis is that it encourages people to understand the interest of others, and to think beyond one's self interest. This may act as a strengthening factor for practicing democracy in the workplace.

Democratic participation can be observed in worker cooperatives, whether it is small or big. Organizational degeneration restricts the controlling mechanism of a firm. It may result from external and internal pressures. There is a fear in direct democracy that in the long run, the elected leaders may try to become the ruling elite. Within a capitalist market, some sort of tensions exists between the employees and the management of the firms. Even for the cooperatives, certain principles like management hierarchy, differentials in wage benefit and minimization of wage costs deter them from functioning in their normative manner. But, to gain political efficacy and participation, co-operatives have to secure a controlling mechanism among their non-active members.

Cooperatives and democracy, though two different institutional mechanisms, tally very well by practicing equal distribution of power to a certain extent. Though cooperatives emerged as a reaction against fast economic mobilization by the capital control firms, but intense marketization and high unemployment led to the growth of cooperatives as a means to prevail upon plant closing, and also for creating new jobs. Cooperatives form an alternative institutional structure that provides a conducive atmosphere for empowerment and social change. If the cooperatives are worker controlled (worker cooperatives), then they can also increase community control of the local economy. If we go by history, in Europe, there has been a phenomenal growth of worker cooperatives, even overriding the growth of capitalist firms (mid-1970s). These cooperatives were primarily concentrated in the construction and manufacturing sector, though it was also found in the service sector. The cooperatives usually avoid capital intensive industries, as they cannot accumulate large amounts of capital, keeping apart the ESOPs.

There are few debates that pointed towards cooperative performance and profitability relation. It is found that the profitability, which is the core of any private firms, is highly unpredictable. Another significant observation was that the survival of workers' cooperative is somewhat more consistent than that of capitalist firms which cannot always make it. But one should not forget that the performance of the cooperative varies within the same sector.

Worker cooperative and democratic governance could be one way to understand democratic practice in the workplace. British worker cooperatives (Cornforth, 1988) were better off; workers had control over their work life. But there were others who were against long, monotonous routine work. Cooperative made up a small sector of the market, especially in the developed western world.

The ESOPs were established with an aim to expand worker ownership, broadening and distribution of wealth, and also to improve the economic performance of American industry. But there were lots of issues regarding the ownership of the workers. It was found that lower and middle ranking workers were excluded, and favors were passed to the high-ranking employees. But whether democratic practices were really practiced in ESOPs was a big question. Well, worker cooperatives face lots of difficulties in their growth, especially with regard to capital input, entrepreneurial support and managerial talent. Dilemmas were evident while raising internal and external finance for the cooperative.

Again, the problem of "cooperative degeneration" may affect cooperative formation like the concentrated capitalistic mechanism. The degenerative tendencies may grow within the cooperatives, as a result of environmental pressure and loss of commitment to cooperative principles. It is a tendency that breaks out between the existing members and the non-members, or when the elites start dominating the cooperative because of their technical expertise or leadership skills. With such processes into play, the cooperative may lean towards a hierarchical system. As against such a tendency, there were other cooperative type structures, like Kibbutzim systems (Israel), where importance was given to social equality, solidarity and commitment to values. It exemplifies a direct democratic system, with some mechanisms of regulation, and specialization.

"Participatory consciousnes" (Bernstein) came up with effective cooperative organization. It is a system characterized by self-reliance, flexibility, and openness to learning and to educate the workers. But practicing this system was a very difficult task. Sometimes, workers look forward to cooperatives out of frustration, not out of choice. They also fear losing their jobs due to plant closings. To have a support system is mandatory for the growth of any organization, be it a business firm, hospital or an educational institute. Worker cooperatives too require a support system, to assist them financially. CDAs were formed (Dickstein, 1988) to stimulate cooperative development especially in Britain. But such developments were not visible across the world, very much restricted to some provinces. And, if CDAs are to really create an impact, then long regular interventions are required. But diverse questions crop up, as to understand the link between cooperative and democratic participation.

If the cooperative system is truly democratic, then it will not turn immediately into a capitalist enterprise. It is often understood that cooperatives are less privileged than capitalist enterprise. There are also ways to raise the status of the cooperatives. Government can take a step towards mandating the cooperatives legislatively or otherwise incentivize the market to take tax initiatives and make social and economic changes.

Industrial democracy brought forth a new outlook towards workplace and democratic governance. Whether it is the producer co-operative, or work councils, or trade unions, shop-floor programs drew up different mechanism for protecting the rights and safeguarding the interest of the workers in the industries.

The eagerness towards democratic practice in the industries was not same in all places. For instance, in Sweden, collective bargaining was pushed forward, with a framework of law on the Joint Regulation of Working Life: the Joint Regulation of Working life Act 1976, a landmark favor towards the union, which was previously dominated by the management. It also established collective bargaining as an instrument for increased industrial democracy. Like collective bargaining, co-determination and work council too did not have universal acceptance. In fact, there were differences in the approach towards industrial democracy or worker participation.

In support of workers' participation in the workplace, the work environment reform movement was started. Even worker voice in decisions related to health and safety, and new technology was given priority. Self-Management, or management of the enterprise by the workers or their representatives, can be considered as another innovation in the line of industrial democracy. Such developments paved the way for humanization of work, especially in late 1960s and early 1970s (in America and Europe).

The projects on humanization of the work was initiated by the management of the firm, as the monotony-driven assembly line production system was not doing enough in the line of production. It is a fact that industrial democracy argued for active role of workers in the decision-making process within the firm, but economic democracy broadened its horizon. It deals with increasing powers of workers in the economy as a whole. Thus, this was considered as third dimension in democratization of society (political, social and economic).

Economic democracy took different forms in different parts of the world. This movement has undergone revisions, changes, but it has set a new trend in worker participations. Economic democracy called for lots of resistance from the part of management, as it touched upon the most vital part of the management system, i.e. capital ownership. But still, such consciousness was welcomed in most of the European countries, and United States. These countries took necessary steps, towards expanded employee rights, and as a result narrowed down managerial prerogatives in decision making. With this, emphasis was shifted from the distribution of economic resources to distributions of power. And, amidst so much of dilemmas, it promoted a way to solve the problems that existed in the workplace.

The existence of a community is very essential for a democratic system to flourish. Then, worker co-operatives, trade unions, work councils, or the ESOPs, all aimed to establish a community within the workplace. For a democratic order to prevail within the community in a firm, there should be a certain degree of rules that prescribe the constitutional order of the firm, or in some form have a collective agreement.

If a democratic order prevails, then it is a norm that every individual should have the same degree of power in the firm's decision-making process. The conventional democratic order is always associated with voting (one person, one vote). In different workplaces, voting rules may work to secure some amount of power. But whether it can deal with the actual distribution of effective power within the community in the workplace is highly doubtful. Voting allows for some to exert power over others. Somehow, voting is avoided from the host of the market practices, like sub-contracting, off-shoring and informal patterns of work. It is not the only essential form of democracy at work.

To practice democratic constitutional order within a firm, the foremost requirement is to enable the constituents to engage in self-governance. But just to rely on such a process would be a bad dream. Democracy can play its role well, when it is supported by the component of fundamental rights. It is also true that all fundamental rights cannot be practiced in the firm. Those rights should be given priority that define the basic structure of the community in the workplace.

Proceduralization or setting up of standards plays an important role in establishing democracy at the workplace. All organizations, both formal and informal, are supposed to be regulated by substantive standards. Process-based standards are better than the result-oriented standards, for they avoid deliberative encounter between individuals and groups who have different interests, and can dispute the norms or use force, or stake, sabotage or even cooperate.

Proceduralization can be created at multiple levels with compliance in norms. The process-based laws attract different ideas of visibility and accountability, and may also lead to convergence at different levels, with workers, the state, trade union or work centres, international organizations, NGOs etc.

To bring out a workable model of workplace democracy, one has to be very cautious. Process-based law first cannot substitute and replace substantive standards. It can aid institutions, individuals, or groups, who can take part in these struggles. The rights component of workplace democracy is very significant not only in present times, but also from before.

Workplace democracy is not against free market, or regulation, or distribution; rather it is an added value to economic inclusion. For an effective workplace democracy, regulations, governance of labor market are very essential and should not be considered as a liability.

The Fordist and post-Fordist discourses have left behind an inevitable mark in work relations, especially in the manufacturing sector, and also in the service sector. Fordism, a result of Gramsci's hegemonistic theory, was very divisive by character. Fordism, or mass production or task fragmentation, came up as a hierarchical authoritative system. It was also regarded as a new form of capitalist mode of consumption. Probably, because of its divisive character, it came into crisis, and then post-Fordism followed. Post-Fordism did not appeal to the scholars as a successful production system. Probably, the disconnectedness was between traditional welfare and labor market policies, and also between labor process and employment relation. It was also identified that there was zero commitment of the employers towards the workers, because of the competitive market, and also too much emphasis on shareholder's value.

After failure of Fordism, other alternatives evolved in the industry. One of the earliest was the socio-technical system; we can say a humanization of the factory work started in Britain. Then, flexible specialization came up with flexibility in machinery, for the highly skilled workers (in Italy). In Germany, customization and quality were placed higher due to strong labor unions. Germany also adopted the socio-technical systems, but in a piecemeal manner. All these systems of production grew as a reaction to the Fordist system. The post-Fordist System of production emphasized on standardization. With internationalization of production, wages became a source of competition, change in employment relations, vertical disintegration of large companies (through outsourcing, sub-contracting etc.), a probable decline in internal labor markets, and a growth of market-mediated employment.

Lean system of production, which is somewhat associated with post-

Fordism, is common across manufacturing and service sector. The diversity under post-Fordism has to be analyzed in the context of dominant tendencies. It is not a simple and straightforward process. In the service sector, the employment relations were organized in a post-Taylorist style and the employment relations were shaped by external forces, such as vertical disintegration, anti-unionism, market-mediated employment.

The JIT delivery system, team work and multi-skilling drew up a synergy between interests of labor and capital, and as a result, Fordism declined. Later on in the 1980s, it evolved with more flexibility, more devolution of responsibility, and more cooperative management and labor relation.

Such developments in the workplace led to some amount of freedom to the workers and also set the congenial atmosphere for democratic practices in the workplace. The Japanese system of work organization, with high-level team work, multi-skilling and a weak hierarchical system, seemed to have created a system of responsibility of the firms towards its employees, shareholders etc. Few objections were raised against the system, but they too agreed that it came as a break from the drudgery of Fordist labor practices. The Japanese system, with its mechanism of team work, timely delivery, flexibility, was able to create an integrative atmosphere, and extend the social organization of work, though at times, flexible work hours may end up with large amounts of overtime.

Normally, the Japanese plants prefer a unitary system, with an integrated, harmonious workplace, and no conflict between the management and the workers, but disdain for unions prevailed. Studies on lean production pointed out that though it give a break from the Taylorist production system, workers' influence in the workplace remained minimal, and teamwork could hardly do little.

Lean production appealed to many for its advantages. The American firms ensured job security by applying this system (Berggren, 1993). Even, Brazil had a positive experience by adopting the Japanese techniques (Fleury and Humphrey, 1993). Lean Production was not bringing first flexibility, greater job security, stable employment, but at times, it is coercive. As part of humanization of workplace movement, several models, like Swedish socio-technical model, Germany's "going our own way" model (as an alternative to

Lean Production), stressed on team work, reasonable production goals, and promotions of workplace solidarity (Roth, 1992). "Going our own way" model, a strategy forged by few powerful unions in Germany (a norm against lean production), spearheaded the "humanization of work" campaign (1970s) with work council playing a leading role.

Studies supporting the discourses on employee relation were not first restricted to European countries. Brazil had a low level of mutual commitment towards employees, with a long history of authoritarian management. Trade unions were bypassed with the introduction of Japanese management techniques. Implicit bargaining followed, workers accepted change, and there was a softening of strategy on the part of management.

South Africa too had to take resort to a new management strategy to come out of its economic problems (1980s). Post-Fordism had a varied assessment graph across societies, but it had a positive influence in South Africa. The Industrial Strategy Project (ISP) that was proposed for economic reconstruction of South Africa (Joffe, Kaplan, Kaplinsky, and Lewis, 1995) came up with a very positive feedback on such post-Fordist firm-level prescription. This prescription aimed at beneficial competitiveness, de-Taylorization of work, and democratization of work through team building. Therefore, a high optimism awaited post-Fordism.

Fordism, with its assembly line production system, high-level mechanization, predominance of technical offices, and standardization and formalization of prescribed tasks, could not create a community with a participatory atmosphere. Rather, it was divisive by nature. There were traces of welfare activities in the Fordist period, but it was not institutionalized at the organizational level. Social responsibility of the organization at that time was not carefully structured, probably, because it was not a part of the core affairs of the organization, but it was not totally ignored. With failure of Fordism, post-Fordism evolved with efficient means of production, with high-level business growth, and more fulfilling work life. It came as a respite to the management of firms for these firms too were tired of worker absenteeism, low production, and the workers were tired of the monotonous, mechanized life.

Post-Fordism started a new movement in the production system. It is also true that post-Fordism too was not bereft of problems, but it came as a hope to the employees, as well as the management system. This can be recognized as a first step towards corporate social responsibility. When in a democratic prospective we talk about democratic workplace, it has to be characterized by a community, a participatory atmosphere, equal distribution of power, and some substantive rights. If these elements are effectively utilized, then democratic practices within a firm can became a reality, and responsibility of the firm will extend to its stakeholders. With post-Fordism, it is argued by some that the shareholder model of corporate governance peeped in. In the shareholder model of corporate governance, shareholders were given priority, because of their investments in the firm. It became the topmost priority of the firm, and that is why profit-driven responsibility was considered to be the first responsibility of the firm. A "Friedmanian CSR" valued the money of the shareholder, and argued businesses to stay within the rules of the game. Though a conservative approach, it was supported by many.

It was Dahl, who argued that denial of democratic right to employees is a violation of the moral rights of the individuals as workers, for he believed that employers of authoritarian firms do not enforce any form of equality in the workplace. That is why a democratic reorganization of the enterprise will bring forth some form of equal distribution power.

Dahl's analogy of political and economic democracy drew attention from different quarters, specially his assertion on the existence of binding decisions. Differential voluntarism of the individual's relationship to politics and to work strongly conditions the force of the individual's claim to a democratic, say in each area. On this count, one can refute Dahl's claim to analogy of political and economic democracy, though we cannot parallel democracy in a nation-state with democratic practices within firm. Democracy in political terms is broad, and the terrain is different, and the takers are the citizens, or the common people. In business, democracy will be determined by the market forces. Within a firm, the canvass is limited and the subjects are the employees. Then, the firm needs to strategize the basic principles of democracy that can govern the enterprise. Principles of equality, participation, power sharing are the basic conditions through which democracy can thrive, not only at the state level, but also at the enterprise level. This will enhance the establishment of governance system which will be democratic by nature. And, it could be rightly termed as democratic corporate governance. Corporate governance is an integral component of corporate responsibility of the enterprise. For the enterprise to function in a democratic framework, there should be participation by all employees (from the topmost professionals to the unskilled workers). Participation will ensure the workers' influence on the community (firm) on which he/she is dependent, for self-development.

Democratic practice is not just for simple participation of the employees, but it is also for the economic well-being of all. All employees work for income and through income, they will be empowered to stand up against any form of hierarchy within the firm. Economic empowerment, which directly results in distribution of income, may not necessarily result in democratization of the workplace. That is why it is argued by some that democratic status of the employees will be strengthened with equal distribution of power.

In order to understand CSR in a democratic perspective, the employees of the firm have to become an inclusive whole; every employee should develop concern for the growth of enterprise. Workplace democracy is when the firm becomes concerned about the growth of the employees (economic, social and psychological), when proceduralization of law takes place, and when the codes of conduct developed by the companies are complemented with international standards. These democratic practices enhance the governance mechanism of the firm, which is in fact the first formidable step towards democratic CSR.

## Employee Participation in India: A Review

Workplace participation and workplace democracy can be understood as an inseparable arrangement, in the democratic atmosphere of the firm. Wages, working conditions were legitimate areas of concern for the employees. But it was not same everywhere; moreover, all concerns do not interest all workers equally all the time. In stable economic situation, employees may be contended with weekly benefits, but in unstable economic climates, employees become concerned with all activities of the organization.

In India, formal bodies were established during the World Wars and after, to give more active participation in the work process. With Gandhi's idea of trusteeship, several forums were created after independence by the Government of India. Various types of involvement with employees were established: whether it is co-determination or participation or information sharing, all these forms in one or another existed in many organizations. Broadly, issues were identified to be classified under different categories of safety and welfare, work, production and business policy. Even at the managerial level, with certain reservations, it was accepted that workers should have some say in significant issues of the organization. A range of issues were identified which required a timely or periodic revision. The issues were mostly pertaining to safety and welfare, work, sharing of gains, production and business policy.

When we talk about participation, one cannot prove it due to lack of concrete and substantial evidence on the link between participation and production. The consultative, administrative and decisive participatory role for the employees geared up in India in the mid-1950s and 1960s. Initially, it was government's intervention that started worker participation in the management system in India.

With the existence of different forms of participation (consultative, associative, administrative and decisive), it is the real participation which gives exclusive control of the productive organization by its workforce on the basis of equality of vote, for the workers not only influence decisions, but they also participate with managers in the management of industry on equal terms. Hence, such influences are not confined to peripheral or minor matters, but are intrinsic to the governance system of the industrial organization (Bhattacharya, 1986).

Participative system, like any other system, has undergone renewals due to globalization. Whether it is for the interest of the organization or for the interest of the workers, enterprises cannot evolve or grow without involving their employees. In the post-globalization era, participative processes were shifted from formal to informal ones, with emphasis on styles rather than forums of participation. But a dilemma existed that some form of superficial participation might replace the real participation system.

The issue of ownership is very significant in the participation system. It was found that many employers and governments across the world have supported workers' stock ownership as a method of participation. This could increase workers' control over matters of the industry, and they can become shareholders of the company (like ESOPs in the US).

In India, such a method of employee stock ownership was started in West Bengal (New Central Jute Mills) with majority of employee ownership (Sen, 1996). Even the Central Government has supported such initiatives, and asserted for employee ownership of some percentage of public sector equity. The government was forthcoming in worker involvement in the participation process.

The participative process was not free from controversies. Generally, the unions sought to promote collective bargaining rather than participation. In fact, in 1952, an argument was generated by All India Trade Union Congress (AITUC) that compulsory recognition of unions by employers and an obligation to negotiate would render participation unnecessary. Another voice of objection was raised by the Hind Mazdoor Sabha (HMS) that participation may enhance the prestige of some leaders, but would not help in protecting labor interests. The Unions in India have preserved their bargaining domain and refused to allow participation on issues which impinge on the matters of bargaining. That is why, despite the absence of all India statutory provisions on union recognition, or right to bargain, collective bargaining had grown while employee participation failed.

## REFERENCES

Adler, P. and Cole, R. (1992), 'Designed for Learning: A Tale of Two Auto Plants', Department of Management and Organization, University of Southern California.

Aglietta, Michel (2000), 'The Socio-technical Perspective: The Evolution of Socio-technical Systems as a Conceptual Framework and as an Action Research Program' in A. H. Van De Ven and W. F. Joyce (eds.), Perspectives on Organizational Design, New York: Wiley, pp. 19-75.

Allway, Max and Stephen Corbett (2002), 'Shifting to Lean Service: Stealing a Page From Manufacturers' Play Books,' Journal of Organizational Excellence, 21: 45-54.

Albrecht, S. L. (1980), 'Politics, Bureaucracy and Worker Participation: The Swedish Case,' The Journal of Applied Behavioural Science, 16: 229-315.

Albrecht, S. L. (1981), The Social and Economic Pre-conditions for Increased Worker's Influence: The Swedish Case, Sociology of Work and Occupations, 8: 252-272.

Albrecht, Sandra l. (1983), Forms of Industrial and Economic Democracy: A Comparison of Prevailing Approach, Mid-American Review of Society, 8(2): 43-66.

Alchian, Armen and Demsetz (1972), Production Information Costs and Economic Organization, American Economic Review, 62(5): 777-795.

Arneson, Richards (1993), 'Democratic Rights at National and Workplace Levels' in David Copp et al. (eds.), Ideas of Democracy, New York and Cambridge: Cambridge University Press, p 138.

Asard, E. (1980), Employee Participation in Sweden 1971-1979: The Issue of Economic Democracy,

Economic and Industrial Democracy, 1 (3): 371-393.

Asplund, C (1981), Redesigning Jobs: Western European Experiences, Brussels: European Trade Union Institute.

Bachrach, Peter and Morton S. Baratz (1962), Two Faces of Power, The American Political Science Review, 56(4): 947-952.

Barenberg, Mark (2009), Sustaining Workers Bargaining Power in an Age of Globalization, Economic Policy Institute Briefing Paper 246.

Batstone, E. (1983), Organization and Orientation: A Life-Cycle Model of French Cooperatives, Economic and Industrial Democracy, 4: 139-161.

Bellas, Carl (1972), Industrial Democracy and the Worker–Owned Firm, New York: Praeger.

Belous, Richard S. (1989), How Human Resources Systems Adjust to the Shift Toward Contingent Workers, Monthly Labor Review, March: 7-12.

Ben-Ner, Avner (1988), 'Comparative Empirical Observations on Worker-Owned and Capitalist Firms,' International Journal of Industrial Organization, 6: 7-31.

Ben-Ner, Avner (1988), 'The Life Cycle of Worker-Owned Firms in Market Economies: A Theoretical Analysis,' Journal of Economic Behaviour and Organization, 10 (3): 287-313.

Berggren, Christian (1993), Lean Production—The End of History?, Work, Employment & Society, 7(2): 163-188.

Berman, Katrina V. (1967), Worker-Owned Plywood Companies: An Economic Analysis, Pullman, WA: Washington State University Press.

Bernstein, R. (1976), The Restructuring of Social and Political Theory. New York: Harcourt, Brace & Jovanovich.

Bhattacharya, J.B. (1986), Participative Management and Industrial Democracy—Concepts and Practices, Calcutta: Omega.

Blasi, Joseph (1988), Employee Ownership: Revolution or Rip Off? Cambridge, MA: Ballinger Publishing.

Blyton, Paul, Cornforth, Chris and Szell, Gyorgyeds (1989), The State, Trade Unions and Self-Management Issues of Competence and Control, Walter De Gruyter Inc.

Boyer, Robert (1990), The Regulation School: A Critical Introduction, Columbia: Columbia University Press.

Bradly, Keith and Alan Gelb (1983), Cooperation at Work: The Mondragon Experience, London: Heinemann.

Bradly, Keith and Alan Gelb (1983), Worker Capitalism, Cambridge, MA: MIT Press.

Braverman, Harry (1974), Labor and Monopoly Capital, New York: Monthly Review Press.

Brown, Clair and Reich, Michael (1989), When Does Union- Management Cooperation Work? A Look at NUMMI and GM-Van Nuys, California Management Review, 31(4): 26-44.

Carter, Neil (2003), 'Workplace Democracy: Training Workers into Citizens?' Paper presented at ECPR Joint Sessions, Edinburgh, March 28 to April 2, Workshop 22: Bringing Citizens Back in: Participatory Democracy and Political Participation. Available at Nicomedia.mathovpatras.gr/ Econ/Dem/resources/EconomicDemocracy/Carter_WorkplaceDemocracy_ Turning WorkersintoCitizens.pdf.

Castree, Noel (2000), Geographic Scale and Grassroots Internationalism: The Liverpool Dock Dispute 1995-98, Economic Geography, 76 (3): 272.

Cleeg, Hugh (1960), A New Approach to Industrial Democracy, London: Blackwell.

Coates, Ken and Topham, Tony (eds.) (1968), Industrial Democracy in Britain. London: MacGibben

& Kee.

Cohen, Carl (1971), Democracy, Athens: University of Georgia Press.

Cohen, Jean (2002), Regulating Intimacy—A New Legal Paradigm. Princeton: Princeton University Press.

Cole, G.D.H. (1920), Self-Government in Industry, London: G. Bell.

Conte, Michael (1982), Participation and Performance in US Labour Managed Firms in Derek Jones and Jane Svijner (eds.), Participatory and Self-Managed Firms, Lexington, MA: Lexington Books, pp. 213-238.

Cordova, E. (1982), Workers Participation in Decisions Within Enterprise: Recent Trends and Problems, International Labor Review, 121(2): 125-140.

Cornforth, Chris (1988), 'Can Entrepreneurship be Institutionalized? The Case of Worker Co-operatives,' International Small Business Journal, 6(4): 10-19.

Cornforth, Chris (1989), The Role of Support Organization in Developing Worker Co-operatives: A Model for Promoting Economic and Industrial Democracy in Szell, Gyorgy, Blyton, Paul and Cornforth, Chris (eds.), The State, Trade Unions and Self-Management: Issues of Competence and Control, de Gruyter Studies in Organization. Berlin: Walter De Gruyter, pp. 107-124.

Cornforth, Chris and Lewis, Jenny (1985), The Role and Impacts of Local Cooperatives Support Organizations, Monograph No. 7. Milton Keynes: Cooperative Research Unit, The Open University.

Cornforth, Chris, Thomas, Alan, Spear, Roger and Lewis, Jenny (1988), Developing Successful Worker Co-operatives, London: Sage Publications.

Cressey, P. (1993), Kalmar and Uddevalla: The Demise of Volvo as a European Icon, New Technology, Work and Employment, 8 (2): 88-90.

Dahl, Ralph (1985), Preface to Economic Democracy, Berkeley: University of California Press.

Dahl, Robert (1961), Who Governs? Democracy and Power in an American City, New Haven, CT: Yale University Press.

Dahl, Robert (1983), Dilemmas of Pluralist Democracy, New Haven, CT: Yale University Press.

Dassbach, C. (1996), 'Lean Production, Labour Control and Post-Fordism in the Japanese Automobile Industry', in Green and Yanarella (eds.), North American Auto Unions in Crisis: Len Production as Contested Terrain, New York: State University of New York Press, pp. 19-40.

Dawson, S. (1978), 'Workers Control', in P. McGuigan and B. Schaeffer (eds.), Developing the Public Economy: Models from Massachusetts. Cambridge, MA: Policy Training Centre.

Deutsch, S and Albrecht, S.L. (1983), Worker Participation in the United States: Efforts to Democratize Industry and the Economy, Labor and Society, July-September, 8: 243-269.

Dewey, John (1988) 'Economic Basis of the New Society' in Jonn Boydston (ed.), John Dewey: The Later Works, Volume 13: 1938-1939, Carbondale: Southern Illinois University Press, pp. 309-322.

Dickstein, Carla (1988), The Role of Cooperative Development Agencies in Developing Worker Cooperatives: Lessons from Philadelphia, Economic and Industrial Democracy, May, 9(2): 197-224.

Dickstein, Carla (1991), 'The Promise and Problems of Workers Cooperatives: A Survey,' Journal of Planning Literature, 6(1): 16-33.

Dobbin, Frank, Soohan, Kim and Kalev, Alexandra (2011), You Can't Always Get What You Need:

Organizational Determinants of Diversity Programs, American Sociological Review, 76 (3): 386.

Doellgast, V. (2010), 'Collective Voice under Decentralised Bargaining: A Comparative Study of Work Reorganisation in US and German Call Centers,' British Journal of Industrial Relations, 48(2): 375-400.

Earle, John (1986), The Italian Cooperatives Movement, London: Routledge.

Edwards, Richard (1979), Contested Terrain: The Transformations of the Workplace in the Twentieth Century, New York: Basic Books.

Ellerman, David (1982), The Socialization of Entrepreneurship, the Empresarial Division of the Caja Laboral Popular, Somerville, MA, Industrial Cooperative Association. Available at www.ellerman.org/wp-content/uploads/2012/12/Soc-of_Entrep.CV_pdf.

Ellerman, David (2009). The Workplace in Deliberative Democratic Theory: A Note on Kant, Mill and Dewey (http: //dx.doi.org/10.2139/ssrn.1389875).

Elster, John (ed.) (1986), The Multiple Self, Cambridge: Cambridge University Press.

Estlund, Cynthia (2003), Working Together: How Workplace Bonds Strengthen a Diverse Democracy, Oxford: Oxford University Press.

Estrin, Saul (1985), The Role of Producer Cooperatives in Employment Creation, Economic Analysis and Workers Management, 19(4): 345-384.

Fleury, A. and Humphrey, J. (1993), Human Resources and the Diffusion and Adaptation of New Quality Methods in Brazilian Manufacturing, IDS Research Report 24, Brighton: Institute for Development Studies.

Fox, Alan (1974), Beyond Contract: Work, Power and Trust Relations, London: Faber & Faber.

Garavito, Rodrigues and Caesar, A. (2005), Global Governance and Labor Rights: Codes of Conduct and Anti-Sweatshop Struggles in Global Apparel Factories in Mexico and Guatemala, Politics & Society, 33: 203.

Garrahan, P. and Stewart, P. (1992), 'Management Control and a New Regime of Subordination: Post-Fordism and the Local Economy', in Gilbert and Burrows (eds.), Fordism and Flexibility: Divisions and Change, London: Macmillan, pp. 107-117.

Gilbert, D.U, A. Rasche and S. Waddock (2010), Accountability in a Global Economy: The Emergence of International Accountability Standards, Business Ethics Quarterly, 21(1): 23-44.

Green, W. and Yanarella, F. (1996), North American Auto Unions in Crisis, Albany: State University of New York Press.

Greenberg, Edward S. (1986), Workplace Democracy: The Political Effects of Participation, Ithaca: Cornell University Press.

Greenberg, Edward S. (1999), Workplace Democracy in the Core Countries: Problems and Prospects, Paper delivered at the Annual Meeting of the European Consortium on Political Research, Mannheim, Germany, March 26-31.

Gregory, Pappas, (ed.) (2008), John Dewey's Ethics: Democracy as Experience, Bloomington: Indiana University Press.

Gutierrez-Johnson, Ana (1984), The Mondragon Model of Cooperative Enterprise: Considerations Concerning Its Success and Transferability, Changing Work, 1: 35-41.

Hammer, Tove, Stern, Robert P. and Whyte, William (1983), Can You Buy Your Job? in William Foote Whyte et al. (eds.), Worker Participation and Ownership, Ithaca: New York, pp. 55-80.

Hancock, M. D. (1981), Modifying Change or Fundamentalist Transformation, The Swedish

Employee Fund Debate: Update and Prospects, Political Life in Sweden, No. 9. New York: Swedish Information Service.

Hanlon, M. D. (1982), Union Responses to QWH: Will It Add to Worker Control? Paper presented at the Society for the Study of Social Problems, San Francisco, September.

Herrigel, Gary and Sabel, F. Charles (1999), 'Craft Production in Crisis: Industrial Restructuring in Germany in the 1990s', in Pepper D. Culpepper and David Finegold (eds.), German Skill Machine: Sustaining Comparative Advantage in a Global Economy, Oxford: Berghan Books, pp. 77-114.

Humphrey, J. (1993), 'Japanese Production Management and Labor Relations in Brazil,' Journal of Development Studies, 30(1): 92-114.

Jain, H. C. (1980), Worker Participation: Success and Problems. New York: Praeger.

Joffe, A., Kaplan, D., Kaplinsky, R. and Lewis, D. (1995), Improving Manufacturing Performance in South Africa: Report of the Industrial Strategy Project, Cape Town: University of Cape Town Press.

Jones, Derek (1979), US Producer Cooperatives: The Record to Date, Industrial Relations, 18(1): 342-357.

Laclau, Ernesto and Mouffe, Chantal (1985), Hegemony and Socialist Strategy: Towards a Radical Democratic Politics, London: Verso.

Lafferty, W. (1985), Decision Making Involvement and Socioeconomic Resource in Norway: A Normative Empirical Analysis, Scandinavian Political Studies, 8: 1-32.

Lazonick, W. and O'Sullivan, M. (2000), Maximizing Shareholder Value: A New Ideology for Corporate Governance, Economy and Society, 29(1): 13-35.

Levin, Henry (1980), Workplace Democracy and Educational Planning, in Education, Work and Employment, UNESCO International Institute for Education Planning, Geneva: UNESCO, 123-216.

Levin, Henry (1982), 'Issues in Assessing the Cooperative Productivity of Workers-Managed and Participatory Firms in Capitalist Societies', in Derek Jones and Jan Svejner (eds.), Participatory and Self-Managed Firms: Evaluating Economic Performance, Lexington, MA: Lexington Books, pp. 45-64.

Levin, Henry (1983) Educational and Organizational Democracy, Vol. 1, Colin Crouch and Frank Heller (eds.), International Yearbook of Organizational Democracy, Boston: Wiley and Sons, pp. 227-248.

Levine, David and Tyson, Laura D'Andrea (1990), Participation, Productivity and the Firm's Environment, in Alan S. Blinder (ed.), Paying for Productivity, Washington, D.C.: Brookings Institution.

Lewchuk, W. and Robertson, D. (1997), Production Without Empowerment: Work Reorganization from the Perspective of Motor Vehicle Workers, Capital & Class, 63: 37-65.

Lipietz, Alain (1992), Towards a New Economic Order, Post-Fordism, Ecology, Democracy, Oxford and New York: Polity Press and Oxford University Press.

Lipietz, Alain (1997), The Post-Fordist World: Labour Relations, International Hierarchy and Global Ecology, Review of International Political Economy, 4(1): 1-41.

Locke, Richard and Romis, Monica (2010), The Promise and Perils of Private Voluntary Regulation: Labor Standards and Work Organization in Two Mexican Garment Factories, Review of International Political Economy, 17 (1): 45-74.

Mathews, J. (1989), Tools of Change: New Technology and the Democratization of Work, Sydney:

Pluto Press.

Maxwell, Elden J (1981), The Political Efficacy at Work: The Connection Between More Autonomous Forms of Workplace Organization and a More Participatory Politics, The American Political Science Review, 75(1), 43-58.

Mayer, Robert (2001), Michael Walzer, Industrial Democracy and Complex Equality, Political Theory, 29 (2): 237-261.

Michels, Robert (1949), Political Parties: A Sociological Study of Oligarchies Tendencies of Modern Democracy, New York: Free Press.

Mill, J. S. (1848), Principles of Political Economy, London: John W. Parker.

Mundlak, Guy (2014), Workplace-Democracy: Reclaiming the Effort to Foster Public-Private Isomorphism, Theoretical Enquiries in Law, 15(1): 159-198.

Offe, Claus (1999), How Can We Trust Our Fellow Citizens?, in Mark Warren (ed.), Democracy and Trust, Cambridge: Cambridge University Press, pp. 42-87.

Padayachee, V. (1997), Progressive Academic Economists and the Challenge of Development in South Africa's Decade of Liberation, Inaugural Lecture, University of Natal.

Pappas, Gregory (2008), John Dewey's Ethics: Democracy, Bloomington: Indiana University Press.

Parks, Susan (1995), Improving Workplace Performance: Historical and Theoretical Contexts, Monthly Labor Review, 118(5): 18-28.

Pateman, Carole (1970), Participation and Democratic Theory, Cambridge: Cambridge University Press.

Paton, R, et al. (1987), Analysis of the Experience of and Problems Encountered by Worker Take-Overs of Companies in Difficulty or Bankrupt, Report to the Commission of the European Communities, Study No.85/4.

Polsby, Nelson W. (1974), Community Power and Political Theory, New Haven, CT: Yale University Press.

Poole, M. (1979), Industrial Democracy: A Comparative Analysis, Industrial Relations, 18(3): 262-272.

Pullman, Buder, Stanley (1967), An Experiment in Industrial Order and Community Planning: 1880-1930, New York: Oxford University Press.

Putterman, Louis (1982), 'Some Behavioral Perspectives on the Dominance of Hierarchical Over Democratic Forms of Enterprise,' Journal of Economic Behavior and Organization, 3: 139-60.

Quarrey, Michael (1986), Employee Ownership and Corporate Performance, Oakland, CA: National Centre for Employee Ownership.

Quarry, Michael, Joseph, Blasi and Corey, Rosen (1986), Taking Stock: Employee Ownership at Work, Cambridge, MA: Ballenger Publishing.

Rodriguez-Garavito, C. A. (2005), Global Governance and Labor Rights: Codes of Conduct and Anti-Sweatshop Struggles in Global Apparel Factories in Mexico and Guatemala, Politics & Society, 33 (2): 203-233.

Roemer, John (1988), Free to Lose: An Introduction to Marxist Economic Philosophy, Cambridge: Harvard University Press.

Rosen C., Klein, K.J., and Young, K.M. (1986), Employee Ownership in America: The Equity Solution, Lexington, MA: Lexington Books.

Rosner, Menachem and Nanni, Cohen (1982), Is Democracy Feasible?, in Menachem Rosner et al. (eds.), Democracy, Equality and Change: The Kibbutz and Social Theory, Derby, PA: Norwood

Editions, pp. 33-60.

Roth. S. (1992), Japanisation, or Going Our Own Way? New Lean Production Concepts in the German Automobile Industry, Frankfurt: IG Metall.

Rothschild, Joyce and Whitt, Allen (1986), The Cooperative Workplace: Potentials and Dilemmas of Organizational Democracy and Participation, Cambridge: Cambridge University Press.

Russel, R. (1984), Using Ownership to Control: Making Workers Owners in the Contemporary United States, Politics & Society, 13: 253-294.

Russel, R. (1985), Sharing Ownership in the Workplace, Albany: SUNY Press.

Schumann, Michael (1998), New Concepts of Production and Productivity, Economic and Industrial Democracy, 19: 17-32.

Schweickart, David (1993), Against Capitalism, Cambridge: Cambridge University Press.

Sen, Ratna (1996), Worker's Management—Some Experiences in Industrial Cooperatives, Kolkata: Subarnarekha.

Shirom, A. (1972), The Industrial Relations Systems of Industrial Co-operatives in the United States, 1880-1935, Labour History, 13 (Fall): 533-551.

Staats, Bradley R. and David M. Upton (2009), Lean Principles, Learning and Software Production; Evidence from Indian Software Services, Working Paper, Harvard Business School. Available at www.edu/faculty/Publication%20Files/08-001.pdf.

Stern, R. N., Wood, H. and Hamner, T.H. (1979), Employee Ownership in Plant Shutdown, Kalamazoo, Michi Upjohn Institute.

Strauss, G. (1979), Workers Participation: Symposium Introduction, Industrial Relations, 18(3): 247-256.

Taylor, Alan (1983), Worker Cooperatives: How Local Authorities Can Help, London: Industrial Common Ownership Movement.

Taylor, P. and P. Bain (1999), 'An Assembly Line in the Head: Work and Employee Relations in the Call Centre,' Industrial Relations Journal, 30: 101-117.

Thomas, Henk and Logan, Chris (1982), Mondragon: An Economic Analysis. London: Allen & Unwin.

Thompson, Paul (2003), Disconnected Capitalism: Or Why Employees Can't Keep Their Seeds of the Bargain, Work, Employment and Society, 17: 359-378.

Trist, Eric L. (1981), 'The Sociotechnical Perspective: The Evolution of Sociotechnical Systems as a Conceptual Framework and as an Action Research Program', in A.H. Van De Ven and W.F. Joyce (eds.), Perspectives on Organization Design and Behavior, New York: Wiley & Sons, pp. 19-75.

Turner, L. and Aver, P. (1996), Diversity of New Work Organization: Human-Centered Lean and In Between, in Deyo (ed.), Introduction: Social Reconstruction of the World Automobile Industry: Competition, Power and Industrial Flexibility, Basingstoke: Macmillan, pp. 233-257.

Vanek, Jaraslav (1977), The Labor-Managed Economy, Ithaca, New York: Cornell University Press.

Vidal, Matt (2011), Reworking Post-Fordism: Labor Process Versus Employment Relations, Sociology Compass, 5 (4): 273-286.

Whyte, William F. and Whyte, Kathleen (1988), Making Mondragon: The Growth and Dynamics of the Worker Cooperative Complex, Ithaca, New York: ILR Press.

Womack, James P., Byrne, Arthur P., Fiume, Orest J, Kaplan, Gary S, John Toussant (2005), Going Lean in Health Care, Cambridge, MA: Institute for Healthcare Improvement. Available at http: //www.entnet.org/sites/default/files/GoingLeaninHealthCareWhitePaper-3.pdf.

Wood, Stephen (1982), The Degradation of Work: Skill, Deskilling and the Labor Process. London: Hutchinson.

Wood, Stephen J. (1991), Japanization and/or Toyotism?, Work Employment and Society, 5: 567-600.

Yanarella, E. J. and Green, W. C. (1996), 'Introduction: Building Other People's Cars: Organized Labor and the Crisis of Fordism', in W. Green and E. Yanarella (eds.), North American Auto Unions in Crisis: Len Production as Contested Terrain, New York: State University of New York Press, pp. 1-18.

# 3

# CSR, Corporate Governance and Ethics: Tracing the Linkages

Be it the confectionary company Cadbury's use of slaves on cocoa plantations in the Portuguese colony of Sao Tome, or the Nike's alleged false claims in a PR campaign about the working conditions in its factories (suppliers), such cases raised a very genuine issue of irresponsibility of business. Was it a beginning or just a sporadic incident of history?

The "business-society relationship" is not just based on profit-driven value system. It has a moral perspective also. If we trace the root of the concept, CSR has a long history; however, it is mostly a product of the 20$^{th}$ century. In spite of its recent growth, there are evidences of businesses' concern for society from a long period of time.

Business–society relations have straddled through different epochs, primarily Industrial Revolution, Welfare State, globalization and many more. Industrial Revolution was an epoch making phenomenon, which brought about a change in human demography and working life of individuals. There was a massive increase in urban population growth in manufacturing businesses. As such factories became centres of fatalities, injuries and child-related atrocities. Women were not left behind. They became an important segment of the workforce, not willingly, but out of necessity.

What was the effect of industrialization? Though it led to the growth of business, money, private property, it also led to civil unrest. Thus, human exploitation spurred various reform movements, especially in the UK. It came to the state notice about the socio-economic unrest. Then, UK had the first Factory Act in 1819 and laws to control and monitor the mines were passed in 1842.

Besides, in US the state's intervention set forth an era of individual philanthropy. Here, we can talk about the Scottish-born Andrew Carnegie, who embarked on a philanthropic cause from the fortunes he made from his manufacturing business (Blowfield and Murray, 2008: 44). The philanthropic quest was not limited to any area. It led to the establishment of educational trusts, or iconic buildings in New York (Carnegie Hall) and the Peace Palace in The Hague.

Every industrial nation has its own history of industrialization, whether it is US or UK. But in contemporary time, the relevance of such phenomena remains, if we analyze the situation in China. A huge influx of people into urban areas from rural areas can be witnessed. This has changed employee composition in the industries.

A huge reform movement took place, especially in the US, whereby the limits on company size was removed. Then company's rights were compared with the citizens. In the early 20$^{th}$ century, a new theme evolved in business, i.e. mergers and acquisitions, and in the mid-20$^{th}$ century, the nature of incorporation underwent major reforms that removed limits on company size, what will be the period of their existence, and what they could own. Thus, company's rights were somewhat compared to citizen's rights.

The conditions before World War I accelerated the global free trade and the market promoted private self-interest that served the public interest or the greater interest. There was a marked change in the idea of creating a new social order. The International Labour Organization (ILO) (1919) also recognized the dangers of an unjust political or economic order. The ILO as a part of the League of Nations brought together three structures: government, business and trade unions and explicitly recognized the dangers of an unjust political or economic order. A new form of capitalism grew after the War. It was also believed that the new form of capitalism was one of the root causes of Great Depression of 1929.

Voluntarism became a norm in business, but such practices did not deter government intervention in business. The "New Deal"[1] influenced the type of Welfare State in different parts of Western Europe, especially the nation's public policies. It was established that business served the common people's needs the best, when it is controlled by the state. In many of the Communist countries in the Eastern Bloc, private enterprises were banned. A new model of governance developed in countries like West Germany and Italy. Such governance systems ensured a steady relation between the workers as well as shareholders. In the USA too, an adaptive relation between business and society emerged.

The changing role of society and business led to a significant change in the thinking about the business-society relation. The concept of Welfare State called for equitable distribution of economic resources. Distribution of resources was the job of the state, and the role of business was to create job opportunities and follow the rules of the game (abide by law and pay taxes regularly). Such consciousness at the national level led to international recognition of human rights especially after the World War II. That is why many national governments came up with an agreement which can be termed as the United Nations Universal Declaration of Human Rights which of course can be rightly referred to as an important corporate responsibility initiative.

Then, in the 1950s, pollution became a real environmental and social concern, especially in USA and UK, when smog killed many citizens. And, then pollution became a political issue. "Silent Spring" sparked the controversy over man-made pollution through pesticides. Thanks to Carlson! People became aware about environmental degradation and business activity. Green Peace (1971) began its movement against environmental pollution outside the political process. During this phase, rights-focused activities became the agenda of many organizations, i.e. worker's rights, indigenous people's rights, children and bonded labour rights. Issues were raised in the workplace in terms of equal treatment of the sexes. Women's right movement rightly fought for equal treatment in the workplace especially in the area of legislation. Its claim over equal treatment of women can be rightly regarded as one of the significant step towards CSR, i.e. companies hesitate to practice any discriminatory practices against women.

Globalization and CSR too share complementary relations. Historically, if we go back, the Bretton Woods Summit set forth the establishment of three major institutions: the International Bank for Reconstruction and Development (IBRD) which is commonly known as World Bank, the International Monetary Fund (IMF) and the youngest being the World Trade Organization (WTO). Why these organizations are important for CSR? Primarily, because they govern international trade relations.

The economic prosperity in North America and Western Europe in 1950s and 1960s was threatened by stagnation in the 1970s, with high unemployment accompanied by inflation. In order to come out of this situation, the governments in US and UK enacted policies supporting private investment, less power to the labor, free markets and government control of currencies. These policies defined the type of governance prevailed in those days. This governance style became the focal point of "Washington Consensus"[2]. Washington Consensus has been able to create an immense impact on foreign investment, global trade, and removal of tariff barriers. Many of the countries from Latin America, Africa and South Asia adopted the policies of the Consensus to have a better economic deal.

## India's Business–Society Relation: Historical Analysis

Like the west, India also has a legacy of business–society relation. Its business–society intersection was unique.

## Corporate Social Responsibility in India

The concept of business's social responsibility or responsiveness is not new in India. In the early Vedic and later Vedic periods, guild systems were the key business centres. During that period, guilds were involved in rich tradition of social giving. These guilds were also drawn to play even broader governance role: "The guilds played an important role in governance during periods of state formation, state consolidation and state dissolution" (Mitra, 2007: 16). The guilds were well formed and they laid down their own rules and regulations. This was possible as they enjoyed the political patronage of the kings at that time. The guilds were not just economic work organizations but shared political roles as well. The stability of the guilds was so great, that they probably endured the dissolution of formed states as well at various periods (Thaplyal, 1996).

In an early stage (600 BC and 320 BC), there was a shifting of loyalty from tribal organization to politico-geographical units. Due to overall development, the guilds had the patronage from the ruler to lay down their own rules. There are references to civil, legislative, judicial and executive powers of the guilds over not just their members, but families and classes of persons living within their jurisdiction as well (Majumdar, 1969). This displayed the overwhelming influences of the guilds.

Even the periods of dynastic rule, say the Mauryan (320 BC-200 BC) or the Gupta Period (300 AD-600 AD), strengthened the role of the guilds. There was relative autonomy granted to the guilds in civic roles, during the Mauryan period, because it was a period of state consolidation. In the Gupta period, systematic rules were set for business, and later the guilds became members of the advising board of the administration at the district level.

The waning influence of the state coexisted with the growth of activities in the area of trade. Guilds were very stable, and in fact they could endure the dissolution of formed states, at different periods.

Spengler opined that the political instability at the macro level let to a natural devolution of decision making and governance roles to the local level through the guilds.

Thus, the guilds were engaged in social and political processes in the wake of the abilities or disabilities of the state for governance (Mitra, 2007). The strong corporate nature of the guilds indicates a joint sharing of resources, profits, and gains. The sources of revenue for the guilds came from member subscriptions, contributions, gifts bestowed by state to individuals in the guild, profits from the execution of orders, price, confiscated property, and permanent deposits of endowment purposes whose interest was to pay charitable works.

Guilds used to partner with large political units for public work, acts of charity, for which they were offered permanent endowments of cash or land. Besides, there was an institutionalization of development activities of guilds. The corporate nature of the guilds was evident from their diligent manner in handling joint holding of resources, sharing of profits, and gains. The guild members accurately documented their social and philanthropic activities.

In fact, the guilds also functioned as banks, and played an important role in the governance of the ancient cities at the municipal level. Monetarily they were substantiated with endowments, in the form of property and deposits in cash. Their services as partners in public works were registered in town halls, or at the record office. Thus, there was somewhat fair formalization of the guilds' development activities. There were internal and external factors to their philanthropy. For its own members, guilds used to provide a congenial atmosphere for creativity and originality. And, for the wider society, they were engaged in charity.

It was also found that such acts included donation for construction and maintenance of public utility services, like assembly hall, water shed, a shrine, assistance at the time of disaster, and other natural and manmade calamities. Thus, it can be argued that guilds were not just guardians, but also helped in fulfilling with material and social needs of the community.

During that time, "endowments came from a wide variety of sources like kings, traders, artisans and other classes of people" (ibid). There was also a fixed system of contribution, which formed the profits of the guilds. A portion of the profits was kept aside for charitable activities. For such activities, guilds were supported with permanent endowments of cash and land by the political authorities and sometimes by individuals as well. Thus, it was found that such development activities were fairly formalized.

Business–society relation took a significant leap with Mahatma Gandhi's concept of Trusteeship. Gandhi viewed the role of business in society through his "Trusteeship theory". He embraced the theory of trusteeship to endorse the fact that wealth in reality belongs to the community. Originally Trusteeship, as envisaged by Gandhi, was most revolutionary in its spirit. It was revolutionary in the sense that it was not just a guide to business functioning in society; it was an integral part of wider world—view of society itself. It was also revolutionary because, it still envisaged a future society, which could (in Gandhi's view) emerge within the parameters of a market economy without violence and on a voluntary basis. Gandhi's belief in trusteeship also draws its strength from the political system at that time. The grip of imperialism and a global economic connectedness threatened to jeopardize a fragile self-sustaining economy into mass impoverishment. His thinking was "instructive in highlighting the great need for thinking economics anew and for bringing the human face centre stage when discussing economic advancement" (ibid: 21). Gandhi's Trusteeship was "essentially a dynamic relationship of confidence between the strong and the weak, governed by an attitude of love and non-violence on their part, the purpose and direction of their efforts being greater equality between them" (Choksi, 1966: 85). He saw capitalism's and its twin forces of technology and mechanization as unbridled by any kind of humanity and morality. Rather "Gandhi's view on property and entitlements were central to the concept of trusteeship" (ibid: 27). He was not much against private property as long as it has potential for all and was not against private entrepreneurs as for trusteeship orientation. In fact, he alluded to the absence of the state and the emergence of a self-regulated society, not like the Marxist state, but a society that has sprung up from the non-violent leadership of the trustees themselves. Gandhi also envisioned a wider role for business, i.e. a business and its endeavor in creating a new society. He spared no class or section of responsibility in creating this new society. This society should be bereft of any kinds of inequalities. If there were inequalities of any kind, both for the dominant and subjugated elements in the relationship, transformation was to be through voluntarism or moral appreciation and effort. The role of business in society, in terms of Gandhi's Trusteeship, can be described as "India's gift to the world". His Trusteeship was influenced by John Ruskin's economic treatise, "Unto This Last", the "non-possession" factor of Vinobha Bhave, the reformist and freedom fighter, especially concepts like *aparigraha* (non-possession) and *samabhavna* (equalizer), from "Gita".

Gandhi's ideas on trusteeship were expressed sporadically in two of his publications, "Harijan" and "Young India", where he wrote clearly, "Enjoy wealth by renouncing it". His trusteeship was somewhat, "Business for giving". Trusteeship provides a means of transforming the present capitalist order of society into an equalitarian one. It does not recognize any right of private ownership of property except so far as it may be permitted by society for its own welfare. It does not exclude legislative regulation of the ownership and use of wealth. Thus, under state-regulated trusteeship, an individual will not be free to hold or use his wealth for selfish satisfaction or in disregard of the interest of society.

As it fixes a decent minimum living wage, the limit should be fixed for the maximum income that would be allowed to any person in society. The difference between such minimum and maximum income should be reasonable and equitable and variable from time to time so much so that the tendency would be towards obliteration of the difference.

The character of production will be determined by social necessity and not by personal need or greed (*Harijan*, 25th Oct, quoted in IIC, Social Responsibility of Business: 105). For Gandhi, Trusteeship was essentially a dynamic relationship of confidence between the strong and the weak, governed by an attitude of love and non-violence on their part, the purpose and direction of their efforts being greater equality between them. Thus, the strong would use his superior position for the good of the weak particularly with a view to strengthening him. The strong could desire only the minimum benefit for himself. The weak would list the ultimate goodness of the man who was strong and try to gain a position of equality by constructive attempts at self-improvement (Choksi, 1966).

Gandhi's concept of trusteeship hovered around his views on "property and entitlements". He associated property closely with exploitation. He was of the view that industrialists were to be paid a commission. What would happen to the successors of the trustees? The state would regulate this commission and the children would inherit the stewardship only if they proved their fitness.

Ruskin's influence on Gandhi's view on entitlement and business was very much evident. It was Ruskin who stated that every profession has certain objectives, "a pastor is to teach, a physician's to heal, and a merchant's (and manufacturer) to provide. It is not their object to seek a fee or stipend" (1907: 128-129). Further, it is no more his function to get profit for himself (merchant/manufacturer) of that provision, than it is the clergyman's function to get stipend.

In Ruskin's opinion, a businessman should not only utilize his energies for not just producing at a cheap cost, but to also distribute the goods at the most affordable price. And, he also acknowledged the fact that during such course of actions, the businessman should be prepared to meet some eventualities like any form of distress, poverty, failure etc.

Gandhi was critical about the role of the state in business. When he returned to India in 1915, he was appalled at the role of state in the affairs of the society. He was against the regulatory nature of the state, but he was also not for the Marxists way of self-regulated society; rather he vouched for a non-violent leadership of the trustees themselves.

Gandhi also argued for a broader role of business. While addressing the

4th Annual Session of the Federation of Indian Chambers of Commerce and Industry (FICCI), Gandhi appreciated the services rendered by the commercial class and requested them to take the Congress as their own and assure they rein only on one condition, by regarding them as trustees and servants of the poor.

Gandhi's views with regard to entitlement in business were somewhat considered to be too extreme. Gandhi spared no class, in creating this new society, not even the labourer. Gandhi opined that wherever there were inequalities of any kind, both for the dominant and subjugated elements in the relationship, transformation should be through voluntarism and moral appreciation.

Thus, there is an overarching role of tradition, spirituality and respect in the evolution of CSR in India (Balasubramanian, Kimber & Siemensma, 2005; Jose, Bandi & Mitra, 2003; Mohan, 2001; Sagar & Singha, 2004).

The eve of independence in India was a time of great deliberation on the type of system that independent India was to put in place. India went in favor of a mixed economic model of development (Mitra, 2007). During this time, business engaged extensively in policy debates. The Government of India also adopted policy resolutions and plans to make the policy of government towards industrial development. This development emphasized on an increase in national wealth, i.e. expansion of production for the emancipation of all sections of people (Gopala, 1992). The post-independence period witnessed a significant change in the industrial relations of the country. Debates and discussions about the models of development that have to be put in place in India were the primary activity at that time. There was an anti-business trend, but India favoured a mixed economic model of development. Planning happened in India with an emphasis on acceleration on economic growth, and ample scope for private sector and a predominant role for the public sector. Even though Government of India emphasized on self-reliance and indigenous production, it was aware of the dearth of domestic savings and entrepreneurial skills, and that is why, it has agreed on the supplementary role of the foreign enterprises in the domestic market. During that period, individual leaders were also engaged extensively in business policy debates. Leaders like G.D. Birla, Purshotamdas Thakurdas, J.R.D. Tata, Walchand Hirachand and

John Mathai worked collectively through the business forum of the time—"the Federation of Indian Chambers of Commerce and Industry (FICCI)" (Mitra, 2007: 30). Through these endeavors, business came out with its own perspective and plan of action for post-independence India.

Business in India took public policy and ideological debate to an unusual stand. G.D. Birla spoke about the fight between pure capitalist organizations against communism; Harish Mahindra and J.R.D. Tata argued that businessmen are to some extent responsible for the poor image of private industry (Mahindra, 1984; J.R.D. Tata, 1980). Tata believed that "Indian business and industry who have adequate means and resources should consider it a part of their social obligations to contribute in some suitable form to the progress and welfare of the community in which their enterprise is located (Tata, 1984: 4). While business was an integral part of policy debates, it did not change the outcomes of national policies: "Philanthropy was primarily directed towards the areas of education and health and was state incentives" (Mitra, 2007: 32). During 1914-1960, the development initiatives were driven towards the establishment of educational institutions. The government also granted incentives for business to be drawn into other development activities, even though there were few takers for the rural areas.

Total engagement in rural development came from the Tatas: "the company had started rural engagement as early as 1949 with developmental efforts among adivasis near Jamshedpur" (ibid: 32). In the early 1960s, Hindustan Levers had begun its rural development programmes. In fact, between early and mid-1970s, "several business houses entered the rural development areas with special tax incentives" (Sunder, 2000: 179-81). Later on, both the government and powerful economic institutions were involved in promoting social welfare and development. Relevance of CSR in India has evolved from the fact that a business cannot succeed by ignoring the human and social needs of the society. And in this age of widespread communication and growing emphasis on transparency, customers of any product or service are unlikely to feel satisfied in buying from a company that is seen to violate the expectations of ethical and socially responsible behavior (Sarkar, 2005: 16).

Progress and welfare of the society is not merely the responsibility of governments alone. And therefore, it involves appropriate actions by all stakeholders, by which the corporate sector is extremely important (Sarkar, 2005). Besides, the engagement of civil society organizations in CSR initiatives is extraordinary. Civil society organizations are involved in disseminating new ideas, and engaging directly with the communities. These organizations are part of the partnership model of community development, followed by the government organizations and also the public enterprises.

In post-independence India, another important development was the Bombay plan. Businesses came out with a new plan of action, and this was, a plan for economic development of India, commonly called the Bombay Plan, published in 1944 and 1945 in two parts.

Due to the depression, and the political instability that was emerging in India, the political leadership at the national level proposed a socialist model of polity. In fact, Birla, a business tycoon, was of the opinion that a "purely capitalist organization is the last body to put up an effective fight against communism" (Mitra, 2007: 30)

The business class at that time was in favour of development, like J.C. Setalvad in 1945 went on to suggest that in agriculture, collective farming should be included with cooperatives for rural transformation (Mukherjee, 2002).

In fact, in Bombay Plan, prominent responsibilities were played by the state in the development process. That is why the National Planning Committee sponsored by the Indian National Congress had a significant participation of business into its sub-committees.

Mukherjee (2002) pointed out that though the industrialists tried to push their class interests, they were forced to plan on overall development of the economy. Tata, Walchand, A.D. Sheriff, and Birla plunged into this endeavour.

To look beyond one's class interests, and to support the development movement, the business supported a public–private partnership. The Bombay Plan also looked for an effective public–private partnership to address the development issues of the nation, but also conceded an important role to the public sector to bring about the first changes required by the nation (Mitra, 2007). In fact, the outcomes of the Bombay Plan and the National Planning Committee were the same, except some of the critical provisions.

The Bombay Plan had two very important provisions: first, a socialist economy under a national government was acceptable, which was primarily to save the local industry from the double impact of socialism and imperialism of the British, and second, an attempt to secure space for private industry, so that the state may consider ownership of the key industries, provided the industrialists are not keen to own it.

Business remained an integral part of the national policy debates, but Gandhi's philosophy and his ideas, and their influence on the business current, were very much visible. Philanthropy reigned over the business exercises, and it was primarily education and health that these businesses pour their resources into. To name a few, the Tatas, Birla, Bajaj, Singhanias, and many others have set up premier institutes, and the state also has supported such incentives.

The government also granted few incentives for business to be involved in these development efforts. Though there were few takers on rural development initiatives, but the Tatas departed from the typical professional temperament, and established the Tata Steel Rural Development Society. Later on, other business conglomerates entered the rural development initiatives, with special tax incentives in 1960s and 70s. "Among these were the 1978 Birla Rural Development Association, the Narottam Lalbhai Rural Development Association (NLRDF) set up in the 1970s, the Lalbhai Group Rural Development Fund in 1984, the Birla Agricultural Farm and the Newata Mandal Village Project in 1979, the Escorts Rural Development and Uplift Division in 1971, Excel Industries Vivekananda Research and Training Institute in Kutch for water resources and health in 1976; and the CC Shroff Self Help Centre in 1978" (ibid: 33). Therefore, it was evident that during that period, business and government went their own directions.

Post-liberalization, new engagements have emerged in developmental activities. A different sort of partnership was emerging between public and private sectors. There were few corporates who went farther ahead than the government with their corporate responsibility practices. The Tata Group of Companies took the lead (see Table 1). In fact, many of the labor laws established by the government were already put in place by the Tatas.

**Table 1: Tata Steel's "First" in Labour Welfare Measure**

| *Labour Welfare Measures* | *Introduction in Tata Steel* | *Enforced by Law* | *Subsequent Legal Measures* |
|---|---|---|---|
| Eight hour working day | 1912 | 1948 | Factories Act |
| Free medical aid | 1915 | 1948 | Employees State Insurance Act |
| Establishment of welfare department | 1917 | 1948 | Factories Act |
| Schooling facilities for children | 1917 | | |
| Formation of works committee for handling complaints, service conditions, and grievances | 1919 | 1947 | Industrial Disputes Act |
| Leave with pay | 1920 | 1948 | Factories Act |
| Worker's provident fund scheme | 1920 | 1952 | Employees PF |
| Workmen's accident compensation scheme | 1920 | 1924 | Workman's Compensation Act |
| Technical institute for training of apprentices, craftsmen, and engineering graduates | 1921 | 1961 | Apprentices Act |
| Maternity benefit | 1928 | 1946 | Bihar Maternity Benefit |
| Profit-sharing bonus | 1934 | 1965 | Bonus Act |
| Retiring gratuity | 1927 | 1972 | Payment of gratuity |
| Ex-gratia payments for road accidents while coming to or returning from duty | 1979 | | |
| Social audit | 1980 | | First in India |
| Pension scheme | 1980 | | |

*Source:* Mitra, Meera (2009), It's Only Business, Oxford and New York: Oxford University Press, p. 37.

It is not only in India, but in some western countries, attempts are made by research foundations to draw attention to the international landmark set by Tata Steel Mill: "The report points out that when the steel mills were still being built, two of Britain's most prominent social scientists and political activists, Sidney and Beatrice Webb, were brought to Jamshedpur to advise on employment and social policy. The report states, by 1912, the Company had instituted the policy of an eight hour working day, long before it was introduced in Europe or in the US, and 36 years before it was made mandatory in India" (David, Delvin & Laurie, 1997: 162). Tatas are considered as the trendsetter for several ethical practices in the industry.

Globalization and environmental expectations have huge implications for business. The business is unmistakably a zero-pollution environment, whatever be the legal requirements. There is a growth in the new environment market in India, including markets for pollution control equipment, or environmental consultancy services.

In order to move to a higher level of social equilibrium, there has been a business move to invest in socially responsible activity. Ashok Leyland, an automobile company in India, was way ahead of environmental legislation. The Company has adopted norms limiting vehicular pollution way ahead of legislation in 1987. Another very interesting initiative of the company was that it has launched a mobile emission clinic which operates on highways and checks vehicles at different entry points in New Delhi. The company has also introduced the first CNG-run bus in India (1997) in collaboration with its foreign partner. Such deliberations have established the fact that business responsibility is not just to benefit society but also to business.

Transparency, accountability became a wave in international business especially in compliance-driven areas, and India too followed the trend. Surveys were conducted to assess transparency in Indian business (UNDP, British Council, CII, PricewaterhouseCoopers Survey of Indian Business, 2002). These surveys showed that enhancing transparency through environmental reporting to investors is gaining ascendancy. Almost 67 percent of the companies in the survey had undertaken such initiatives. However, it is clearly competition and market driven because an overwhelming majority of these companies (85 percent) were public-listed companies. The trend however has been set for the remaining 15 percent who were not public-listed companies, but also moved in the direction of disclosure.

There has been a trend towards environmental compliance, but there is a continuing avoidance of compliance. Even there is a lack of responsibility in legal requirements, with non-compliance to environmental responsibility.

The government mechanisms should be efficient enough to practice compliance so that all the players abide by it. If the environment ends up being polluted, then government's regulatory role should rise above all, and ensure that corporate responsibility is maintained. It is observed that the regulatory bodies in India are understaffed, underqualified, and hence failed to play any regulatory role. The monitoring mechanism had plenty of loopholes. That is why, innovative compliance measures were initiated by the community and civil society organizations.

Business chambers and associations that grew up around 1980s and 1990s were primarily established to address policy issue that is economy driven. But, later on, they tried to address wider social concerns.

The Social Development Council (SDC) of the Chamber of Indian Industries (CII) and the FICCI Socio-Economic Development Foundation (FICCI-SEDF), the Rural Development Foundation and the Family Welfare Foundation, all of these associations of business formalized their social initiatives way back in 1980s and 1995.

In India, the business chambers ascertained their role as facilitators of CSR through research. The research was selected in some fields of development like education and health. Both were identified as not only important for national development, but for business growth as well (Mitra 2007).

Even CII at that time, through its education and few literary committees developed a document for planning and designing school projects. This was further argued to be a project for social development around the workplace, and was more or less value-added educational initiative to the existing system, but not a parallel system.

Developmental projects sometimes serve as rescue models for people who are affected by disasters. We are aware that India is the home to major national disasters and health epidemics. For instance, The Gujarat earthquake in 2001 left 20,000 dead, several thousand injured, and over a million homeless. FICCI entered into a strategic alliance with CARE India to form the FICCI–CARE Gujarat Rehabilitation Project (FCGRP) in collaboration with Government of Gujarat (project initiated by FICCI-SEDF under Chairmanship of P.M. Sinha) and raised over 57 crore for reconstruction efforts. The intervention model adopted by FICCI was very unique, as it was a quick action, multi-stakeholder partnership initiative.

Again, in 2004, CII plunged into disaster relief for Tsunami victims in Tamil Nadu. CII in collaboration with Tamil Nadu Government engaged in a multi-stakeholder partnership from relief to rehabilitation. Then, 2004 Mumbai flood also drew the attention of CII, and in association with the police of Maharashtra started relief camps, and participated in procuring medicines, clothes, and medical services to the victims. The association between business and social development is very old. Institutional involvement in the pursuit of corporate social initiative had added a new momentum to this relation.

There are numerous institutions who were involved in social developments along with their corporate goals, like the International Lions and Rotary Clubs with their branches across India. In the early 1900s, these two organizations were started by individuals, who were keen to integrate extra business activity with community orientation[4] (http: //www.ri3240.com/RI/roindia.htm). If we revert back to John. H. Paterson's National Cash Register, which set the course of industrial welfare movement in America in 1800s, in India professional social responsibility by individuals—started in the 1900s. Probably, this was an effect of the Trusteeship philosophy of Gandhi.

That is why any discussion on business initiatives in social development in India would be incomplete without mentioning two organizations, i.e. the Rotary Club and Lions Club. These two organizations went past all the challenges and were successful in reaching their goals. One among these was to eradicate Polio. With new confirmed cases of Polio across the country appearing, Rotarians, worldwide and in India, committed to deliver a Polio-free world. Another significant point here is that the institutions were committed to eliminate the disease within a time frame. There were joint initiatives, at both the national and state levels to curb the disease. Such joint initiatives were between the WHO, Rotary International and the Centre for Disease Control and Prevention, and other funding bodies and the government. At the international level, "the Rotarian contribution was more than US$ 500 million, with an additional US$ 119 million raised by Rotary as resources in 2003. In addition, Rotary's Polio Eradication Advocacy task force has played a major role in decision by donor governments to contribute over US$ 1.5 Billion to the effort" (Mitra, 2007: 51). Such positive consequences pointed towards benefit of alliances between players from different background.

In India, the results were positive. The India Expert Advisory Group for Polio Eradication (IEAG) consisting of medical professionals, government representatives, other partnering organizations reviewed the efforts of the joint initiatives (WHO, Rotary International and the Centre for Disease Control and Prevention, CDS and few other collaborate bodies). Their review indicated that India has made an important progress from 2004 and early 2005 in this initiative.

A business association that took beyond the firm is looked at as a long-term business interest. Government's partnership with business also provided an incentive for social development.

## Corporate Governance, Business Ethics and CSR

When we are arguing, debating on social responsibility, we must not forget that governance-driven ethics must be an integral part of it.

Well, corporate governance is an area that has grown very rapidly in the last decade. It became a very concerned topic of discussion, especially in Europe and USA, with the failures of businesses. It is believed to have started with the collapse of the Enron. And, the subsequent financial problems of other companies in various countries (Mallin, 2001). It refers to the internal functioning or operations of business. It also implies specified rules of business decision making that apply to the internal mechanisms of companies. Certain sets of norms, rules, laws operate within the companies. These norms and laws, shape the relations among different groups of employees, say the board of directors, shareholders, and managers and also solve conflicting situations within the organization.

A business organization operation revolves around a set of contracts between three principal actors, i.e. the corporation, shareowners and the stakeholders. It relates to the internal mechanism by which corporations are operated and controlled. A good corporate governance mechanism helps to assure that corporations use their capital efficiently. It ensures that they take into account the interests of a wide range of constituencies, as well as of the communities within which they operate, and that their boards are accountable to the company and the shareholders. This, in turn, helps to assure that the corporation operates for the benefit of society as a whole. Such wide range of linkages is not simplistic enough, so preferences are given to some, while others are ignored.

If we go by the evolutionary perspective, corporate governance has undergone changes in terms of ownership and control. Then, one can analyze three major periods of corporate governance with its own models of reference (Frentop, 2003).

The first period is typified by the dominance of the founding family and stretched from the Industrial Revolution to the 1920s; the second period is marked by the rise of the professional manager and prevails from the 1920s to the 1970s, and third period, with its origin in the 1970s is characterized by increasing accountability to society. These three periods are presented as distinct stages in the history of the corporation, each with its own model of reference for corporate governance (Gomez and Korine, 2005: 743).

The historical record shows that the four western economies, i.e. France, Germany, UK and USA, in each historical period of development of corporate governance, are somewhat in congruence with democratic principles. The birth of the new economic order led to establishment of two significant developments, the establishment of property rights for industry, and the removal of the requirements of public authorization for incorporation. In fact, the American legislation on general incorporation (1811 for New York) and the English Joint Stock Company Regulation and Registration Act (1844) represent the first step towards economic sovereignty. It has opened the individual right to ownership of corporation, especially to those who can afford it, independent of status, class or heredity, and also established that every owner of property is equal before law.

Till the end of the 19$^{th}$ century, the incorporation of the limited liability company was subject to public authorization. The removal of the public authorization for incorporation started some time in 1850s, for instance, United Kingdom (1856), France (1867), Germany (1870), but also Spain (1869), Belgium (1873), Hungary (1875) and Italy (1882). The developments were significant to the tune of shareowners' power with the removal of the public authorization. Thus, shareowners acquired sovereignty over the corporation. They can freely create, buy and sell their shares. But, this doesn't imply that the corporation in the 19$^{th}$ and early 20$^{th}$ centuries was governed by the procedures of democracy. Even, the businesses at that time were predominated by family-owned business. The corporate governance was dominated by the founding families.

As the family owns and manages the assets of the corporation, there is no separation of powers in the corporation. And, since decisions are made in secret family meetings, there is no representation of outsiders and public debates. Gomez and Korine (2005) opined that the new entrepreneurs, who more often are not commoners benefitting from the new legal order, appear to recreate the institutions of the old regime, constituting veritable dynasties of industry: the DuPont de Nemours in the US, the Siemens or the Haniel in Germany, the De Wendell or the Boussac in France, and the Courtaulds in the United Kingdom.

But towards the end of the 19th century, there was a decadence of family-owned business, especially after the World War I. The reasons behind this was firms are becoming bigger, more complex, requiring more resources to maintain the growth. That is why there was a large-scale transition towards managerial form of governance. In many instances, familial governance cannot cope with the changed economic condition of the 20th century and managerial governance arose to take its place (Birla, 1932; Chandler, 1962).

There were also changes in the laws and codes, which favored the managerial control and separation of ownership in Europe and in the US, e.g. securities laws were passed concerning the obligation of disclosure in the US in 1933 and 1934. In France, company laws were passed in 1940 and 1943, making a board of directors compulsory, and—and, in 1947 and 1957, laws were established in Germany for the two-tier board in the companies. With this type of legislation, it was believed in many business circles that democratic practices epitomized corporate governance.

Therefore, most general structure for a publicly held company includes an annual shareholders' meeting that votes on major corporate issues, an elected board of directors that oversees professional management, and in some jurisdiction, like Germany, owner and worker representatives on the board (Roe et al., 1993).

However, adoption of the corporate governance is not a straightforward process. Though corporate board is supposed to be independent of management, but in practice, the board is often dictated by the managerial technocracy.

Managerial governance faced resistance. Challenges approached business due to the dramatic changes in the technology, deregulation and globalization. Even centralization of managerial authority has not proved to be fruitful, when

MNCs need to work fast in the global market besides, the state has withdrawn from large activities, and economic weight has fall on very large corporations.

Sometimes, too much centralization of authority bestowed on the managerial system may prove to be inefficient. This is related to MNCs that need to be active and swift in the global markets.

Wartick and Cochran (1985) argues that the withdrawal of states from large activities, and concentration of economic weight on large companies raise new questions about corporate responsibility in decision making.

When the professional managers are struggling with such challenges, the nature of ownership also undergoes a significant change. Here, the important role can be credited to equity-based retirement financing, employee stock plans, privatization of large enterprises across the world, and increase in individual ownership of shares. This increase is not just limited to the advanced countries like US, Germany, France, but also the developing countries. But the wave is still to pick up.

Mass ownership and pension reform in corporate governance have led to the growth of a new class of institutional shareholders. In the opinion of Gilbert (1956), these shareholders are immensely motivated to take their concerns to management.

With the increase in the share-owning individuals, a new force was adding to corporate governance, a force which we can call mass ownership. These groups of shareowners fought to gain more information and rights over management, even engaging in public debates that have engulfed the courts, the legislations and the press (Davis and Thompson, 1994). The shareowners became a decisive force in the governance system of the firm and the state.

Although institutional investors engagement is increasing, but their roles in corporate governance are not clear. However, the individual shareowners are not the only players in the governance system. There are other stakeholders, unions, NGOs, and international forums, like the United Nations.

In fact, O'Sullivan (2001) argued that these stakeholders are reoccupying the space abandoned by national governments in the successive waves of trade liberalization and industry deregulation that characterized the half century following World War II.

## Theoretical Analysis

There are theoretical discourses on Corporate Governance which lie beneath corporate activities in a liberal democracy. Mostly, large companies are not run by their legal owners. It is the board of directors and the management that run the company on behalf of the owners. Corporate governance primarily reflects the owner–agent relationship. The Neo-Classical economics points at the individuals acting rationally to maximize their own utility. It is assumed that individuals will move their investments to obtain the highest possible return. Firms will also act to maximize their profits, and eventually it will lead to economic efficiency, and benefit all the stakeholders.

Agency theory articulates some of the conflicts of interest that exist between an agent and owner. It is a synthesis of accountability and transparency between the managers and all the stakeholders in any business enterprise. In an agency relationship, the principal, i.e. one party, delegates work to another party, i.e. the agent. But agency relationships may have a number of disadvantages, such as opportunities or self-interest of the agent (Mallen, 2004). It may also happen that one party gets all the opportunities, and the other party is left out.

A numbers of dimensions can evolve from such a relationship; say, the agent may misuse one's power for some advantage. Even, the agents may view the risks undertaken by the principal, as not being appropriate. Again, problems may also arise when there will be asymmetry in the accessibility of information. It is found that the principal is at a disadvantage because the agent usually has more information.

In the context of issues of corporate control, the Board of Directors plays an essential role as a monitoring device, to control the problems that arise from the principal–agent relationship.

Adam Smith (1838) in his book, *Wealth of Nation* argued that the directors of companies (especially the joint stock companies) act as managers of other people's money than of their own, but it cannot be expected that they play the role of a watchdog, as if it was their own.

Berle and Means (1932) worked on investor and corporate relationships. They highlighted that as countries industrialized, market system also became advanced, and the ownership and control of corporations also became separated. This is somewhat followed in USA and UK. It is also possible because the legal systems have provided protection of minority shareholders in these countries.

But in places, where there is a code of civil law as opposed to common law, the protection of minority shareholders is not strong, and as a result there has been less enthusiasm for a broad shareholder base.

There is a growth of a new form of corporate governance, particularly an institutional shareowner with dispersed ownership.

In the last few years, there has been increasing pressure on shareholders, and particularly institutional shareholders also own shares on behalf of the "man in the street", to act more as owners and not just as holders of shares. The drive for more effective and efficient shareholders, who act as owners, has come about because there have been numerous instances of corporate abuses.

That is why, when shareholders act like owners, then they will be able to exercise direct influence on companies management and the boards.
And, eventually the boards will be more accountable for their actions.

However, Useem (1996) argues that institutional investors will ultimately become accountable to the millions of ultimate owners, who may come to question the policies of the new powers. Then, the question may expand from whether they are fostering maximum public good. Their demands for downsizing and single-minded focus on shareholders benefits—whatever the costs—may come to constitute a new legal of ownership charge.

But there is a shift from shareholders to a wider stakeholder group, such as employees, customers, suppliers, government, and the local community, and then, the shareholder value becomes less evident.

When we talk about the stakeholders, it is not just the managers or the shareholders of the firm: "It includes its employees, customers, supplies and other individuals or groups that could influence or, if a broad definition of stakeholder is adopted, be influenced by the decisions of the company" (Freeman and Read, 1983). The shift from shareholders to stakeholders is a rational development, because it is not just the shareholder, but the entire gamut of employees, customers, suppliers are affected by the business decisions, influences and their outcomes.

The stakeholder perspective of corporate governance is much wider than the shareholders' interest. Only catering to the interest of the shareholder might prove to be counterproductive. This will never foster sustainability of the organization. Thus, the convergence of all stakeholders' interest will lead to a productive and sustainable organization.

The stakeholder perspective of corporate governance is far broader than the shareholders. The stakeholders represent families of economic agents or otherwise who have legitimate rights and obligations in the company. It is true that shareholders run the risk of losing their financial capital invested, but other stakeholders are equally likely to suffer more or less significant losses. Hence, the broader perspective of corporate governance should accommodate the interests, needs and demands of all the stakeholders.

An alternative approach to Corporate Governance was introduced by Donaldson and Davis (1991) as Stewardship Theory. It stresses on the beneficial consequences for shareholder returns of a facilitative authority structure, which unifies command by having roles of CEO and the chair held by the same person (refer to Mallin, 2004, for elaboration).

For an effective growth of corporate governance, codes are very essential, and then next is the compliance with the codes. The compliance is on a voluntary basis. The development of corporate governance in the UK is related to the Cadbury Report (1992). Before the report, the Cadbury Committee was set up to examine the concerns about the general sinking confidence in financial reporting and auditing. The London Stock Exchange (LSE) and the Consultative Committee of Accountancy Bodies convened a committee to consider "the financial aspects of corporate governance".

The new road to transparency involved structural changes. One such change was setting up of committees to prepare the grand future course of action. Thus, a committee met under the chairmanship of Sir Adrian Cadbury, first chairman of Cadbury Schweppes: "The Committee sat for over 18 months and, when the Cadbury Report was actually published, it was in the form of a code of conduct for companies. It recommended that company boardrooms be constituted in such a way that they would feature appropriate sub-committees dealing with matters of remuneration, audit, and nomination, with independent non-executive directors, and more crucially a separation in the rules and functions of the CEO and the Chairman" (Blowfield and Murray, 2008: 216).

This implies that a company should comply with the code, but if it cannot comply with any particular aspect of it, then it should explain why it is unable to do so. This disclosure gives investors detailed information about any instance of non-compliances and enables them to decide whether the company's non-compliance is justified (Mallen, 2004). Disclosures in the governance system of the company signal a new direction of transparency.

Debates were going on regarding the size of directors. And then, in 1995, the Greenburg Committee was set up in response to concern about the size of directors, remuneration packages and anomalies in the company's disclosure process. Blowfield and Murray (2008) argued that the pay and benefits awarded by board of directors to themselves were disapproved by many.

The core of the Greenburg Report was strengthening accountability and enhancing the performance of directors. And, these two aims were to be achieved by presence of a remuneration committee comprising independent non-executive directors who would report fully to the shareholders each year about the company's executive-remuneration policy. Since then, disclosure of director remuneration has become quite a prolific exercise.

Then, implementations of the recommendation of both the committees became the biggest challenge. To speed up the implementation of the Cadbury Committee and Greenburg Committee recommendations, the Hampel Committee was formed. A number of companies have decided not to implement the Cadbury recommendations.

The Hampel Report (1998) stated that the directors as a board are not only responsible for retaining stakeholders, but are also accountable to the shareholders. Directors can also meet their legal duties to shareholders.

As Hampel was reporting, then an attempt was made by LSE to consolidate all the three reports (the Cadbury, the Greenburg, and the Hampel Report). It tried to tabulate the recommendations of the three committees, on the one hand and institutional investors on the other hand. All the issues of audit, remuneration, shareholder relation are covered.

Hereafter, many reports and codes were developed with the acceptance of the fact that business needs a controlling mechanism.

## Corporate Responsibility and Corporate Governance Relation

Corporate failures are not just the concern of government, professional bodies, or investors, but also the public at large. Various agencies have worked at large to refine the governance mechanism so that it can minimize the probability of future crises. By and large, the terms like "accountability" and "transparency" have become a guiding procedure for CSR.

Engaging with stakeholders is an important part of how corporate responsibility is managed. From a corporate responsibility perspective, shareholders have very limited rights under the regulations governing company administration in most countries with a liberal economy. Resolution on which vote can be cast at general meetings tends to be restricted to rather functional, and administrative matters.

There is an understanding that institutional investors can play a bigger role in such a situation and few company boards may act against the desires of such organizations. But, for private shareholders, their power to influence corporate behaviors is limited and to be effective would require a level of concerted action that is beyond the will of the most investors.

Corporate responsibility as the ethical drivers of corporate governance mechanism can call for more control of the audit firms, which seem easily to escape accountability in cases of corporate collapse.

## Corporate Governance and Public Governance Relation

Corporate sector has been engulfed with failures and scandals. How much the governance codes could make a difference in the findings of the corporate world is yet not clear, because these codes were primarily voluntary in nature. But, there could be a new way, through which corporate governance can enhance itself, especially from the way democratic government and public administration are administered and organized.

Corporate governance can learn from public governance. But how? Benz and Frey (2007) propose that corporate governance can learn from four cornerstones of public governance. Corporate governance can gain from realigning manager's compensation with the practice prevalent in the public sector, especially, fixed compensation not necessarily depending on pay-for-performance relying in the democratic idea of division of power in corporate governance. And, the rules of succession prevalent in the political space can be applied for better governance in the corporate sphere. Even, corporate governance can be improved by bringing in institutionalized competition in core areas of the firms.

The concept of fixed salaries for public officials was primarily developed to set the regulation so that the officials do not get the opportunity to manipulate such principles. But if such principle of the public sector is followed in the private sector, then some fundamental problems connected with pay-for-performance can be avoided. A system of fixed compensation is the principle in public governance differs substantially from pay-for-performance. There are arguments for, and against fixed pay.

One such view is that fixed income has the important advantage of serving as redistribution constraints (Frey and Osterloh, 2005). But there are other arguments against fixed pay or compensation for top managers. We have to admit here that firms acts in a different environment than governments and public bureaucracies. And, entrepreneurial incentives are more important in the market than in democratic decision making (Dahl and Lindblom, 1953). Therefore, the distinction between government and business bureaucracies is part of the modern political economy.

Again, it shouldn't be assumed that the public governance approach is against managerial growth. It does not imply that managers should be badly paid or say, they shouldn't be given any incentives. It is also true that sometimes low wages in the public sector may lead to problems of its own.

It is seen that managers usually work in shareholders' interests, and fixed pay can be a suitable way to remunerate top managers while the lower level managers can be offered fixed compensation (Murphy, 1999). A weak relation was discovered in the decade-old research between management's compensation and firm performance.

Division of power is an important aspect of the public governance system which primarily relates to control and discipline. In a democracy, disciplining the public servant is a central task. If seen historically, democracies have developed various effective institutions to restrict accumulation of power. A very significant element of democracy is the idea of division of power.

In a democratic state, there are three classic decision-making bodies: the executive, legislative, and judiciary. This does not prevent one branch from dominating for a period of time, but it ensures that the other branches can reassert themselves in due time (Benz and Frey, 2007). Even attempts are made to draw an analogy between a private corporation and the public sector.

The CEO corresponds to the head of government, company board correspond to the members of the cabinet, and the shareholders to citizens convening in a town council meeting (Kesner and Dalton, 1986). But the political structure of the private and the public sector differs in fundamental respects, and especially division of power is applied less strictly in corporate governance than in public governance. For example, in US, France and Switzerland, it is a common practice for the CEO of a firm to be the chairperson of the board. Hence, it negates the division of power between the top agents (CEOs) and the principal, i.e. shareholders.

But not much attention has been paid, until recently to a clear separation of the control over core aspects of the firm, like the independence of compensation and audit committee (Benz and Frey, 2007). Due to the numbers of scandals that broke out in the corporate system, new government rules in many countries separate the executive from the auditing branch.

In the United States, all members of a company's audit committee, rather than management, are directly responsible for the appointment, compensation, retention, and oversight of the work of the auditors (see the Sarbans-Oxley Act). This is an area where corporate governance has co-opted inclusion applied in public governance, but only after having incurred huge costs.

It so happens that in some companies, the CEO enjoys duality of power, i.e. a person is CEO of a firm and also the chairperson of the board. If we see it from a public governance perspective, it is a case of too much power without any control. But some empirical evidences share that CEO duality leads neither to positive nor negative consequences. Beasley (1996) opined that some researchers have found a weak relationship between CEO duality and the incidence of corporate fraud.

There are other areas where corporate governance can earn from public governance. It is the institutional competition. There are two primary features of institutionalized competition: voting rights and competitive process.

Voting and representation have found their alliance to both public sector and stock companies. In both the spheres, there is a collective action problem, primarily related to disperse ownership. Most corporations use elections by shareholders to determine the members of the board, and the board then elects the top management and the external auditing firm.

Usually, each share in a company has one vote. But this is violated by the privileged shares. Such devices are used to prevent unfriendly takeovers (Grossman and Hart, 1988). But voting right shouldn't be limited to the shareholder groups and should also include the employees.

In a competitive election process, the voters can choose among the relevant alternatives. If we follow the democratic process, then the persons with the voting right will choose among various persons, the director. Again, they can also have the option of choosing among several competing firms offering external auditing.

In both the cases, the competitors must be willing to clearly state their interests and program, and they must be able to convince the corporate votes that they are capable of fulfilling the required tasks (Benz & Frey 2007: 99).

Competitive election is the best for position on the board. The Board members are the representatives of shareholders, and it is hardly conceivable that shareholders should not have the possibility to exercise their rights of free choice (Belechuk: 2003, 2005).

But again, the question is, whether competitive election is only applicable to board members. Corporate governance can be strengthened if shareholders are given the rights to choose the board members. Here, Benz and Frey argue that such election would greatly improve the independence of the shareholder, vesting them with institutionally based legitimacy to take an independent stand. And, at the same time, it would secure their (Board members) accountability to shareholders in important corporate matters. Accountability of the board members will enhance the solidarity of the firm.

Capitalism and industrial society too have their own morality and solidarity. Emile Durkheim, in his classic treatise, "Division of Labour in Society" (1933), rightly points out to the emerging order of solidarity in a complex advanced world, characterized by specialization, differences, and of course complexity.

Even the complex societies bond people, though differently from the simple societies.

Durkheim stated that in society whose solidarity is mechanical, social cohesion is based on common roots of identity and similarity (Morrison, 2006). In such a society, the individual is linked directly to society through various points of attachment. Collective rules and social practice are predominately religious in nature and tend to define and encompass all aspects of social life and social activity.

In Durkheim's (1933) argument, all sorts of circumstances were used as reasons for joyful gatherings. Moreover, distribution of food stuffs and money often took place at the community's expense.

At that time, there have been discussions, as to whether, the corporation has a sick fund. It may help those members who need it the most. Unfortunates are also aware that they could count on it at the time of need. It so happens that all the fairly rich corporation had a collective columbarium and when the organization had no funds to buy a burial plot, there was at least the certainty that its members would have honorable burial at the expense of the common fund. So, it implies that the common fund is an essential for business to fall back upon in the time of crisis.

The Roman Corporation resembles a great family. Here, community of interests took the place of the community of blood members and they looked upon themselves by that name. Familial life was very developed and the members shared a strong bond; this was replicated in the workers' corporation. Associations were principally for the pleasure of living together, for finding outside oneself distracted from fatigue and boredom, to create an intimately less restrain than the family, and less extensive than the city.

In an organic society (advanced, complex society), specialization is ingrained in the system. It is also apparent in business. The commercial code which regulates the contracts is special to business: Contracts between commission agent and principal, between carrier and shipper, between the holder of a letter of exchange and the drawer, between the owner of a ship and his creditors, between the first and the captain and crew, between the granter of a charter and the charterer, between the lender and the borrower, in gross, between the insurer and the insured (Morrison, 2006). It exemplified a relation based on specialization and contract.

Thus, with more complexity, and specialization, the solidarity losses its collectiveness and it drives more towards goal-oriented solidarity and purposive solidarity. As the societies approach the new social type, the degree of determination of collective states will slowly vanish.

Corporate governance has been established in Britain, through a series of committee formation one after another to arrive at an accurate code for the governance mechanism with the company.

But it was US which brought in regulation called Foreign and Corrupt Practices Act of 1977 followed by Securities and Exchange Commission's tightening of mandatory reporting of internal financial controls in 1979. The Tradeway Commission was formed in 1987 after the collapse of several savings and loan institutions in US. The Tradeway Report highlighted the need for a proper control environment, independent audit committees and an objective internal audit function.

Sarbanes–Oxley Act of the US (2002) was a wakeup call. It is a call to get back to fundamentals and it identifies 58 separate provisions that affect internal auditing and the question of Directors of Boards looking the other way is unacceptable and must change. It is applicable to the public and private governance and economic development deeply related with each other.

## Corporate Governance in India

In terms of corporate laws and financial systems, post-independence India emerged far better than the other colonized nations. With the 1956 Companies Act, a movement towards governance system was started.

The beginning of corporate developments in India was marked by the managing agency system that contributed to the birth of dispersed equity ownership, and also gave rise to the practice of management enjoying control rights disproportionately greater than their stock ownership.

The 1956 Industrial Policy Resolution put in place a regime and culture of licensing, protection and widespread red tape that bred corruption. In the following years, it grew bad to worse. Then, without a developed stock market, financial institutions like the Industrial Finance Corporation (IFC) of India, the Industrial Development Bank of India (IDBI), and the Industrial Credit and Investment Corporation of India (ICICI) became the providers of long-term credit to companies. But later on, these organizations were evaluated on the quantitative growth rather than on qualitative lending and as such didn't have any incentive for credit appraisal and monitoring.

Financial disclosure norms in India have been superior to most Asian countries, but fell short of those in the USA and other advanced countries. Non-compliance with disclosure norms and even the failure of auditors' reports to conform to the law attract nominal fines with hardly any punitive action (Chakrabarti, 2005). Though the Company Act provides clear instructions for share register, but in reality, minority shareholders have suffered from irregularities in share transfers and regulations, be it deliberate or unintentional.

In the post-independence era, the Indian equity markets were not sophisticated enough to exert effective control over the companies. But minority shareholders and creditors in holding remained effectively unprotected in spite of an established codified law.

Since liberalization, there has been a wide-ranging change in both laws and regulations, to start general consciousness of corporate governance. In this regard, we have to mention the Securities and Exchange Board of India (SEBI; 1992), as one of most important development in the field of corporate governance. It was established primarily to regulate and monitor stock trading. It also played a crucial role in establishing mining ground rules of corporate conduct in the country. In fact, like any other nations reason to consider an adequate governance system in business, India's urgency to establish a system of transparency and accountability took off with the Harshad Mehta stock market scam in 1992 followed by incidents of business discriminations, and preference to promote at a very high discounted price and also those companies who disappeared with investors' money.

With so many in discrepancies in the backdrop, several investigations took the lead. Code for Desirable Corporate Governance was developed by a committee chaired by Rahul Bajaj.

The CII (India's largest industry and business association) came up with first voluntary code of corporate governance in 1998. The second was by the

SEBI, now enshrined as Clause 49 of the testing agreement. The third was the Naresh Chandra Committee which also submitted report in 2002 (National Foundation for Corporate Governance, 2004).

The CII took a special initiative on corporate governance, the first ever institutional initiative in Indian industry in 1996 (Dasaraju and Murthy, 2011). This initiative by the CII flowed from public concerns regarding the production of investors' interest, particularly small investors, the promotion of transparency within business and industry.

The objective was to develop and promote a code of corporate governance to be followed by both the Indian public and private sectors. Towards the end, a National Task Force was created to oversee the desirability of corporate governance, and funding the finalized code of desirable corporate governance. With this, corporate India started recognizing the role of disclosures in creating corporate value in the market-oriented economy.

In 1991, the SEBI appointed a committee under Kumar Mangalam Birla, in order to promote the raising standards of corporate governance.

The committee's terms of reference were as follows:

> (a) to suggest suitable amendments to the agreements executed by the stock exchange with the companies and any other measures to improve the standards of corporate governance in the listed companies in areas such as continuous disclosure of material information, both financial and non-financial, manner and frequency of such disclosures, responsibilities of independent and outside directors, (b) to draft a code of best corporate practices, and (c) to suggest safeguards to be instituted within the companies to deal with insider information and insider trading. (ibid: 104)

The recommendations were both mandatory and non-mandatory.

The collapse of Enron (2001) and the enactment of the Sarbanes–Oxley Act (2002) had an immediate sparkling effect on Indian business. The Department of Corporate Affairs formed a committee to examine corporate auditing, and role of independent directors (IDs) under Naresh Chandra.

It concerned or focused on auditor's relationship with the company that touches upon some of the compulsory audit partner rotation, its disclosure of contingent liabilities, disclosure of qualification and the eventual actions, task certification by the management on the eve of auditor's replacement, its annual certification of independence, appointment of auditor, certification by the CEO and CFO on annual auditor accounts, and audit committee charters. Its recommendation were reflected also on the independence of directors, and their training exemption of non-executive directors from certain liabilities, establishment of corporate fraud office and of course, on SEBI and subordinate regulation (National Foundation for Corporate Governance, 2004).

Thus, it can be inferred that the Naresh Chandra Committee took few essential recommendations from the Kumar Mangalam Birla Committee setup by SEBI, especially, the representation of ID on a company's board, and the composition of the audit committee. Though SEBI instructed companies to comply with Birla committee's recommendations, but finally, its observations pointed towards a huge variance in the extent and quality of disclosure made by companies in their annual reports.

To further improve the corporate governance practices, SEBI formed a committee chaired by N.R. Narayana Murthy of the Infosys Technologies Ltd., an IT company. The Committee (2003) was in total concurrence with the Naresh Chandra Committee Report, especially on the following counts: disclosure of contingent liabilities, certification by the CEOs and CFOs, definition of IDs, and then, the independence of audit committees.

The committee came out with two sets of recommendations, both mandatory and non-mandatory. The mandatory recommendations focused on strong responsibilities of audit committees; improved quality of financial disclosures including those pertaining to related party transactions and proceeds from initial public offering, requiring corporate executive boards to assess and disclose business risks in the annual reports of companies, calling upon the boards to adopt formal codes of conduct; the position of nominee directors and disclosure relating to compensation to non-executive directors and shareholders.

In a significant development, the Government of India constituted an expert committee on company law under the chairmanship of Dr. J. J. Irani. It took a dramatic stand, which was in variance with SEBI, and recommended on the composition of IDs (one third of the board of a listed company should comprise IDs).

Every organization functions under certain norms, rules, and procedures.

Here, Richard E. Nisbet (2003) rightly observes that organizations have certain structures that function under certain rules and procedures. But you need people to run them, and people are a part of a society. Hence, organizations are social units, where social norms and structures, cultural practices, philosophies, and value system influence them.

Corporate governance is deeply rooted in India's philosophy and culture. India is a land of convergent philosophies, be it Hindu, Christian, secular, liberal, or Gandhian.

If we go back further, Kautilya, the celebrated ancient philosopher, in his treatise "Arthashastra" (Science of Political Economy) viewed the state as an economic organization ruled by the king. Kautilya referred the king's role to that of a trustee. Say, it is in the welfare of the subjects that the king's welfare lies.

If we equate the state to a corporation, the king to a corporation, the Chief Executive Officer or board, and the subjects to the shareholders, we could interpret Kautilya's words to mean that a corporation's resources are to be used only for the well-being of the corporation and its shareholders—not for the personal benefit of the Chief Executive Officer, the board of directors, and managers.

It was Kautilya's observation that effective economic activity brings prosperity. In the medieval period, it was Emperor Akbar who uphold reason over blind faith. In fact, through his secular religion "Din-E-Illahi", he tried to build a secular state. Thus, it can be inferred that Indian governance system drew inspiration from its own culture, customs, laws which in fact influenced the Indian business also.

In the era of globalization, Indian governance also seeks to expand worldwide. Its ability to pursue acquisitions overseas and attract foreign capital depends on its adoption of the West's approach (Afsharipur, 2010). The urgency of accounting principles intensified the Indian business to adopt the Western best practices.

India has a distinct corporate governance practice, probably originating from the family-owned companies. Khanna and Palipu (2004) argue that "concentrated ownership" is a unique characteristics of Indian business sector (private sector) for the last seven decades. They could not find any valid reasons for "concentrated ownership" or business apathy towards competition. According to them, in some Indian families, concentrated owners have consistently tried to use their business group structure to launch new ventures. In the process, they have either failed to turnover in identity or reinvented themselves.

In another analysis, it was found that one third of Indian companies are controlled by one or more family members in consent with one another (Sapovadra and Patel, 2009). Though the ownership share is decent enough, but the controlling family may dominate by using dual classes of ownership.

There are fully functional stock market and an active manufacturing sector, and a well-established English-derived system of corporate practices. Then, from 1947 to 1991, Indian Government followed semi-socialist policies. The nationalized banks became the primary provider of both debt and equity capital for the private sector. There was a huge gap here, where the government agencies that provided assistance to private firms were evaluated on the basis of the amount of capital invested rather than on their returns on investment (Pande and Kaushik). Even the private debt provides for equity capital faced serious obstacles regarding control over managers due to long delays in judicial proceedings and also difficulty in enforcing claims in bankruptcy, and the public companies were required to comply with limited governance and disclosure standards put forward by the Companies Act of 1956. Besides the companies have to refer to the listing agreements, and the accounting standards put forwarded by the Institute of Chartered Accountants of India (ICAI).

But in 1991, with a huge fiscal crisis at the backdrop, the Indian Government responded to the crisis with a series of reforms which precisely inclined towards economic liberalization. The formation of the SEBI in 1991 was one of the biggest breakthroughs at that time. It became the first securities' market regulator. By mid-1990s, the Indian economy grew steadily and the Indian private firms began to seek equity capital for financial expansion and the growth of outsourcing.

Since the mid-1990s, there was a growth of initiative focusing on improving the governance system in corporate India, but it was essentially very much rudimentary. Well, the first step towards the codification of the corporate governance was started by the CII, the India's largest industry and business associates. Immediately, after the East Asian crisis of 1997, the CII went ahead and set up a committee to examine corporate governance issues, and recommended a voluntary code of best practices. The voluntary code drew its basic structure from the Anglo–Saxon Model of Corporate Governance. The code was voluntary, detailed and focused, especially on listed companies. The Desirable Corporate Governance: A Code (CII Code) was publicly released in April 1988. Though it had overwhelming response, but some felt that Indian situation is far more conditioned for a statutory system than a voluntary code. The SEBI took up the second major corporate governance initiative by setting up the Kumar Mangalam Birla Committee to raise the standards of corporate governance. The Birla Committee made few specific recommendations regarding board representations and independence, support law, audit committees, and also the function and constitution of the board audit committees.

SEBI ratified some recommendations and incorporated those into Clause 49 of the listing agreement of the stock exchange. With corporate failures in the US, there was a growth of consciousness in the industry and the Government. The Department of the Company Affairs (DCA), under Ministry of Finance and Company Affairs, appointed the Naresh Chandra Committee. It made recommendations in terms of two key aspects: financial and non-financial disclosure and independent auditing and board oversight of management. Besides, it also made few recommendations pertaining to certain matters: the grounds for disqualification of audition from assignments, the type of non-audit services that auditors should be prohibited from performing, and concern for compulsory rotation of audit partners.

In order to create more positive corporate governance, SEBI again set up a committee under the chairmanship of N.R. Narayana Murthy, in order to review Clause 49, and also suggested measures to improve corporate governance standards. Both, the Birla Committee, and the Narayana Murthy Committee examined a range of corporate governance issues relating to corporate boards and audit committees as well as disclosure to shareholders and, in their reports, focused heavily on the role and structure of corporate boards; they argued for strengthening the definition of IDs mentioned in Clause 49, specially to address the role of insiders on Indian Boards.

Most of the committees, considered the Anglo-American standards of governance, and its imprints were evident in the provisions. Though it did not directly cite the Anglo-American model of governance, but its reaction followed few months after the enactment of the Sarbanes–Oxley Act (SOA), 2002. Then, in 2011, the revised Bill was presented in the Lok Sabha (14th Dec.). In fact, there were striking similarities between Clause 49 and the leading Anglo-American corporate governance standards—specially, the Cadbury Report, the OECD Principle of Corporate Governance, and Sarbanes–Oxley.

With Clause 49, the corporate governance did not put an end to its reform efforts. Rather, the Companies Act, 1956, was revised by the Ministry of Corporate Affair (MCA) under the chairmanship of Dr. J. J. Irani on 2nd Dec. 2004 to advance on new Companies Bill. Then, based on recommendations of the Irani Committee, the Government of India introduced the Companies Bill, 2008. It sought to enable the corporate sector in India to operate a regulatory environment. Due to the dissolution of the Fourteenth Lok Sabha, the Companies Bill lapsed. Most of the provisions of the Bill were broadly considered to be suitable for addressing various contemporary issues relating to corporate governance. The Government re-introduced the Companies Bill, 2008, as the Companies Bill, 2009 (no changes were made in the provision, except the year).

One very interesting observation is that the corporate governance movement in India was being initiated by SEBI till the last decade. The recent developments have been taken by the MCA. The Companies Bill, 2011, contains several aspects of corporate governance which have hitherto been the mainstay of Clause 49. This represents a trend towards legislating on corporate governance rather than leaving it to the domain of the risky agreement.

This also signifies that there is a shift in corporate governance from SEBI to the MCA.

India has a new Company Act, i.e. the Companies Act, 2013. With the passing of the Companies Bill, 2012, several things changed in the Indian corporate sector. The basic recommendations are as follows: the corporate boards will have to have a third of their members as independent members;

same boards will have to include more women; auditors will have to be compulsorily changed after 10 years; directors of a company will have to become more accountable and most important, minority shareholders and depositors in a company. The main issue that the Act focused on was Independent Directors (IDs). The provisions to make companies have one third of their board members as ID is fine in principle. IDs are also more stringently defined; their times will be limited to the team adding up to 10 years. IDs can also hold a maximum of 20 directorships.

The Bill doesn't make two percent spending on CSR mandatory, but it somewhat comes close to it. The Bill does not define CSR, but the only obligation is to earmark the funds, form a committee, and formulate a CSR policy. The company can donate or spend money, but have to be clearly indicated in the annual report. The new act is very bureaucratic; to make the directors accountable, it mandates that every director shall register himself or herself with the government and obtain a Director Identification Number (DIN).

But the most innovative part of the Act is the enabling of tort action and class action suits. Jagannatha argued that if such provision had been on the statute book in 2008, Satyam Indian Shareholders could have filed a class suit against the Rajus, or even the Mahindra-run Company that took over Satyam assets.

### Significance of Corporate Governance Reform

A very crucial aspect of the corporate governance reforms in India is its voluntary nature and the public-listed companies endeavour in improving the governance standards.

CII, a non-government, industry-managed organization primarily dominated by giant public-listed firms, had played a very active role in the development of India's corporate governance norms. Though it started as a voluntary exercise, but it acquired a mandatory status through the adoption of Clause 49, which means that, companies listed on stock exchange were required to comply with these norms, and it was further reinforced by stringent penalties for violation of the prescribed norms. But the voluntary corporate governance guidelines of 2009 was a move back to a voluntary perspective, whereas the consolidation of corporate governance efforts into the Companies Act, 1956, can be regarded as reversal effort. Thus, the corporate governance norms in India are an oscillation between the voluntary and the mandatory approaches.

Like any other territory, corporate governance in India had certain basic issues. According to Varma (1997), the governance issue in the US or the UK is essentially that of disciplining the management that has ceased to be effectively accountable to the owners. As against this, the problem in the Indian corporate sector (be it the public sector, the multinationals or the Indian private sector) is that of disciplining the dominant shareholder, who is the principal block-holder, and protecting the minority shareholders. In the Indian context, it is not possible to resolve the conflict between the dominant shareholder and the minority shareholders.

In Varma's view, abuses of corporate governance in India have been defined on the principle of "shareholder democracy", as they are sanctioned by resolutions of the general body of shareholders, and Board of the company has been powerless to prevent such abuses. He feels that remedies against corporate governance abuses lie outside the company. That is why reforms in governance system are essential for equal significance to all shareholders.

## Corporate Governance, Business Ethics and Corporate Social Responsibility

The word "Ethics" is derived from a Greek word "ethos", which means character or custom. But in contemporary lines, the word ethos is referred to distinction, character or attitude of a specific people, culture, or group.

It refers to the rational and responsible person who finds himself or herself obliged and constrained to act by virtue of the position or office one occupies, and the function one is called upon to discharge. If it is put simply, it means the rational person obliged to act by virtue of the duty, situation, position or office (Agalgatti and Krishna, 2001).

## Philosophy behind Ethics

Socrates (469-399 BC), Plato (C.427-347) and Aristotle (384-322), these legendary philosophers, tried to connect ethics to a meaningful life. According to these three philosophers, ethics is played successfully through the functions of human beings or activity which is peculiar to them. In such context, Aristotle's "eudaimonia" (good life) consists of successful performance of that function. And then, nothing can perform its peculiar function successfully unless, it is good of its kind. For Plato and Aristotle, the content of "good of its kind" depends on some prior notion of what it is to be human. It is not just morality, but the nature of the good life of man.

Here, how do we as common people perceive, what are right actions? Socrates doesn't have proper account of justice, and also not aware who could do so. Then, Plato treats such knowledge as special knowledge, accessible to only a few. He in fact tells what sort of person one should aim to be. But Aristotle tries to locate the source of ethical insights into experience of life. He believed that a combination of training in the right habits and direct experience with practical situations will enrich an individual's ethical insights.

Kant confirms the existence of an absolute moral law. Kant's moral principles do not rest on contingencies, but on defined actions, as inherently right or wrong. He believed that moral rules can, in principle, be known as a result of reason alone and are not just based on observation.

Kant wrote that moral obligation must not be sought in human nature, (nor) in the circumstances of the world. Rather, it is a prior, by which he meant that moral reasoning is not based on factual knowledge and that reason by itself can reveal the basic principles of neutrality (Shaw, 57). Thus, from here, one can draw the basic moral principles of Kant's ethics, i.e. actions are morally defensible to the extent they respect the freedom, dignity, and autonomy of people. He gave utmost importance to the rational character of human personality and provided another basic guideline to the effect that the principles of human action must be able to be applied universally and be free from internal contradiction and inconsistencies.

If we see from utilitarian philosophy, it is the majority that determines what is moral? Or what is immoral? It states that each person votes on the basis of his or her pleasure or pain, but it goes by the majority ruling. Utilitarians argue that almost anything might, in principle, be morally right in some particular circumstance. For instance, breaking a promise usually produces unhappiness, but in some circumstances, more happiness would be produced. Under such circumstances, utilitarians would pursue to break the promise.

Utilitarians also wish to maximize happiness not just immediately, but in the long run. The indirect effect of an act should be taken into account. Utilitarians also acknowledge that future consequences of human actions are uncertain. That is why, one has to act accordingly, and the expected result will be as great as possible. When one has to choose among possible actions, utilitarians do not ask people to disregard their own pleasure.

Utilitarian ethics in an organization system promote an organizational policy, decision or actions which promote the general welfare more than any other alternative does. Utilitarianism stands as an alternative for resolving self-interest and it contrast with egoism.

By proposing a standard outside self-interest, Shaw argued that utilitarianism greatly minimizes and may actually eliminate such disputes. Such standards provide a flexible, result-oriented approach to moral decision making. By recognizing no action of a general kind as inherently right or wrong, utilitarianism encourages organizations to focus on the results of different actions and policies and it allows them to tailor their decision to suit the company's situations.

Do Kantian ethics have any form of applicability for organization? Kantian ethics provides an organization with firm rules to follow in moral decision making. Kant introduced humanistic dimensions into business decisions. As we have seen, both utilitarianism and egoism treat humans as means to an end, but Kantian ethics strictly forbid this.

Well, many would argue that respect for the inherent worth and dignity of human being is much needed today in business, in which increasing technology and computerization tend to dehumanize people under the guise of efficiency. Kant's theory puts the emphasis of organizational decision making where it belongs to individuals. Organizations, after all, involve human beings working in concert to promote goods and services for other human beings. For Kant, an action has a moral value, when the person doing it is morally motivated, i.e. either on principle or out of moral conviction.

He makes a logical demonstration of categorical imperative which is core to his ethics. A person making a false promise using someone else as a means is equivalent to imposing your will on him or her, against his will or interest. Otherwise, another way of viewing "categorical imperative" is that we should make a general principle to govern our action, and test its validity, in the light of reason (Agalgatti and Krishna, 2001: 54).

The basic moral principles in Kantian ethic are that actions are morally defensible to the extent that they respect the freedom, dignity, and autonomy of people.

## Ethics and Morality in Business

Moral standards, human welfare, high levels of spiritual perfection are all attached to the doctrine of morality. Moral standards are different from non-moral standards as they are based on ethical conduct. Again, moral standards are different because they concern behavior that is of serious consequence to human welfare that can hurt people (Shaw, 1999). Moral judgments are very strong, by nature, and such judgments are primarily very strong and can be overridden only by a stronger moral consideration. It can be observed that moral praise plays a crucial role in our social life, while making moral coercion, an effective instrument in social change (Agalgatti and Krishna, 2001).

Levinas argued that ethics is not just oneself, but recognition of other people, i.e. a person's responsibility towards others (Bergo, 2017).

Ethics comes into its own, when people recognize that in the pursuit of individual excellence, there are other people who have to be treated with respect (Krygier, 1997).

Morality unlike ethics can be privatized, and indeed it often is. Morality does not demand acquiescence from others the way ethics does. In other words, it is possible to be moral alone. In fact, many times a moralist gets a charge by being in a sea of immoral people (Gupta, 2006). If we see morality from another angle, it may also compel to abide by norms of purity and pollution, racial and religious appetite. The prejudices attached to such kind of morality are not open for scrutiny.

We can also perceive morality as good in itself, and not because of its ability to do collective good. And, even if others do not participate in a particular moral consideration, a person's moral standard will not change.

Morals are not pressurized to objectively demonstrate the efficacy of morality, which is unlike ethics. Ethics must always, without exception, translate its norms into policies that have demonstrated positive effects. This is why, ethics is so important in the making of organization norms.

## Merging of Corporate Governance and Ethics

Max Weber (1905) in his epoch-making book *Protestant Ethic and the Spirit of Capitalism* draws upon the hardworking Protestants as the epitome of new capitalism in Europe. Protestants were disoriented with the Church, because the Church drifted from the Cardinal principles of Christianity. A new philosophy of Protestantism was born with novel orientation. This novel orientation is that the utter despair made them hardworking, and they called it duty. The duty is the hard work on this earth that will get a better place in heaven after death. So, the origin of ethics in business (in Europe) and growth of Protestants in capitalism is very much linked.

Ethics, religion and business, though are three different phenomena, but connectivity between them is very significant. With the loss of faith in Christianity, people leaned towards new sects, such as the Protestant sects. It is believed that admission to congregation is an absolute guarantee of the moral qualities required in business, such as "Baptism secures to the individual the deposits of the whole region and unlimited credit without any competition" (Gerth and Mills, 2009: 305). It so happened that, if a sect member travelled from one place to another, he carried the certificate of his congregation. Sect membership meant a certificate of moral qualification and especially of business morals for the individuals.

The extraordinary moral discipline was unavoidable because of the interest in the purity of the sacramental community. In this respect, the sect resembles the monastic order; persons expelled because of moral offences were often denied any contact with other members of the sect. The sect thus invoked an absolute boycott against them, which included business life.

The members of the sect have to possess certain qualities to enter the community circle. Being endowed with such qualities was important for the development of rational modern capitalism. This can be considered as the origin of ethics in business.

The ascetic sects formed one of the most important historical foundations of modern individualism and ethics. Sects are usually united through ethically qualified fellow believers. Their membership was not based upon apprenticeship or upon the family relations of technically qualified members of an occupation. The sect controlled and regulated the members conduct exclusively in the sense of formal righteousness and methodical asceticism. It was devoid of the purpose of material subsistence policy which handicapped an expansion of the rational striving for profit.

In modern world, ethical issues are pervasive in business and in the field of corporate governance, awareness of ethical issues ensures that managers avoid abusing their power. Sharing of power amongst the different actors makes up a company's structure. In this way, the relationship between ethics and corporate governance humanizes the exercise of power and renders it more transparent and credible not only to the shareholder in particular, but also to stakeholders in general (employees, clients, suppliers, trade unions, NGOs, public opinion) (Dessain et al., 2008).

Ethical behavior in governance is the way in which a company's stakeholders try to manage collective action in the interest of the majority. In the area of governance, ethics aims at raising awareness of the other rights and common needs, by imposing some principles of minimum requirement. Hence, ethical governance must be seen as a system of shared and transparent governance which seeks to establish the general frameworks and guidelines for managers of large companies, by enforcing the value of transparency, responsibilities and professionalism (ibid).

To be ethical is not a spontaneous process and it requires different stakeholders to transform their mindsets, behavior and actions. In this regard, Enriquez (1993) identifies four main ethical challenges. First, it is the ethics of conviction that entails the courage of affirming and defending one's own opinions and principles. Second is the ethics of responsibility which emphasizes on autonomy and free will and asks individuals to reflect on the context and consequences of their decisions or actions. For this reason, this kind of ethics brings about tensions between organizational and personal responsibilities. Third, Enriquez identifies the ethics of discussion, based on sharing information and on defining interests around the issues of reciprocity. Finally, Enriquez identifies the ethics of purposefulness focused on the goals of an action, for which ethical decisions take into considerations widely shared missions and values. If we see the last one, it is an attempt to integrate the other three and change their principles to make them compatible.

However, organizations should reflect upon all these challenges and transform into operational guidelines, which will formalize an ethical approach to corporate governance. And, this will probably match professionalism with citizenship and principles of action with rules of conduct (Dessain et al., 2008).

This ethical formalization appears to respond to a dual need. It allows the company to act as a tool for reacting to external pressures and also for establishing internal rules. Hence, monitoring and controlling system should be established in every organization.

Dessain asserts that these systems should aim at establishing relationships of trust as well as constructive transactions. However, creation of codes of conduct is just one aspect of the process of ethical institutionalizations within companies. Companies also need internal ethics committee at the board level, the appointment of personnel in charge of ethics, and the organization of periodical ethic audits.

With these positive actions in command, the organization should be an integral part of the corporate world, and has to create value and generate profits. The economic objective of the organization should not be criticized. Porter and Kramer (2006) argue that a company should carefully select the social and environmental issues it wants to address and select those more likely to bring about benefits to both society and itself. In the areas of sustainable development and social responsibility, ethical needs have also to support the growth of companies. It should have the capacity to innovate by anticipating foreseeable situation and a more rigorous and global management of the risks, especially environmental and social ones. Respecting ethical principles is also at the core of companies' efforts to preserve their reputation and valuation, especially with respect to public opinion and their clients.

### Stakeholder Perspective in Ethics

Stakeholders are a boon to company's well-being. There is no doubt that the shareholders put their money in business; employees contribute through their expertise and performance on the job; customers buy the goods and services that a business enterprise offers; the community supports the enterprise as a corporate citizen. It shows that stakeholders have a legitimate claim and genuine interest in the firm. All the stakeholders expect value in return. What is this "value"? For the shareholders, it is the proper utilization of the money that they have put in the shares (profit): then employees want recognition of their work, a just working environment and responsibilities of the company towards their services, through remuneration, but also concern for their families, and above all, transparency and accountability, with well-organized corporate governance system; customers aspect quality products at appropriate prices, that will add value to the money, and the community values, environmental responsibility, and if possible contribute to social change.

What constitutes values for different categories of stakeholders is business ethics all about. Then again, what is the stakeholder view of business? It is important to know how employees at different levels in the hierarchy view the rules and norms of the company. Then, the company should not forget the creditors and dealers, who are external to the organization, but are very integral to the organization. Then, the customers should be satisfied with goods and services of the business.

There is a shift in concern in the corporate world from shareholders to the stakeholders, and this shift has made a huge difference even on pure business consideration: "Successful corporate houses in the west have developed acute sensors to pick up the faintest seismic rumble among customers, and indeed, in the community at large. This is how leaders in the business field broke away from the pack and set up an entirely different set of standards" (ibid: 38). By giving the public a feeling that they matter, such companies reject the more traditional ones that focused only on shareholders returns.

Stakeholder orientation recognizes the multiple objectives of the company, not just maximization of shareholders' wealth. Sometimes, the connection between shareholders and managers is nothing more than an existing contract between productive entities. The company is considered to be a specific set of contacts applicable to customers, suppliers, employees, investors and so on. In this regard, changes turn out to be particularly significant concerning consumers that would like to consume products manufactured under conditions corresponding to the principle of sustainable development, or for investors that would like to invest in companies that position themselves for their objective. And, hence one can argue that the desire for equilibrium between the interests of the various stakeholders of the company and the investors will manifest itself in a way that the value is appreciated more broadly across a multi-stakeholder vision of the company and its governance.

## CSR, Corporate Governance and Ethics—The linkages

CSR should have a business interest, without too much obsession with profit. Ethics should be given top priority, with positive corporate governance into place. CSR is not just obeying the law; it is more than that. Its primary concern is the stakeholders (customers, employees, suppliers, and clients) and they are viewed quite differently than the way they were perceived decades ago.

An organization must have a governance mechanism within the organization. But how do the governance mechanism work? Does it follow any procedures or codes?

With so many corporate frauds, failures, it has become essential to strategize the mechanism of the firm, so that all the stakeholders' interests are recognized. When we discuss governance, ethics comes into the foray automatically. Ethics aims at raising awareness of others rights, needs, and interests. Ethical governance is a system of shared and transparent governance which seeks to establish a general framework for its high-ranking managers, by enforcing the values of transparency, accountability, responsibility, and professionalism. It is also necessary to know which values are essential, which ones protected and defended. Materialization of interests and transformation of guidelines for operational purpose formalizes the link between ethics and governance.

Freidmanian understanding of CSR was very instrumental, and narrow, for it was primarily profit driven within the rule of law. Any other responsibility has to be shouldered by the state, for it is not businesses' responsibility. But, Friedman's view of social responsibility was very narrow, and CSR has gone beyond charity or donor mentality.

To exercise the best possible CSR would be to incorporate the cardinal principles of democracy within the organization and outside. CSR within the organization will be top driven: from the top executives to the most unskilled personnel will be given equal priority. But the implication here is not all employers will be at par with each other. Principles of transparency and accountability will replace exclusiveness of higher ranks. Corporate governance can draw some inspiring concerns from public governance, like fixed compensation, democratic division of power, rules of successions, and institutionalized competition. Adoption of these steps will set up a governance system within the organization. Companies are shifting their concerns from shareholders to stakeholders. Companies have to build their reputation on ethics and public concern. They are into more employee relation, and consumer practice. And, as a positive development, these new motives have aligned business with dominant social concerns. Ethics is not just contented here; it believes in a participative corporate culture. The participative corporate culture consists of effective communication between different levels, gainful remunerative policy and protection of whistle blower; the workplace democratic system entails to look at workplace practices and the workers' plight seriously. They are the force behind the growth of business.

Democracy is a universal value. It enriches the lives of the citizens in different ways. Be it political freedom, or social freedom, it perpetuates political and social participation. Applicability of democracy in workplace is complex, but cannot be denied. Democracy in the form of participation increases group and community identification through shared interest. Individuals are expected to cooperate in work and also in arenas outside work. But can democracy work in a workplace and outside? Yes, workplace community is different from the nation-state. To take part in the competitive system of the market and compete according to the dictates of the market is not easy. Probably, it can sustain among the territorial communities of the workplace.

The indistinct boundaries of the workplace can deter the growth of a democratic system in a workplace, but it cannot outrightly, write off democratic process in the workplace and beyond. That is why, it is important to rethink about the association of democracy and workplace governance system.

The rules in an industrial or occupational order are different in form and substance, from the typical constitutional order of the state. The firm is the shareholders' democracy, and if it intends to extend its boundaries, the management should be made accountable to a more extensive set of interests. The principle of democratic order implies that each individual or constituency should have the same degree of power to affect the outcomes of the firm's decision-making processes at all levels of decision making.

An all-participative mechanism is essential to establish a democratic order within a firm. This will ultimately culminate into strong corporate governance, which will bear implications not only within the firm, but outside as well.

## NOTES

1. As it became an alarming situation in business in 1934, Franklin D. Roosevelt started the New Deal Measures, which are primarily designed to limit the power of the corporations. There was strong opposition from the industry, but the government did not change the provisions of the New Deal. It was only when oil shortages crippled the economy, the US Government was forced to rethink its economic policies.
2. John Williamson, an English economist, coined this term in 1989. To him, it refers to a set of ten relatively specific economic policy guidelines which he thought as a kind of standard package for crisis-ridden developing nations. And these policy prescriptions were mainly developed by Washington-based institutions like IMF, World Bank and the US Treasury Department. However, today, the term is used more commonly to refer to market fundamentalism or neoliberalism.
3. According to David Henderson, the "Salvationist Illusion" states that globalization has transferred power from governments to business. And, it also confers on business and NGOs the same status which they have no claim on, because they are neither elected nor politically accountable. CSR holds that businesses should assume a leading role in making the world a better place: they should demonstrate corporate citizenship. This is taken to mean endorsing and pursuing the objective of sustainable development. CSR supporters presume mistakenly that the notion of sustainable development is well-defined and universally agreed (Henderson, 2001).
4. The commercial infrastructure was drawn to bring innovations in the bottom of the pyramid. Shaping aspirations, innovations of sustainable product in the Tier 4, will promote consumer education, which will benefit the people at the bottom of the pyramid, but will also shape the future of those in Tier 1. *Improving access:* Better distribution and communication system will improve the accessibility of those in Tier 4. *Tailoring local situations:* To produce global products is not enough; in order to stay in business one has to cater to the needs of local markets, culture, and then only one can generate wealth at the lowest levels of the pyramid, creating buying power. As more than one third of the workforce in the world are low paid or unemployed, neither they can support themselves nor their families. Creating buying power of those will help to elevate them, and will also prove to be a valid business opportunity.

## REFERENCES


Afsharipour, Afra (2010), 'The Promise and Challenges of India's Corporate Governance Reforms,' Indian Journal of Law and Economics, 1(1): 33.

Agalgatti, B. H. and Krishna, S. (2001), Business Ethics, Delhi: Nirali Prakashan.

Balasubramanian, N.K., Kimber, D. and Siemensma, F. (2005), 'Emerging Opportunities to Traditions Reinforced,' Journal of Corporate Citizenship, 17: 79-92.

Beasley, M. S. (1996), An Empirical Analysis of the Relation between the Board of Director Composition and Financial Statement Fraud, Accounting Review, 71: 443-465.

Bebchuk, L. A. (2003), The Case for Shareholder Access to the Ballot, Business Lawyer, 59: 43-46.

Bebchuk, L. A. (2005), The Case for Increasing Shareholder Power, Harvard Law Review, 118: 833-914.

Benz, Mathias and Frey, S. Bruno (2007), 'Corporate Governance: What Can We Learn from Public Governance?', Academy of Management Review, 32(1): 92-104.

Bergo, Bettina (2017), Emmanuel Levinas, The Stanford Encyclopaedia of Philosophy, Fall Edition, in Edward N. Zalta ed., Available at: https: //plato.stanford.edu/archives/fall2017/entries/levinas/.

Berle, A. A. and Means, G. C. (1932), The Modern Corporation and Private Property. New York: Macmillan.

Birla Committee Report. Available athttp: //www.sebi.gov.in/commreport/corpgovhtml.

Blowfield, Michael and Alan, Murray (2008), Corporate Responsibility: A Critical Introduction, Oxford: Oxford University Press.

Bowman, Edward H and Haire, Mason (1975), 'A Strategic Posture Toward Corporate Social Responsibility,' California Management Review, 18: 49-58.

Carroll, Archie B. (2009), 'A History of Corporate Social Responsibility', in Andrew Crane et al. (eds.), The Oxford Handbook of Corporate Social Responsibility, Oxford: Oxford University Press.

Chakrabarti, Rajesh (2005), Corporate Governance in India: Evolution and Challenges, Social Science Network. Available at http: //ssrn.com.

Chandler, A. D. (1962), Strategy and Structure: Chapters in the History of American Industrial Enterprise, Cambridge, MA: MIT Press.

Chandler, A. D. (1977), The Visible: The Managerial Revolution in American Business, Cambridge, MA: Harvard University Press.

Choksi (1966), 'The Gandhian Concept of Trusteeship', in Social Responsibility of Business-IIC, Bombay: Manaktala & Sons Pvt. Ltd., pp. 85-100.

Committee for Economic Development (1971), Social Responsibilities of Business Corporations, New York: Committee for Economic Development.

Dahl, R. A. and Lindblom, C. E. (1953), Politics, Economics and Welfare, New York: Harper & Row.

Dallas, G. (ed.) (2005), Governance and Risk: An Analytical Handbook for Investors, Managers, Directors and Stakeholders, New York: McGraw Hill.

Dasaraju, Himachalam and Murthy, Kota Srinivasa (2011), 'Corporate Governance Mechanism and Issues in Emerging Economies: A Case of India in Global Scenario,' International Journal of Management and Business Studies, 1(3), http: //www.ijmbs.com/13/himachalam2.pdf.

David, Logan, Delvin, Roy and Caurie, Regelbruggie (1999), Global Corporate Citizenship-Rationale and Strategies, Washington, D.C.: The Hitachi Foundation.

Davis, G. F. and Thompson, T. A. (1994), A Social Movement Perspective on Corporate Control, Administrative Science Quarterly, 39: 141-173.

Davis, K. (1960), Can Business Afford to Ignore Social Responsibilities?, California Management Review, 2 (3): 70-76.

Davis, G.F. and Greve, H.R. (1997), 'Corporate Elite Networks and Governance Changes in the 1980s,' American Journal of Sociology, 103: 1-37.

Desirable Corporate Governance: A Code (CII). Available athttp: //www.acga-asia.org/public/files/CII_code_1998.pdf

Dessain, Vincent, Meier Olivier and Salas, Vincente (2008), Corporate Governance and Ethics:

Shareholder Reality, Social Responsibility or Institutional Necessity?, Management, 11(2): 65-79.

Donaldson, L. and Davis, J. H. (1991), 'Stewardship Theory or Agency Theory: CEO Governance and Stakeholder Returns,' Australian Journal of Management, 16 (1): 49-64.

Drucker, Peter (2001), The Essential Drucker, New York: Harper Collins.

Emile, Durkheim (1933), The Division of Labor in Society, New York: Macmillan.

Freeman, R. and D. Read (1983), Stockholders and Stakeholders: A New Perspective on Corporate Governance, California Management Review, 25: 88-106.

Frentop, P. (2003), A History of Corporate Governance, Amsterdam: Deminor.

Frey, B. S. and Osterloh, M. (2005), 'Yes, Managers Should be Paid Like Bureaucrats,' Journal of Management Inquiry, 14: 96-112.

Friedman, Milton (1962), Capitalism and Freedom, Chicago: University of Chicago Press.

Gerth, H. H. and Mills, Wright C. (2009), From Max Weber, Essays in Sociology, New York: Routledge.

Gilbert, L. D. (1956), Dividends and Democracy, New York: Freedom House.

Gomez, Yves and Harry, Korine (2005), Democracy and the Evolution of Corporate Governance, Corporate Governance, 13(6): 739-752.

Gopala, Krishna (1992), Corporate Social Responsibility in India: A Study of Management Attitudes, New Delhi : Mittal Publications.

Grossman J. Sanford and Oliver Hart (1988), 'One Share/One Vote and the Market for Corporate Control,' Journal of Financial Economics, 20 (1/2): 175-202.

Gupta, Dipankar (2006), Ethics Incorporated, Top Priority and Bottom Line, New Delhi: Response Books.

Henderson, David (2001), The Case Against Corporate Social Responsibility, Policy, 17 (2).

http: //www.ri3240.com/RI/roindia.htm

http: //www.rotary.org/aboutrotary/strategic.html.

Jagannatha, R., New Companies Bill: Here Are the Pleasure and Pain Points. Available at https: //www.firstpost.com/business/companies-bill-here-are-the-pleasure-and-pain-points-1022453.html.

Johnson, Harold L. (1971), Business in Contemporary Society: Framework and Issues, Belmont, California: Wadsworth Publishing Co., Inc.

Kar, Pratip, Culture and Corporate Governance Principles in India: Reconcilable Clashes? Private Sector Opinion, Issue 23, A Global Corporate Governance Forum Publication. Available at: www.ife.org/wps/wcm/connect/1fe292804a4785e6824d9faa52ef3b86PSO_23_Pratip.pdf?MOD=AJPERES.

Khanna, Tarun and Krishna, G. Palepu (2004), 'Globalization and Convergence in Corporate Governance: Evidence from Infosys and the Indian Software Industry,' Journal of International Business Studies, 35(6): 485-507.

Krygier, Martin (1997), Between Fear and Hope: Hybrid Thoughts on Public Values, Sydney: ABC Books.

Levitt, Theodore (1958), The Dangers of Social Responsibility, Harvard Business Review, 36(5): 41-50.

Majumdar, R. C. (1969), Corporate Life in Ancient India, Calcutta: K. L. Mukhopadhya.

Mallin, A. Christine (2004), Corporate Governance, Oxford: Oxford University Press.

Mitra, Meera (2007), "Its Only Business!" India's Corporate Social Responsiveness in a Globalized

World, New York: Oxford University Press.

Moon, Jeremy (2005), 'An Explicit Model of Business-Society Relations', in Andre Habisch et al. (eds.), Corporate Social Responsibility Across Europe, Berlin: Springer.

Morrison, Ken (2006), Marx, Durkheim, Weber Formations of Modern Sociological Thought, Los Angeles: Sage.

Mukherjee, Aditya (2002), Imperialism, Nationalism and the Making of Indian Capitalist Class 1920-1947, New Delhi: Sage.

Murphy, K. J. (1999), 'Executive Compensation', in O. Ashenfelter and D. Card (eds.), Handbook of Labor Economics, Amsterdam: Elsevier, pp. 2485-2563.

National Foundation for Corporate Governance (2004), Corporate Governance in India: Theory and Practice, Discussion Paper. Available at www.nfcgindia.org/library/cgitp.pdf.

Nisbett, Richard E. (2003), The Geography of Thought, New York: Free Press.

O'Sullivan, M. (2001), Contests for Corporate Control-Corporate Governance and Economic Performance in the United States and Germany, Oxford: Oxford University Press.

Organization for Economic Co-operation and Development (OECD) (2001), Corporate Responsibility: Private Initiatives and Public Goals, Paris: OECD.

Pande, Santosh and Kaushik, Kshama V. The Study on the State of Corporate Governance in India: Evolution, Issues and Challenges for the Future, Calcutta: Indian Institute of Corporate Affairs, Thought Arbitage Research Institute, Indian Institute of Management, Calcutta. Available at https: //www.academia.edu/6310145/Evolution_of_Corporate_Governance_in_ India?auto =download

Porter, M. E. and Kramer, M. (2006), The Competitive Advantage of Corporate Philanthropy, Harvard Business Review, 23(2): 185-197.

Prahalad, C.K. and Straut L. Hart (2002), The Fortune at the Bottom of the Pyramid, Strategy and Business, Issue 26, First Quarter.

Preston, L. E. and Post, J. E. (1975), Private Management and Public Policy, The Principle of Public Responsibility, Englewood Cliffs, New Jersey: Prentice Hall.

Roe, M. J., Ramseyer, J. M. and Romano, R. (1993), 'Some Differences in Corporate Structures in Germany, Japan and the United States', Yale Law Journal, 102: 1927-1950.

Ruskin, John (1907), Unto This Last and Other Essays, London: J. M. Dent & Sons Ltd.

Sapvadia, Vrajlal K. and Patel, Kandarp (2009), Is Blood Thicker Than Water? Appraising Adequacy of Indian Corporate Governance for Family Based Companies: A Case Study of Satyam Computers, Working Paper Series, Social Science Electronic Publishing (http: //ssrn.com/abstract=1347868).

Sarbanes–Oxley Act 2002 (US). Available at: https://pcaobus.org

Sarkar, C. R. (2005), Social Responsibility of Business Enterprises, New Delhi: New Century Publications.

SEBI Committee on Corporate Governance (2003), Narayana Murthy Committee Report. Available at: https: //www.sebi.gov.in/reports/reports/mar-2003/the-report-of-shri-n-r-narayana-murthy-committee-on-corporate-governance-for-public-comments-_12986.html

Shaw, W.H. (1999), Business Ethics, Boston, MA: Thomson Wadsworth.

Smith, Adam (1838), An Inquiry Into the Nature and Causes of the Wealth of Nations, Edinburgh: Thomas Nelson.

Sundar, Pushpa (2000), Beyond Business From Merchant Charity to Corporate Citizenship, New Delhi: Tata-McGraw Hill.

Thaplyal, Kiran Kumar (1996), Guilds in Ancient India, New Delhi: New Age International Limited.

Teach, Edward (2005), Two Views of Virtue, CFO, Dec: 31-4.

The Naresh Chandra Committee Report. Available at: http: //www.nfcg.in/library-page-4

UNDP/British Council/CII/PWC (United Nations Development Programme/Confederation of Indian Industry/PricewaterhouseCoopers), 2002: Corporate Social Responsibility Survey 2002: India.

Useem, M. (1996), Investor Capitalism: How Money Managers are Changing the Face of Corporate America, New York: Basic Books.

Varma, Jayanth Rama (1997), Corporate Governance in India: Disciplining the Dominant Shareholder, IIMB Management Review, 9 (4): 5-18.

Walton, Clarence C. (1967), Corporate Social Responsibilities, Belmont, CA: Wadsworth.

Wartick, Steven L. and Cochran, Philip L. (1985) The Evolution of the Corporate Social Performance Model, The Academy of Management Review, 10(4): 758-769.

Weber, Max (1905), The Protestant Ethic and the Spirit of Capitalism, London: Routledge.

# 4

# Corporate Social Responsibility (CSR): A Democratic Perspective

The term CSR has no clear definition, and hence, it is a complex phenomenon. The canvass of CSR ranges from the spirit of law, covers workplace practices or beyond that. CSR can be a preventive, or promotive initiative, which deals with social issues in the course of business functioning.

To understand CSR from a democratic perspective, one has to analyze several aspects of business like business performance directed towards its core activities; workplace practices within the firm (sharing of power, participation in business making process); stakeholder engagement; performance towards the communities (workplace community, business-affected community, large community) and performance towards the environment.

CSR to be strategically oriented, has to be integrated with core business objectives and competencies of the firm. It should be directed towards creating business value and positive social change, and has to be embedded in the business culture and the operations of the company. It implies that CSR needs to be embedded within the firm and should reflect the core values of the firm. It has to be linked to the mission, vision and values of the firm. CSR has to be treated and managed as a core business strategy just like the strategies of marketing, research and development. A clear performance metrics should be in place that measures reputation, achievements, gains in market share, brand perception, increased sales, decreased operational expenditure, employee satisfaction as well as increased focus on society and environment.

Active participation of the employees in the firm is the key to a successful liberal democratic practice of the business. In management-driven forms of participation, it often involves strategically devised attempts to increase loyalty and commitment from the employees, rather than seeking genuine decisional input. It is also observed that absence of appropriate forums results from constrained decisional contexts, inadequate or distorted information. As a result, employees tend to suppress their own needs and internal value conflicts. Even team-based decision making is constrained by self-generated limits to open participation. Normally, managements are reluctant to include employees in crucial decision making, sharing power or granting autonomy.

Effective CSR can't rely on only managerial goodwill, government regulation, or consumer choice alone. But the efficacy of CSR should be motivated by employee participation, incorporation of social values, and operation within a process that constructively comes up with creative solutions.

CSR of business can be practiced with business motive, but without much obsession with profit. Businesse's primary concern should be its stakeholders, customers, employees, suppliers, shareholders and investors. Then, if we broaden the stakeholder responsibility, the larger community and society automatically get aligned with it.

How to make all the stakeholders an integral part of the organization?

An organization must have a governance mechanism which should be ethically oriented. To be ethically oriented, the governance system has to be democratic by nature. If we broadly analyze it, the democratic framework in a workplace can be primarily characterized by the existence of a community, a participatory process to ensure equal distribution of effective power among the constituents of the community, and a substantive amount of rights to be guaranteed to the workers so that there is no misuse of power.

Such a democratic framework can be enhanced through a systematic corporate governance mechanism. This mechanism helps the organization in its internal functioning, or in the operations of its business activities. The business, to flourish in its core craft, has to shoulder its responsibility to different types of communities aligned with its functioning. The firm cannot do without the employee community, supplier community, investor community or so to say the whole stakeholder community.

The stakeholders are the essential communities of business. That is why, it is important for business to engage with its stakeholders continuously. Stakeholder engagement entails direct or indirect interaction with investors, customers, shareholders, employees, and the unskilled or contract workers.

The firm should keep stakeholder expectations, demands and needs at the top, without being too much concerned with business gain. Like the stakeholder community, the environment too is an important stakeholder of the business.

The natural environment is very much aligned with business like the work environment. Business policies should be driven in such a manner that it causes least impact on the environment. Its business activities have to ensure an eco-friendly environment. Like any other environment, the natural environment has a certain setting and order. In order to sustain, it requires least disturbance and utmost preservation and maintenance. The democratic behavior of the firm has to ensure that its activities do not disturb the natural functioning of the environment. It is the democratic right of the environment to behave in the manner that it has been naturally destined. Democratic CSR clearly establishes the fact that engaging, involving and encouraging participation of the stakeholders is essential for the democratic system of an enterprise. Exploring the existence of such a system of governance in different industries, whether it is public or private, will validate its applicability.

In this regard, I have examined the role of the Bharat Petroleum Corporation Limited (BPCL), one of India's reputed Public Sector Undertakings.

## BPCL

Industrial development and growth swept away almost all the countries of the world. The growth of petroleum refineries all over the world took a leap in 1860s, and India's search for petroleum products was started in 1886.

BPCL, a pioneer in the Indian petroleum sector too joined this drive. It grew out of the alliance between Asiatic Petroleum (India) and Burmah Oil, known as the Burmah Shell Oil Storage and Distributing Co. of India Ltd., dealing mainly in kerosene. As Liquefied Petroleum Gas (LPG) was introduced to Indian homes in the mid-1950s, urgency spurred up to establish a permanent system that will produce, refine and distribute petroleum products. In 1951, the Government of India and the Burmah Shell Group of Companies signed an agreement to build a modern refinery at Mahul, near Chembur in Mumbai. Then, on 1$^{st}$ August 1977, the Burmah Shell Group of Companies was taken over by the Government of India, and renamed as Bharat Petroleum

Corporation Limited. It also established the first refinery in India to process the newly found indigenous crude oil from Bombay High.

## The Company's Core Responsibility

BPCL's core functions relate to the production of diverse range of products from petro-chemicals and solvents to aircraft fuel. Bharat Petroleum started a journey of growth and expansion, following nationalization in 1976. Due to the expansionist drive of the company, large-scale training and recruitment took place. Liberalization of the Indian economy in the 1990s introduced competition and performance. Challenges also appeared in the form of the phased dismantling of the administered pricing mechanism (APM) for petroleum products and emergence of new capacities in private refining and marketing (http: //www.bharatpetroleum.com). Initially, the steps were directed towards a selective group of stakeholders, i.e. the employees with a welfare-driven motive.

Later on, an appropriate business culture, with a social motive, was created. Its operations, marketing, financial endeavors not only entailed—an economic gain, but were also socially beneficial. This can be regarded as a step forward in the democratization of the CSR process of the organization.

When the Indian Government in 1990s urged the Public Sector Units (PSUs) to adopt a market-driven approach, BPCL got consultants to restructure its vision and mission. During that time, the Company had about 12,000 employees. Several initiatives were launched by the Company to consolidate the ideas of the employees.

Based on the realistic situation at that time, BPCL aspired to make a global presence by adopting environment-friendly measures in its operations. The Company restructured itself into two primary divisions: marketing, which is dispersed all over India, and refining. Thus, it dismantled the function-based structure and replaced it with a process-based one.

With this, restructuring different units were established across India: corporate centers, strategic business units (SBUs) and shared services and entities. Marketing has been diversified into five SBUs: aviation, industrial and commercial, LPG, lubricants and retail. It was spread across four regions of the country: Mumbai (west), Kolkata (east), Delhi (north) and Chennai (south). The strategic planning of the Company at that time did not view social responsibility as an integral aspect of its activities. Be it operations, marketing, or finance, the Company performed in all these activities with a pure business motive. But only solace was their concern for the employees of the organization. The Company facilitated various innovative initiatives for the employees, so that they could understand the complexity of the market and needs of the customers.

The Company focused on the development of organizational capabilities of the employees through performance management, competency modelling, identifying competency gaps and bridging such gaps through appropriate training and development programs, and multi-skilling. Besides, the Company also adopted welfare measures for the employees.

Business has broadened its horizon by incorporating a stakeholder model of engagement. From shareholders to stakeholders, business has to pass through a process that involves debates, discussions to establish the fact that besides the shareholders, others, in the form of employees, investors and suppliers, are equally important for its growth. It is the responsibility of the business to understand how important business is for them and how important they are to business. There has to be direct or indirect interactions with investors, customers, shareholders, employees and the unskilled workforce.

CSR can be best when it keeps its stakeholder expectation at the top. Due to globalization, modernization and technological innovation, the outlook of business towards the stakeholders has changed and the stakeholders' expectations from business too have multiplied. BPCL as a petroleum-manufacturing company has continuous engagement with its stakeholders in the market.

The Company engages with its stakeholders on issues that affect the Company's operations. It has a wide range of stakeholders that comprise customers, employers, investors, suppliers and non-governmental organizations.

### Customers

The SBU initiatives undertake capacity-building for safe use of the products for the customers. The Company has initiated the CUBE or Customer

Undertaking for Business Excellence. It allows the Company to obtain an overall view of the customers' understanding of products, equipping the business units to make databases available to them. The Company maintains a resolution to attend to customers' complaints promptly.

Company involvement with different communities in a proactive manner accelerates the democratic governance system. Community involvement or community engagement can be at three levels. Firstly, it is the employee community; secondly, the project-affected or business-affected community and thirdly, the larger community.

Community involvement can act as a strategic thrust upon firm to redefine its connection with it. In this front, communities are residents of societies which qualify to be considered as stakeholders to business on one or more of the accountability, management or ethical perspectives. There are employees, who have the responsibility to gain profit for the firm, or there are people on whose lands manufacturing plants get located, and their lifestyle gets changed due to the fact that business is located there. There are other communities which tend to migrate to other stakeholders as consumers, and they therefore provide the strategic link. There is more than one single association between business and communities. Employee engagement or involvement in business is not new to India. It has a long pedigree.

## Employee Community Involvement in India

In the mid-1950s and 1960s, the Government intervened for workers' participation in management; till then, there was no urge among unions for greater involvement in the management of industrial organizations. In fact, the introduction of works committee by the Industrial Disputes Act of 1947 was an important step towards participation.

The Section 3 of the Act states that the works committees aim is to promote measures for securing and preserving good relations between the employer and the worker. By then, it was established that works committee is an industrial relation tool to resolve or reduce differences between management and labor. It was not first a participation body.

In the 1950s, joint management councils (JMCs) were proposed to be set up, and works committees were meant to deal with small issues, so these committees could not enter the domain of the JMCs. Initially, three lists were prepared, one each for JMCs, collective bargaining, and works committee.

Works committees discussed issues pertaining to basic facilities, like sanitation, drinking facilities, medical and health services, safe working conditions, administration of welfare funds, education and recreation activities etc. Employees showed some excitement for the committees, but later on they lost interest, as other forums developed. The committees served as forums for addressing grievances of the workers. Then, the JMCs were formed to promote cordial relations between management and labor. The aim was also to build trust, secure welfare, and train the workers. There were some specific functions of the JMCs: to have equal representation from workers and the management; to be consulted on certain matters, like the economic situation, the state of the market; sales, profit, loss, as well as expansion. But JMCs were not free from biasness. All matters for collective bargaining such as wages and allowances were to be excluded, and the creation of new rights between management and unions was to be avoided. The JMCs had a good start, where managements were not averse to the concept of sharing decisionmaking with workers, like the works committee, but the JMCs fell into disuse in mid-1960s, due to inflation. There are few reasons behind their failure: reluctance on the part of management to accord equal status to worker representatives, non-implementation of the decisions of the council, blaming the workers and their lack of rationalization in addressing the grievances of the workers.

With the failure of the JMCs, government started a new form of participation in PSUs. In 1971, Government announced provisions for worker directors on PSU boards, but the implementation was very slow. Most of the unions in the PSUs were affiliated to Indian National Trade Union Congress (INTUC).

In 1975, the government came up with a "20-points agenda", related to participation in the workplace, and workers' participation was one of the points. A new policy of shop council and joint council was formulated. This policy was applicable to all enterprises in manufacturing and mining. In 1976, the Constitution was amended to include the workers' participation as an objective of state policy. This article guaranteed appropriate legislation, to secure participation of employees in the management of different undertakings, and establishments. The functions of the shop council were to assist the management in achieving production targets, improving production, efficiency, utilizing manpower to the highest level, and eliminating wastage.

The Joint Council's constitution was same like the shop council with the Chief Executive of the plant as chairman. The function of the joint council was almost same like the shop councils. The PSUs started implementing the schemes, but they didn't turn out to be successful. Later on, the government recommended a statute on participation. This was highly contested by employer organizations.

In 1980, the government appointed a committee to go into details on company governance. Like the previous initiatives, it too could not make much headway. But the efforts to bring changes within the organization went on. Final step towards the introduction of participation were taken in 1990. The new government incorporated a participation of workers' section in the Management Bill. The structure was not that different from the previous ones, but measure taken on was that the workmen of the industrial establishment were either voted by secret ballot or nominated by the registered trade unions. Board-level participation was compulsory and the number of workmen and non-workmen would constitute 25 percent of the total board strength. A monitoring agency was to be appointed to review the progress of implementation.

But, this step of the government too suffered a setback like its previous initiatives. Thus unending succession of schemes and the regular emergence of new ones led to confusion. Participation of the workers could have been possible, if the policies were implemented. But companies, both public and private, have installed Human Resource Management (HRM) practices, which are nearer to participation, but remain as HRM strategies. The company also maintained a responsible behavior towards its investors, dealers, contractors, and NGOs.

The company took precautionary steps towards safe product handling and also delivery of the products and also ensured a cordial atmosphere for all its stakeholders.

## Investors

The Company ensured that all the valuable suggestions of the shareholders, accelerated to the functioning of the company, are examined, discussed and acted upon.

## Dealers

The Dealer community considered community initiative, communication, environment, health, safety as important areas for partnering with the company.

Distribution of the company appreciates promoting safety at customer premises, increasing reachability of LPG to rural markets. They are also attracted towards the community initiatives of the company. In fact, they are for tie-ups with NGOs for community initiatives, and also prescribed welfare activities for distributor staff.

## Contractors

Contractors also believed that safety standards, worker welfare, water management etc. are important initiatives for which they are aligned with Bharat Petroleum. They also emphasized on capacity development and promoting environmental awareness.

## NGOs and Foundation

The Company has been interacting and engaging with the NGOs and different private and government foundations for implementing various CSR initiatives, and also to gain from their expertise in community projects.

## Employees

The Company's concern towards its workforce is apparent through its policies which are directed towards creating an energized workforce. The health and work environment are given top priority.

Community involvement is an extended form of stakeholder engagement. Being a business organization, it has primarily diverse form of community involvement. As a manufacturing company, its highest responsibility was towards the project-affected people.

As a petroleum-manufacturing company, BPCL always tried to involve with the community, especially those who are displaced, due to its business. Displacement of people due to acquisition of land, and finding an alternative livelihood pattern for the displaced people is a huge responsibility of the company.

When the Mahul refinery was built in the Mahul Village (Bombay), an entire community was displaced. To deal with the issues of the displaced community, a social welfare department was established within the refinery. The company assigned the task of rehabilitating and resettling the community to the welfare department. The rehabilitation polices of the company were in the form of providing employability, training, financial support and vocational guidance to the displaced community. Mahul is a tiny village, located in Bombay (Now Mumbai) and predominantly dominated by fisherman communities. After the refinery was set up, these communities had a very bad plight. They had to give up their age-old livelihood pattern and look out for an alternative mode of livelihood. The company partnered with few NGOs, who were well versed with the problems and issues of the communities, and devised a rehabilitation programme that focused on employability and training, giving financial support, vocational guidance to the villagers.

The partnering NGOs used to assist the company in the implementation of the programmes. But the company somehow failed to deliver the initiatives in an adequate manner.

Some of the beneficiaries pointed out that the schemes and programmes devised by the company could not incorporate all the affected members of the community villagers. Few of them were roped in for the development work of the company; training was provided, but providing employment, especially to the youths, became a daunting task.

The company's partnership strategy with the NGOs, for the implementation of the programmes, was not clear. In fact, it was difficult to ascertain the genuineness of this partnership, as there was no clear agenda to assess the impact of the programmes from the company's side. Some argue that this displacement or uprooting has created business for some by causing disadvantage to others. The company in fact did not have a monitoring mechanism to check the implementation process.

The Company's community involvement at this level was very business specific and the initiatives were not all comprehensive. It's not just delivery or implementation of the policies, but the strength lies in effective monitoring and impact assessment of the programmes. Moreover, it is imperative that business needs to uphold its genuineness in its functioning by engaging with the affected stakeholders. This is possible only when business recognizes its role as a development player in society.

The other form of community involvement is in the form of a participative workforce. Participative mechanism should help the employees to influence the community on which they depend. It can be argued that equal influence should be granted to those who are affected by it.

To function as a democratic institution, the existence of a community is very important. One may argue that the way organization of work is instrumental to the democratic quality of the state, the workplace can be a basic unit within which democratic practices can take place. Worker-owned economy and workers' co-operative trade unions may create a system of co-governance in which labor and capital are placed in a situation of coherence.

## Employee Involvement and Relations

Bharat Petroleum has a network of unions in all the different regions and refineries, with negligible industrial unrest. The company has devised one common agreement for the entire marketing division in all SBUs, which was achieved through negotiation with 10 unions.

There is one condition for union representation: the union should have at least 25 percent employees of that region as members. There is a policy that welfare and social security are not up to bargaining. Safety and healthy work practices are topmost agendas of the company.

Employee involvement of the company is confined to safety and caution measures. Every location of the company refinery, depot and LPG bottling plants has safety committees. Caution committees have been set up at all locations, but cautions are primarily operated by the company. The members of the union are mostly employees of the company. A continuous consultation process is held between union and the regional management on issues such as holidays and uniforms. If new policies are launched, for instance, voluntary retirement, new pension scheme, and new loan facilities, then the unions have to handle all these policies. Besides, the unions have to be consulted for feedback, modification and announcing the changes formally to avoid bureaucratizing of the system. The company usually preferred discussions on a need-based basis. The unions have constant interactions with the management pertaining to issues which they feel are really problematic or need some corrections. Continuous consultations take place between the management and the unions for certain issues, like productivity, wastage and cost reduction. Meetings are held on a quarterly basis and are held between the unions and the management on any issues jointly or separately.

Employee involvement is very high at the Wadilube plant within the Mumbai refinery. The Wadilube plant, located in the dock area of Mumbai, manufactures lubricants, but the base oil for lubricants is supplied through a pipeline from the refinery. The works in these locations are carried out in shifts. There are three trade unions affiliated to different organizations: Shiv Sena (Bharat Petroleum) Karmachary Union, the MNS (Petroleum Karmachary Union) and the INTUC (Petroleum Employees Union). All the office bearers of the trade unions are employees of the company.

### Employee Involvement in business

Employee involvement is not just suggestive of simple involvement but a rationalized and meaningful commitment from both the sides. Several employee involvement procedures are there in the plant and the refinery. There are some procedures which are structured; others are unstructured. But a work committee was set up as per the Industrial Disputes Act, 1947, and in such committees, workers were elected from among the employees. Thus, employee involvement in workplace became an integral part of the participatory process of the workplace in India.

The committee system had representatives from all divisions, one from the operative, one from clerical, one from the service and maintenance divisions. Work committees are set up for a period of 2 years. Meetings are held on a quarterly basis and are used mainly for discussions related to welfare activities, working conditions and counseling workers who are addicted to drugs or alcohols.

The alliance of the union and management resulted in various committees.

The relation between the unions and the management relations suggested a cordial relation between the two.

There are no regular meetings held to discuss the unstructured initiatives. The management tries to spread awareness about performance and the competitive environment by utilizing various plant events. The plant management conveys all major issues to the union representatives, so as to increase the utilization of capacities of the workers, deployment of workers, and improving the packaging unit to improve work performance. The plant management organized training-cum-workshop programme, called Vertical Integration Training for Harmony. A good number of employees participated in this initiative from different divisions, without disrupting the production process. The union members supported the Vertical Integration Programme, because everybody got an opportunity to express himself or herself. The achievements of the programme have to be assessed in the backdrop of the recession that the economy was passing through (2008-09). It had a minimal effect, and fortunately there was no layoff.

Mumbai Refinery remained one of the successful endeavors of the company. It has a successful record of implementation of various projects. The refinery has sophisticated systems, in the form of a microprocessor-based digital distributed control system (DDCS) and has been accredited with ISO 9002 (quality management system). The laboratory of the refinery has been also accredited with a unique quality certification from National Accreditation Board (NAB) (http: //bharatpetroeum.com).

The nature of production in the refinery requires high-skilled employees. The systems are highly automated, and there is hardly any room for deviation from standard procedures. This is reflective of the collective effort that every employee endures.

The refinery has four plants with strong employee union presence, the Bharat Petroleum Corporation Refinery Employees Union (BPCREU), BPC Process Technicians and Analysts, Petroleum Workmen's Union (PWU) for clerical grade employees, and for the technical and non-technical employees, especially in maintenance and general operation, there is the Bharat Petroleum Technical and Non-Technical Employees Association. The office bearers of the unions are employees of the company. Negotiations engaging in debates and discussions formed various democratic mediums of union–management relations. If there are issues regarding wage settlement, the unions do not take any abrupt decisions. Rather, the union leaders always interacted directly with the employees, before finalizing any settlements.

Here too, employee involvements are both structured and unstructured like the plant. There is a safety committee in each department and one joint safety committee for the plant as a whole. Members in the joint committee are from both the union side and the management side. Meetings are held on a monthly basis to discuss safety in the whole refinery as well as the unresolved issues from the departmental safety committees.

Regular consultations are held with employees in all cases of routine plant shut-down, for maintenance and repair. It also includes the extent of work by contractors, contract workers, supervision of actual work, maintenance, repairs etc. All these matters are discussed with respective employees. Meetings are also held jointly with all the unions. The issues that are raised by the management and union pertain to manpower optimization, comparison of manpower with other refineries, lightning of pricing margins due to continuous rise of crude oil prices and constraints on pricing in the Indian market.

In the unstructured involvement, specific issues are discussed. The company consults the unions, where SBUs were introduced. It sends union office bearers to five refineries to see for themselves the nature of the changed operation. And then, it outlays a plan for upgrading the plant. Consultative sessions are held with the process technician unions, and the members of this union are there in all operation points of the plant. Whenever a modernization process is undertaken in the refinery to increase the capacity, it also adopts the technology to upgrade the process to produce environment-friendly products and reduce pollution. There was an agreement signed between the unions and the management; it included clauses on union cooperation, manning for new and modernized sections and redeployment of existing manpower from positions with comparatively low job load and elimination of a few positions (Sen, 2012). Regular consultations between the management and the unions imply a continuous participative process.

The company maintains a regular consultation with all the unions before any planned manpower study. In fact, the unions are also very ambitious about the company's future. They also aspire that the company should emphasis more on exploration, diversification into other products like gas and biodiesel, and also improve it as the best pay master. Hence, the instrumentalist goal of the company didn't forbid it from demonstrating a democratic atmosphere.

## Stakeholder Responsibility

The Company's stakeholder approach compelled it to adopt measures that accentuate its responsibility towards its customers.

## Customers

Stakeholder engagement also entails responsibility towards customer needs. In order to be responsive to customer needs, the company started a corporate initiative called CUBE. CUBE tends to achieve its goal, through its level of governance structure comprising the CUBE Steering Committee, CUBE Core Team and CUBE Customer Care. These initiatives aim at fostering a culture of collaboration at the field level. This is possible through core business units, customer innovation councils taking note of customer views and understanding them better. The company used a strategy of meaningful analysis of the existing data, and engaged with channel partners to deliver a consistent service to the customers.

The company adopted a customer-centric approach while designing the products and services. The levels used for the production have all the national and international specifications on the product. The company conducts regular customer surveys to get customers' feedback and their needs. After that, compliance and marketing are done in a responsible manner.

There are few initiatives started by CUBE: one-point contact, a new customer care centre, which intends to act as a single-point contact for any information, feedback or grievance handling; BPCL platform, a consolidated BPCL loyalty card was started for all sets of customers and can provide knowledge-based management solutions.

Democratic workplace is not just active employee involvement; it requires a safe and healthy atmosphere. The workplace should be adaptive to the physical and psychological abilities of employees.

Safe and healthy atmosphere is the utmost responsibility of a company towards its employees. Safety and healthy atmosphere pertains to a firm's working conditions. It also relates to those companies whose manufacturing process requires a strict adoption of measures that can assure the workers a healthy workplace. The company has recognized that safety for the employees is not a cost, but an investment towards sustainable business.

Given the nature of operation of Bharat Petroleum, health and safety issues are topmost in its business units. The Company has actively adopted the oil and gas industry standards and norms which include emergency handling system, safety and environment management system etc.

All the employees of the company have access to health advisors through the medical support services. When the employees travel overseas, they are advised and counseled regarding any health risks by providing appropriate training and the essential vaccination.

There are constant initiatives from the company to promote wellness amongst the employees, especially about the ills and preventive measures of various diseases. In fact, frequent cancer screening camps are organized in association with Indian Cancer Society and SRL Religare Diagnostics.

The new employees of the company have to undergo health and safety orientation programmes before they are assigned any job. The programme includes familiarization with courses covering health and safety policy; potential hazards inside the plant, unsafe conditions and causes for accidents, incident identification and reporting; safe operating; operation and availability of operation, maintenance, safety manuals, guidelines, rules and regulations.

The company has devised few policies for the contractual employees and ensures that these employees are properly trained and are acquainted with the procedures before being put on the job. The company also has detailed guidelines for the contract management, transport safety management and construction safety.

Business and the environment are always linked to each other. In order to sustain, business has to care about its environmental performance. Business should develop products that reduce resource consumption and then replace them with more environmental friendly products.

Bharat Petroleum as a petroleum-manufacturing giant requires adopting environment-friendly policies in its operation maintenance. It has accepted environmental pollution reduction measures.

### Pollution Control through Coal Gasification and Coal to Liquid

Due to the rise in crude oil prices in the international market, the company adopted the measures for producing liquid fuels from coal. In compliances with the Auto Fuel Policy of Government of India, BPCL has started a rolling plan to upgrade Auto Fuel from Bharat Stage II, to III and IV. It is found that as the stage progresses, the fuels are expected to give better performance during their use in the vehicle leading to lesser fuel consumption and reduced pollution. Here, special emphasis is laid on the reduction of sulphur, which is a pollutant and also has harmful effects on the system during its storage, transportation and use. When there is a reduction in sulphur, it will automatically lead to decrease in sulphurdioxide ($SO_2$) and trioxide emissions.

Bharat Petroleum started a venture called Bharat Renewable Energy Limited (BREL) that made significant investment in the renewable energy projects (2012-13) and was able to generate about 2689187 HWH energy through these projects (Sustainability Development Report, 2012-13: 51). It has adopted few energy conservation measures like chemical closing of heat exchanges, advanced process control in furnace operations, maximum heat recovery from process steams etc. And these measures resulted in reduction in Green House Gas (GHG) emissions.

### Product Life Cycle

There have been few remarkable changes in the product value chain by Mumbai Refinery. In line with sustainable development principles, the company has started production and supply of auto-fuels meeting Bharat Stage IV specification and is in the process of developing plans for meeting the emerging Euro-V specifications. Even the transportation of the petroleum products has been intensified through pipeline, and as a result there has been lowering of GHG emission. Liquid fuels were replaced with Re-gasified Liquefied Natural Gas, and this helped in reducing $CO_2$ and $SO_2$ emission from the refinery. The company is in the process of installing energy-efficient crude and vacuum distillation, which will produce higher yield products as compared to earlier days.

## Waste Management

As it is a manufacturing company, its operation generates a wide variety of waste, which has the highest probability of having a negative impact on the environment. Every location has a waste management system in place. The company gives preference to the waste being generated through operational efficiency, instead of treating waste from other sources. It reuses and recycles the waste.

In the year 2012-13, the refineries generated 15402-24 tonnes of waste, of which 69 percent was hazardous (BPCL Sustainable Development Report). The waste disposal is done through certified vendors who are authorized by the pollution control board. The non-hazardous waste is disposed of to the secured landfill using specified methods.

In Mumbai Refinery, a business waste-to-energy project was started in 2011-12. It was expanded to use waste consisting of hardwood and soft or loose biomass materials like jatropha plantation waste for the production of energy. It allowed for the use of bio-diesel waste as the fuel source, and reduction in effluents and improving the specific fuel consumption process. In the oil and gas sector, companies' real concern lies in their avoidance and management of oil spills. Bharat Petroleum established an advanced spill response management system which aims at mitigation and restoration plans. The company has partnered with other oil authorities to establish a Tier I Oil Spill Response facility at the Mumbai harbor, to avoid ecological and economic problems caused by an oil spill. The primary focus is to prevent any spilled oil from coming into contact with oil-sensitive resources. Another significant drive in this context was the management of waste water. The company has installed Effluent Treatment Plants (ETPs) and oil-water separators in different locations to ensure the waste water is being discharged outside, with regulatory requirements and stipulated limits.

Waste water from Kochi and Mumbai Refinery is discharged to Chithrapuzha River and sea, respectively (BPCL Sustainability Development Report, 2012-13: 54). The company monitors the waste water based on various quality parameters, and takes necessary measures whenever required.

The company officials claimed that the discharged water quality from both the refineries was well within the permissible limits specified by state and central pollution control boards.

The company operation requires a significant amount of water, and its installations are situated all across the country and some of them are situated in water-stressed zones. The type of water source depends on the locations of the units. Though surface water, ground water and municipal supplies cater to the water requirement of the company, but its usage is guided by regulatory norms. To minimize the use of fresh water resources, the company has adopted site-specific water conservation plans and water intensity targets. The water intensity targets have been intensified, as demands for water vary from site to site. Even recycling of waste water has been implemented across different locations. The company has made significant investments in rain water harvesting especially in 2012-13.

The company's effort to increase the recycling and reuse of water is driven towards reduction of fresh water in its operations.

### Material and Energy Utilization

The company's core operations initiate extensive use of materials. That is why there is an urgent drive to establish process improvement aimed at reducing and recycling of the material use. While a significant share of material usage occurs in the refineries, the company focuses on opportunities to recycle packaging and other materials used. Even the LPG SBU continues to minimize the use of new LPG cylinders by reusing used cylinders for several refilling cycles.

### Community Responsibility

The company's community involvement extends to the communities near its operations. Its community initiatives concentrate on health, education and few capacity-building initiatives for the business-affected communities. There have been investments in the community in the form of capacity-building initiatives for women (especially widowed women). It has set up "Soil Testing Lab" to help the women farmers understand the quality of the soil before undertaking farming.

The company has initiated few programs: a Service Education Programme in Collaboration with Agastya International Foundation, an NGO, for children of government schools near Solur, Bangalore (Karnataka); digital literacy and life skills projects were started in Mumbai in partnership with NGO Pratham, and were able to reach out to 25,000 children.

The company also started a project in support of Read India initiative to reach out to 50,000 children in the district of Nandurbar, Maharashtra, and also carried out skill- based intervention programmes for women in collaboration with NGO Seva in Lucknow, Uttar Pradesh. Water harvesting being their forte in community involvement, the company started this initiative in villages suffering from acute problems of water scarcity.

It initiated a project for training parahealth workers in Bastar region of Chattishgarh. This project benefitted more than 5000 tribals in villages with acute problem of in accessibility to health facility.

Corporate governance is an essential mechanism that helps the company to attain its corporate objectives, internal control, and its external relationship. It ensures that an adequate and appropriate system of control operates within the company. It is concerned with the relationship between a company's management, the board of directors, shareholders and other stakeholders, and encourages transparency and accountability. Bharat Petroleum has systematic corporate governance mechanisms in place.

## Analysis

CSR to be perceived from a democratic perspective considers responsibilities as very essential, whether it is economic responsibility, or employee responsibility or environmental responsibility. All the responsibilities foster constant stakeholder engagement, be it the customers, stakeholders, suppliers, investors, employees, environment and the society at large. Business organizations' constant engagement with stakeholders helps them to excel in their core activity.

BPCL as a petroleum-manufacturing giant has tried to primarily direct its business towards its core functions. Since its nationalization in 1976, the company has been on an expansionist drive. To keep up with the challenges and opportunities in this drive, it established a system of consolidation of its workforce. Its social concern was also directed towards the welfare of its employees.

The core functioning of the company required a very strong strategic system that coordinates its operation and finances marketing, research and development, and human resource management. In its initial years, these functions were purely business driven, with least socio-cultural leanings. Welfare and social activities were primarily directed towards the employees. The company also realized that to keep pace with the development and expansionist trend of other enterprises, it has to totally rely on its employees. Besides, it was essential for the employees to understand the market situation and the requirement of the customers.

The company understood the importance of all its stakeholders. The initiatives developed for its customers, like CUBE, allow the company to give an overall idea of the products to them. Its record of attending to customer complaints was fulfilled through the governance system of CUBE. A customer-centric approach was apparent in its designing of products and services also abiding by the international standards.

Other stakeholders like the investor dealers and distributors were positive about their relation with the company. They were appreciative of the community initiatives (for the business-affected people), and also health and safety initiatives of the company. In fact, the distributor community feels that welfare measures of the company should not be restricted to one section of the stakeholder community, but should be diffused to all the stakeholders.

It is not just the business interest that aligns the stakeholders with the organization. Because of the company's compliance to various standards, be it safety, worker's welfare, or water management, the contractor community has become highly ambitious about the company.

The company also realized that to deal with the communities, it is essential to rope in NGOs and research foundations, because these organizations are aware about the issues, problems of the communities, and their contact mechanism.

As a manufacturing company, its core activities lead to displacement of the communities at different sites. The company has initiated measures for rehabilitation and resettlement of the displaced communities. It has been observed that though the company has adopted measures by partnering with the local NGOs in this endeavor, it did not have a clear monitoring mechanism that can evaluate the impact assessment of the measures. Even some community members argued that the welfare measures were not encompassing though. It is also a stark reality that due to the company's business, the community has been forced to give up its age-old profession without any adequate replacement. But the initiatives for all its stakeholders were not uniform, as some of the displaced communities are in a precarious situation.

The company's employee involvement is not just confined to safety and health strategies of the company. Employees are members of union bodies recognized by the company, in different location (plants refineries). To make the employee involvement more democratic, discussions are held constantly between the unions and the management. The alliance of the union and management were able to keep bureaucratization of the system at bay.

Employees' involvement procedures are both structured and unstructured. The structured procedures ensure formation of committees, where workers are elected through a democratic process, and representatives are there from each division of the workforce. Both the unions and the management offer suggestions, and preference is given to those which have a future implication. Not just limiting itself with a structured involvement, the company also initiated an unstructured initiative. Here, the management with the help of the union representatives spread awareness about the performance of the company through various plant events.

As it is a manufacturing company, BPCL requires a very efficient disciplined workforce in all its locations. Each site of the company is equipped with sophisticated systems. To run these systems, it requires high-skilled employees, whose collective effort matters the most to the company.

To maintain an efficient system of operation, the workforce is divided into technical and non-technical groups. Both the groups have their representatives in the union. Suppose there are issues pertaining to wage settlement, the unions directly interact with employees before arriving at a final decision. Besides permanent employees, the company's involvement with its contractual workers is in positive footing.

There has been active participation of the workers at various levels, through the union management system. Decisions pertaining to core function are restricted to employees at a certain level. But the governance system ensures that information of crucial decisions is passed to all the employees of the company.

Community involvement at the employee level is very encouraging. Then, with the business-affected communities, it requires an urgent consideration by the management of the company to seriously think about them. They are equally important, if is not less, like other communities (customers, suppliers, investors, NGOs). In order to excel in their core functions or to make projects successful, there is a huge contribution from these communities or stakeholders, if not directly, but indirectly. The company should devise a clear policy of implementation, monitoring and impact assessment of the measures adopted for their participation.

Due to their nature of operations, health and safety issues are topmost concern in the company's responsibility towards its stakeholder's workplace. The company has initiated measures to promote wellness amongst the employees. It is also conscious about the fact that its operation can cause pollution on a wider level; that is why, the company has adopted energy conservation, waste management, management of oil spills measures in the most scientific manner. Even the waste water released from the refineries (Kochi and Mumbai) was within the permissible limits, as confirmed by company sources.

Thus, from the above analysis, it is very clear that the company has given top priority to employees, as well as the larger environment. It has adopted a scientific approach for controlling pollution of the environment. It has devised various mechanisms to engage with all its stakeholders. But still, such measures are far from all- encompassing. The project-affected communities are far away from the ambit of the development process. Democratic CSR to be part of the governance system has to consider the significance of all its stakeholders, and make it participatory for all of them in the functioning of the company. It should encompass every segment of the stakeholder community. Their contribution in different ways has made the company a frontrunner in the petroleum-manufacturing sector of the country.

## REFERENCES

BPCL Sustainability Development Report 2012-13. Available at https: //www.bharatpetroleum.com/pdf/sustainability/SDR_2012_2013.pdf

http: //www.bharatpetroleum.com.

Sen, Ratna (2012), Employee Participation in India, Working Paper No. 40, ILO Publications, International Labour Office, Geneva. Available at https: //www.ilo.org/wcmsp5/groups/public/—ed_dialogue/—dialogue/documents/publication/wcms_187873.pdf.

# 5

# A Democratic CSR Framework

The universe of CSR comprises people (stakeholders), profit (economic performance) and the environment (environmental performance). Based on interaction and engagement with its stakeholders, the democratic CSR model can be developed, especially, by stressing on basic economic responsibility of the firm, its stakeholder responsibility and environmental responsibility.

Economic responsibility of business is what business does for itself. It is the economic performance of the firm, or performance to pursue profit. Economic responsibility is not just pure financial performance, but performance with social inclinations. To enhance the economic performance, the organizations require an effective finance, marketing, disciplined manpower, research and development of the products and services. All the activities aligned with economic performance of the firm have to be socially oriented. Economic performance also promotes the development of the knowledge base, skills and networks of the firm and also accelerates the profit. It should be integral part of the mission, vision and values of the organization. Then, it will become a development effort of the company and the existing management and performance system. On this basis, the firm can develop clear strategic economic performance metrics, which will signify reputation, achievements, profit in market share, increased sales, decreased operational expenditure, brand perception and employee satisfaction.

Drucker (1980) drew upon the relation between business and society based on the performance perspective. It is business's prime responsibility to perform its core activities, i.e. economic performance. This performance can be achieved within the limits of its competence, accountability and measurability. Drucker argued that if the business enterprises are lacking in these principles, then they are outside their own value system. He argued that business enterprises need to align themselves with the social problems. If it is possible, the enterprises can convert these problems into an economic opportunity for performance and contributions. Organizations cannot escape concern for society, for they are all based on society.

But, there are few "don'ts" that the business organization should keep in mind. Management of a firm should be cautious to resist responsibility for a social problem that may compromise or impair the performance capacity of its business. All organizations within a society are performing institutions with their own autonomous management. They can make the greatest social responsibility by performing their functions accurately and adequately. If the company is genuinely interested in the social problems, then it should take the help of expert advice without compromising on its core performance.

How to deliver economic performance?

- To accelerate economic performance, the firm has to make necessary arrangements to concentrate on the core activities, and make economic gain.
- Managers of enterprises have to maintain an optional balance between the performance capacity of the firm and the social issues.
- Initiate clear performance metrics to assess reputation achievements, profits in market share, increased sales, decreased operational expenditure, and employee satisfaction.
- If possible, convert social problems into economic opportunity, for firms cannot escape concerns for the society, as they are based on it.
- Accumulate capital through economic performance and do not assume social responsibilities that it cannot support, or the firm sooner or later might end up in trouble. The managers should avoid such irresponsibility, which might affect the economic performance of the firm.
- Encourage to concentrate on the firm's specific mission, because it is also society's first need and interest.
- Initiate social investment which is within the competence of the firm. Business can draw the link between economic and social performance, when social investment doesn't hamper or negatively impact the economic performance of the firm.
- Encourage to take opinion or advice from experts to deal with social issues, but with no compromise on business core functions.

## Environmental Responsibility

Environmental Performance is the performance which has an impact on the environment. Such performance ensures clear democratic practices in terms of the ecology. All members of the earth family are inter-connected. Earth democracy is an ancient world view and also an emergent political movement for peace, justice and sustainability. Vandana Shiva, a supporter of Earth Democracy movement, argues that all members of the earth community, including humans and other species, have the right to sustenance. These rights are not given by the states or corporations, and so they cannot extinguish these rights.

Shiva's *Earth Democracy* (2006) primarily stresses on the performance of the firm towards the environment, through its core activities. This responsibility is derived from the existence of the business with the environment. It is not always that business and the state cause intentional harm to the ecology.

With a departure from Shiva's line of protest against the corporate and the state, it is the state and business that can take lead in causing least harm to the environment, in pursuance to their core goal of economic profit.

Environmental responsibility scores over the environmental implication of the company's operation; products and facilities; elimination of waste and emissions; maximizing the efficiency and productivity of its resources and minimizing practices that might adversely affect the enjoyment of the country's resources by future generations.

Internet and news media and the information revolution shine light on business practices around the world, and companies are judged on the basis of their environmental stewardship. Partners in business, and customers want to know what is there inside a company. Even a growing number of companies in a wide range of sectors and geographic regions have discovered concrete values and competitive advantages from taking environmental initiatives, in areas such as pollution prevention, energy efficiency, environmentally oriented design, supply chain management and industrial ecology. It is also found that the environmental initiatives have produced positive financial results.

Environmental performance also helps firms to establish savings in input costs, waste disposal costs, labor costs through reduced absenteeism, increased loyalty, reduced costs of compliance with regulation, and other benefits like attracting quality investors. Firms also benefit through greater cooperation from their communities, and from building political capital that has been useful when community decision may affect the enterprise. By reducing the use of energy and raw materials and limit emissions and waste from product processes, firms can make business tackle the environmental challenges facing the world.

Environmental performance of business should be preventive and precautionary.

### Preventive Approach

- The Company needs to take necessary actions before scientific proof is available on the grounds that a delay in the action will cause damage to nation and society.
- Refraining from unnecessary use of resources so that the assimilative capacity of the natural environment can be widened.
- It should demonstrate care. It is the duty of those undertaking active changes or carrying out changes to demonstrate no environmental harm.
- Compensating for past errors of judgments, why preventive measures should be adopted?
- Preventive environmental measures entail both opportunities and cost cuts, because remediating environmental harm after it has occurred can cost much more.
- Investing in a production method that is not sustainable may depute resources and degrade the environment. It will lower the long-term return which can be anticipated from investing in sustainable resources.
- Improving environmental performance means less financial risks.
- Research and development for more environment friendly products that can have long-term benefits.

Firms need to have a thorough understanding of potential environmental impacts, as well as the baseline environmental condition within their influence. It essentially requires an approach to business activities that can manage uncertainty and ensure transparency.

With a precautionary approach for business, the following range of actions can be possible:

- Install safety margins while setting standards in areas where significant uncertainties still exist.
- Restrict or stop an activity whose impact on the environment is uncertain.
- Use of the best technology.
- Implement a cleaner production process.
- Initiate constant communication and engagement with the stakeholders.

These actions can be adopted in the following areas of business.

- Environmental management system.
- Waste management and resource conservation.
- Water and waste water management.
- Product innovation and process improvement.
- Green workplace practices.

### Environmental Management System

Corporates have to develop a management system to reach a situation where companies operate in a way that is consistent with the concept of sustainable development. That is why, the significant step would be to develop an environmental management system that promotes quality, commitment by the management as well as the employees to environmental issues, and to also ensure that there would be periodic assessment of environmental performance. An environmental management system not only helps the company to meet the legislative requirements, but also implement, manage and foster voluntary initiatives at the corporate level. The management system is not only meant for management responsibilities, but also the responsibilities of all the employees.

### Water and Waste Water Management

Water management practices should integrate the use of water-efficient technologies and treatment system which includes the following:

a. Mandatory water conservation such as rain water harvesting, ground water recharge, waste water reuse and recycling. The aim is to save and preserve water for sustainable use.

b. Water pollution control measures: Install adequate segregation, collection and centralized treatment facilities for waste water set by national and international standards.
c. A modern ETP with equipped treatment facilities.

### Waste Management and Resource Conservation

Best possible ways to manage the hazardous constituents of the waste and to reduce their impact on the environment are as follows:

a. Ensure recycling or reuse of the waste.
b. Ensure thermal energy recovery.
c. Ensure land filling of waste with utilization of land fill gas.

### Green Workplace Practices

The impact of daily activities on the environment has spread from individuals to groups, and family to organizations. Organizations are also volunteering to operate in a responsible way. The non-state actors, NGOs, transnational actors, trans-governmental bodies are encouraging business to become greens, sometimes by offering incentives. Green workplace explores types of practices that organizations practice, or encourage its employees to practice environment-friendly practices.

### Demonstrate Environmental Responsibility by the Employees

- Environmental responsibility as a part of the organization's mission and vision.
- Environmental responsibility efforts should be covered in the organization's annual report/sustainable development report.

### Encourage Environmentally Responsible Practices by Employees

- Management can possibly donate used office furniture to employees or local communities.
- It can set up a reuse facility, whereby employees can take unused supplies rather than drawing them away.
- Using energy-efficient lighting system and equipment.

- Encourage recycling of office products (papers, plastic, glass, cans).
- Encourage employees to use more environment friendly methods (e.g. making double-sided photocopies, powering down computers after few minutes of inactivity, using energy-efficient lights, ensuring blinds are lowered in the summer to conserve energy).
- Promote car-pooling for employees.
- Use recycled materials in the construction of building.
- Offer recycling program for selected personal products.
- Minimize water consumption by using water-conserving plumbing fixtures.
- Install automatic shut-off for equipment.

(*Source:* Adapted from *SHRM Survey Brief: Green Workplace*)

Business has to have strategies for its environmental performance in such a manner that with least harmful impact, it can cause sustainable growth. For adequate implementation of these measures, the government and non-state actors like NGOs, Civil Society Organizations and other corporate can play a significant role.

## Role of Governments

Governments may have a strong inclination towards promoting CSR initiatives, for it will serve a long-term national interest. With the support of local NGOs, governments can play a big role in building a framework for CSR through a goal-driven approach.

It may also want to bear environmental responsibility with a minimal conflictive manner, with less cost and more impact on job creation, competitive position with respect to trade and finally making economic and social gain.

## Governments' Responsibility Practices

- Inform and engage business in dialogue concerning mandatory compulsory initiatives and institutionalizing this process.
- Develop incentives and assistance to firms seeking to adopt environmentally responsible business models.
- Monitoring of environmental conditions and enforce sanctions.

Government can engage the private sector by providing funding for research, disseminating information and raising awareness. The public forums can develop appropriate management tools and mechanisms, environmental agreements, benchmarks, and guidelines for company management and reporting systems. The public sector too can play an important role by partnering in environmental initiatives.

### Business Responsibility

CSR initiatives differ from company to company, or even sector to sector. Manufacturing companies are confronted by a wide range of environmental challenges, while those in the service sector, or retail sector, face these to a lesser extent. Some companies address environmental issues on facility-wise or department-wise basis, while some others integrate environmental responsibility into all aspects of their operations.

### Corporate Environmental Policy

Companies who intend to reduce their environmental impact usually create a set of environmental principles and standards. And, it expresses the company's intention to respect the environment in the design, production and distribution of its products and services. The company has to be fully compliant with all laws and sanctions that go beyond compliances. Even the companies should have a policy whereby employees, community members, business-affected people and others can be informed of any potentially adverse effects the company's operations might have on the environment.

### Environmental Audit

The company can develop a policy of environmental audit. The aim of environmental audit is to understand the type and amount of resources used by a company, product facility, and type of waste and emission generated. It tries to quantify the data in monetary terms to understand the bottomline impact.

### Employee Involvement

Companies also recognize that to be effective, every employee needs to embrace an environmental policy. Then companies need to educate and help employees understand the environmental impact of their job. Companies can also assist employees to become environmentally responsible on their level by helping them build an environmental ethic. Even the companies can create incentives, rewards and initiate recognition programs for employees who demonstrate their environmental commitment.

### Green Products and Procurement

Companies buy greener products and material from their suppliers to ensure that their products and processes are environmentally responsible. Sometimes, companies can participate in buyers groups in which they can leverage to push suppliers to consider alternative products or processes.

### Role of NGOs

NGOs play an active role in implementing the social responsibility initiatives of business. In order to induce compliance, the NGOs may take an adversarial approach, threatening harm for no compliance, or otherwise a cooperative approach offering the firm a reward for compliance. The firm might decide to regulate itself (self-regulate) by taking volunteering action in order to avoid a threat or harm. In an alternative arrangement, firms may participate in its regulatory effort.

### Adversarial role

If the NGOs adopt the adversarial path and the firm rejects the NGOs demands, then the NGOs may attempt to deliver its threatened harm, or spread negative propaganda about the firm, or initiate a customer boycott of the firm's product.

### Demand for Transparency

On one hand, the firms face grave pressure from NGOs to undertake CSR activities, and on the other hand, they may face growing demands for transparency, and complete disclosure of their environmental profiles.

### Active Vigilance and Fight against Selective Disclosure

NGOs tend to remain vigilant about the perceived corporate hypocrisy known as corporate green wash. Green wash or selective disclosure goes back to the theory of Green Wash (Lyon and Maxwell, 2011). This theory states that firms with poor reputation tend to disclose fully because they gain a lot by trumpeting their success or lose little by disclosing a failure, because it is known that they are expected to fail. But firms with excellent reputation disclose nothing because they hardly gain anything by disclosing success. They are always expected to succeed, and firms with moderate reputation may choose to selectively disclose, because it may produce a significant improvement in public view, and also intend to withhold information about a failure, to avoid a negative public perception.

### Endorsement and Welfare Implication

If there is an unregulated market, then there is a high probability that NGO certification would lead to increase in sales of environment-friendly products. Suppose there is a probability of government regulation, NGO certification does not enhance social welfare.

Once social welfare regulations of the government agencies go higher, it can force all products out from the market which normally do not adhere to these standards. As against this, if the industry supports NGO label as a substitute for governmental regulation, then the existence of the NGO label intensifies. If it coexists with a government standard, then the NGO certification enhances social welfare, because it certifies environment-friendly products.

### Stakeholder Responsibility

It was in 1963, the word "Stakeholder" was used for the first time in an international memorandum at the Stanford Research Institute, although the constitution of a company had existed before (Freeman, 1984, Preston and Sapionza, 1990).

Stakeholder perspective takes into account the individual or groups with a stake in or claim on the company. Thus, stakeholders are groups and individuals who benefit from or are harmed by corporate action, and hence, it can be argued that corporations have an obligation to constituent groups other than shareholders, or stockholders. Corporations have a responsibility to all the constituent communities affected by business activity. A firm is not just based on set of contracts/contractual relations, but on a variety of interests that converge.

The purpose of the firm is to serve as a vehicle for coordinating stakeholder interest (Evan and Freeman, 1988). The legitimacy of the stakeholder perspective lies on two ethical principles: Principle of Corporate Rights and Principle of Corporate Effects. Both the principles take into account respect for persons. The first establishes that the firm and its managers cannot violate the legitimate rights of others to determine their future. The second establishes that the firm and its managers are responsible for the effects of their action on others.

There are other principles which can guide managerial decision making for stakeholder management.

### Stakeholder Management Principles

- The corporation needs to be managed for the benefit of its stakeholders: customers, suppliers, employees, owners, project affected communities, and local community at large.
- The management of the corporation shares a fiduciary relationship with its stakeholders, and the corporation. It must act in the interests of the stakeholders as their agent, and also in the interest of the corporation to ensure the survival of the firm, by safeguarding the long-term stakes of each group.

Based on the above-mentioned two principles of stakeholder management, its practical appropriation can be assessed as follows:

- Managers should acknowledge and monitor the concerns of all legitimate conflicts between their own roles as corporate stakeholders, and their legal and moral responsibilities for the interest of all stakeholders. They should address such conflicts through open communication, appropriate reporting, incentive systems, and a social audit review.
- Managers should avoid activities that might jeopardize inalienable human rights or give rise to risks.

(*Source:* Adapted from *Principles of Stakeholder Management* proposed by the Clarkson Centre for Business Ethics, 1999)

These principles can act as guidelines for respecting stakeholders' legitimate rights and interests.

### Human Rights and Stakeholders

To understand different issues within the company, the company needs to respect human rights. It is always advisable to incorporate human rights in the core values and overall culture of the organization. The company has to establish appropriate guidelines based on human rights principle, and wherever, and whenever possible, include input from stakeholder groups.

### Strategies for Protecting Human Rights

- Develop a health and safety management system.
- Initiate staff training on human rights issues and how they are affected by business.
- Facilitate staff training on internal company policies as they relate to human rights.
- Perform human rights impact assessments of business activities and renew them.
- Discuss human rights impact with business affected groups
- Improve working conditions in consultation with the workers and their representatives.

How companies can assure human rights through their daily activities?

### Workplace

- Provide safe and healthy working conditions.
- Guarantee freedom of association.
- Ensure non-discrimination in personal practices by avoiding direct or indirect use of forced child labor.
- Provide access to basic health, education and housing for the workers and their families.

### Community

- Prevent forcible displacement of individuals, groups or communities.
- Protect the economic livelihood of local communities.

(*Source:* Adapted from UN Global Compact)

Corporate governance and CSR are significant aspects of ethical business. To instill a democratic perspective, the corporate governance mechanism of the firms should also adopt democratic principles of management and governance.

Social democracy refers to the welfare state, industrial democracy refers to the decision making in the workplace, and economic democracy relates to the control over capital in a corporate system. Democratic corporate governance focuses on employees controlling and managing the organization.

Business to practice CSR in a democratic manner has to engage with its employee community in proactive way. The company needs to be responsible to all the members of the employee community, at all levels, be it the highest ranking official of the firm, or the lowest unskilled or the contractual workers. The company's responsibility towards all its employees should be equal. It is usually found that such responsibility does not percolate downwards. It is essential to establish a dialogue with employees to understand each other's problems better and find ways to resolve them.

The governance mechanism of the firm should be such that its rules, practice and procedures are held accountable to those who have a legitimate claim in the enterprise.

Major issues of corporate governance include the duties of directors, methods of financing the corporation, compensation to the manager acquisition and divestments and the monitoring of decision making at the strategic and operating levels. These issues are not only important for the company, but to all stakeholders as well: shareholders, employees, customers, distributors, contractors, business-affected communities, and the community at large.

Democracy is always justified in governing economic enterprise, the way democracy is justified in governing the state. Though the situations are different, still with the integrated constituencies of stakeholders, democratic practices are feasible with a well-planned participatory process.

Collective decision making is an essential part of any association. In order to reach a collective decision that will be binding on all members, decisions should be made by all those people who are subject to the decision. In fact, each person in the association is entitled to be the final judge of his or her own interests. Each adult individual is equally well qualified to decide which matters should be directly intervened and which matters should be delegated to others for intervention.

Participation by employees should be enjoyed by all autonomist agents. Work is an important part of one's life. It is time consuming, and is also the centre for personal development.

It can be argued that democratic practices in the workplace enhance the economic well-being of the employees. In a state without a distributive system, workers remain dependent on government, owners of capital being only concerned with maximizing profit, and hence, economic mobilization and distribution of economic power is resisted systematically. That is why, instead of providing the workers with social welfare incentives, it is always beneficial to provide workers with influence and controlling mechanism.

Within the democratic perspective, the existence of a community is very important. It requires a participation process which aims at the equal distribution of effective power in the community, and also needs the rights to protect individuals and groups from unwarranted use of power by others.

The workers' ownership seeks to establish a community in which only workers or employees exist. Initially, trade unions were viewed as creating a system of co-governance in which labor and capital are rationally placed in a situation of parity. This can be termed as internal democracy.

## How Democracy Exist in Firms?

It is an established belief that democracy is the structure for the governance of common people. It is the state in which those who govern are selected by, and govern as the representatives of the governed.

In an economic organization, the managers are those who govern. So, then who are going to be governed? It is the stakeholders who are either governed by the enterprise, or whose interests are affected by the enterprise (Ellerman, 1990).

The employment system divides a person into two categories: (i) the owner and seller of labor and (ii) the person who performs the labor services. In a large firm, the employees play more than one role, i.e. his or her labor seller role, or another input, supplier role. When the worker plays the role of an external input, supplier has direct control over his labor-selling activities. Workers are not governed in that role. If the employee is working, then the person is governed by management.

In direct control, rights are entirely directed towards making the decision of the enterprise. Managers take the sole decisions, but they do so as the representative of those who ultimately hold the direct control rights. In a corporate organization, the shareholders hold the direct control rights; other stakeholders, like suppliers, customers, dealers, contractors, NGOs, Research Foundations, Communities (Project-affected Communities/Larger Community) have an indirect role. Since they are affected by the operation of the enterprise, they have effective means to exert direct control on the operation of the enterprise, to protect their legitimate claim, probably in a collective form or as an individual claim.

The boards of directors exercise direct decision-making rights, but the affected interest groups are assigned with indirect decision-constraining rights. The democratic principle assigns ultimate direct control over an organization to the people who are governed. The affected communities are under the authority of the enterprise. It is the workers who are assigned the direct control rights by the democratic principle. But the same person can have several functions, as a worker, as consumers, or as capital supplier.

Self-determination is an important component within the democratic framework, but it excludes the right to violate the rights of outsiders. A democratic state does not have the rights to intervene in its neighbors activities. Direct control rights are to be exercised within the limitation established by the indirect control rights of the externally affected groups. Under such a system, each group will be self-governing. The workers can self-manage their work and the consumers can self-manage theirs, based on the constraints established by the other with either of them having direct control rights over the other.

A firm has to establish a system of governance that ensures equal rights to the workers, so that they can actively participate in the activities of the firms. Participation is essential for the workers, because it guarantees confidence, security and above all a feeling of belongingness to the firm. The management should possibly comply with the various processes of involvement of the workers, freedom of association and collective bargaining. Such arrangements can spearhead the internal democracy of the firm. Management should not muddle in an employee's decision to associate, or discriminate against the employee or a representative of the employee.

The freedom to form association involves employers, unions and worker representatives freely discussing issues at work in order to reach agreement that are jointly acceptable. These freedoms will allow the industrial process to function smoothly, because both the workers and organizations can defend their economic and social interests.

Collective bargaining is a voluntary process which determines terms and conditions of work and the regulation of relations between workers and their organizations. An effective recognition of the right to collective bargaining is the principle of good faith. This principle asserts that the partners work together and make effort to reach an agreement through genuine and constructive negotiations. Then, both the parties avoid unjustified delay in negotiation.

### Strategies for Collective Bargaining and Freedom of Association

- Encourage all workers to form or join a trade union of their choice without fear, or reprisal.
- Encourage union-neutral policies and procedures in such areas as application for employment and record keeping, decisions on advancement, avoidance of layoffs and transfer.
- Provide the opportunity for the worker representatives to carry out their functions within the company's needs, size and capabilities.
- Provide the facilities to collect union dues on company premises, posting of trade union notices and distribution of union documents related to normal trade union activities in the enterprises, and time-off with pay for union activities.

### Collective Bargaining

- Encourage collective bargaining as a constructive firm for addressing working conditions, terms and conditions of employment and relation between employers and workers.
- Initiate preventive measures with the interest of workers and management, including restructuring, training, safety and health,

grievances and dispute settlement procedures, disciplinary rules, family and community welfare.

- Provide accurate information for meaningful bargaining.
- If there is insufficient legal protection, take steps to preserve the safety and confidentiality of trade unions and their leaders.

## External Democracy

Internal democratic practices have their effects outside the organization, its employees, and the larger community.

A democratic state has to function in a different context, but in an organization, it has to assume the existence of communities, starting from shareowners, customers, investors, suppliers, and above all the employees. This can be termed as an external democratic practice. Democratic practices of a firm essentially try to restrict themselves to workforce and its participation, presentation, within the organization. When the workforce of a firm is considered, it is mostly the skilled, and the semi-skilled employees.

What about the unskilled laborers/wage laborers/contract workers?

Workers care about the organization or firms they work for. There are plenty of concerns for the workers. It can be alienation, participation, wage, job security, risk etc. Alienated workers are unlikely to contribute their best efforts to the firm.

These groups of workers except their contractual agreements, and their labor, have nothing to gain from the firm, with which they have been informally associated with. But there are instances of labor controlling the mechanism of firms (labor control firms).

Economic systems vary from private and public ownership and control with the firm organization. If we go back to the pedigree of the laborist control firm, then it is important to throw light on such firms.

The laborist controlled firms in the private sector are those in which the assets are privately owned, and are primarily controlled by their workforces, rather than investors.

The self-managed firm or the Yugoslavia Model of worker firms, developed during 1949-91, considered the assets of the firms as social property. But in practice, they are owned by the state. The workers within each firm had large control over their use.

The idea of workers' control motivated a diverse assortment of organization experiments since the Industrial Revolution. In contrast to public ownership, there were few attempts to impose workers' control on the entire society through political clout. A very good example in this line is the Yugoslavia Model. But this experiment was confounded with lots of problems, like price regulation, poorly defined property rights, and political authoritarianism. It is somewhat difficult to use the Yugoslavia experience to determine the workers' control in a setting of free markets, private ownership and political democracy (Dow, 2003).

In an economic system, large enterprises are under the ultimate control of capitalists, so to say, individuals or groups who supply capital to the firm. It is important to stress that private ownership does not always imply capitalism; rather it means that firms are actively managed by the suppliers of capital or their agents. In a worker-controlled firm, workers retain control over the firm's activities, except in extreme circumstances such as default on contractual obligation. Workers could also draw upon their personal savings to finance collective asset ownership by the firm.

In modern economic theory, firms are seen as a set of incomplete contracts among input suppliers (Williamson, 1985; Grossman and Hart, 1986; Mailgram and Roberts, 1990). In the light of such a view, the right to make decisions, not previously by contracts, must be assigned to some person or group. Such control rights are either used to determine a firm's product line, or investment strategy, or wages and employment, or production methods, and working conditions. In the large enterprises, these decisions are mostly made by managers, who are at the mercy of the board of directors (either hired/fired by the board of directors). This is somewhat related to typical capitalist-governed firms.

In the labor-owned firms, managers are either hired or fired by the board of directors, but the difference here is that they are accountable to the workforce.

A capital-managed firm is the one in which the ultimate control is allocated by virtue of capital being supplied by the capital supplier. The labor-managed firms assign control to those by virtue of or in proportion to labor supply.

In reference to control over the firms, if the shareholders can agree among themselves on the objectives of the firm, their control over the board of directors is limited and directors have limited control over top manager. This is the separation of ownership and control, put forward by Berle and Means (1932). But workers can influence the decisions of their superior in capitalist firms; for instance, employees might pressurize the management through committees, or they might exert social pressure on managers, positively or negatively (giving false information, or bribe them).

Worker predominance lies in both. The workers can exert pressure on the governance mechanism of the firm, and can influence in a varied manner, and can also strengthen their respective positions within the firm.

### Strategies for Democratic Participation of the Unskilled/Wage Laborers

- Encourage all the workers to form associations.
- Encourage them to keep records on various issues of the company, decisions, alternative to layoffs, and transfers.
- Provide guidance and, if possible, orient them to raise their concern about the company and themselves.
- Facilitate training to run such associations effectively.
- Provide the facilities to collect association fees on company premises.
- Encourage collective bargaining as constructive forums for addressing their issues: working conditions, terms and conditions of employment.
- Encourage preventive measures like restricting, safety and health, insurances, grievances and dispute settlement, disciplining rules, family and community welfare.
- Provide adequate and accurate information for meaningful bargaining.
- If there is insufficient legal protection, take steps to provide them.

Business-affected communities, or project-affected communities, are part of the affected stakeholder constituencies. They are an integral part of business, not only because of their business operation but also for the growth of business. The democratic practices of CSR of a firm should be based on policies that strengthen their performance towards the project-affected communities or business-affected communities.

A firm's business operation and activities affect the community. Either the community is displaced, or projects are located in the vicinity of the community settlement. It is the firm's responsibility to rehabilitate and resettle the displaced people (if the firm's operation does), and cause least negative impact on their lives.

How to strategize responsibility towards the project-affected communities?

- Provide all the required help to the communities to regain their previous life.
- Create employment avenues for the educated youth.
- Offer training and orientation for the unskilled community members so that they can be absorbed by the firm.
- Provide vocational assistance training to the members of the community, so that they can strengthen their interests and acquire qualification to lead a dignified life.

Business cannot be restrictive; so that Shareowners, Suppliers, Customers, Dealers, Distributors, Contractors, NGOs and CSOs do not feel alienated from the stakeholder community, business has to have constant engagement with them.

### Investor Community

The firm has to undertake discussions with the investor, and accept suggestion from them. It is very important for the functioning of the firm which can be acted upon in the future. Communication, health and safety measures should be given top priority while engaging with the dealer community.

### Distributor Community

Distributor communities are concerned about their relation with the company. Companies have to establish strategic policy towards them as product distribution is one of their core functions. That is why to keep the confidence of the distributors, the firm has to engage constantly with them.

### Contractor Community

Welfare and safety standards of the firm should be extended to the contractors. Firm's business policy, capacity development and environmental awareness programmes need the active participation of the contractors.

The proposed CSR model duly recognizes the core profit-making responsibility, stakeholder responsibility and finally environmental responsibility as the basis for the establishment strategic CSR.

This is all about how an enterprise can strategise its responsibilities towards the stakeholder community . Democracy within the enterprise is not just about the enterprises' responsibilities towards its stakeholders . It is also about stakeholders responsibilities towards the enterprise -be it employee responsibilities towards the enterprise ; shareholders responsibility in ethical spending and displaying concern about it: suppliers adhering to the various contractual arrangement with the firms; and other stakeholders varied engagement with the enterprise.

## REFERENCES


Berle, Adolf and Means, Gardiner (1932), The Modern Corporation and Private Property, US: Transaction Publishers.

Clarkson Centre for Business Ethics (1999), Principles of Stakeholder Management, Toronto: Joseph L. Rotman School of Management. Available athttp: //www.mgmt.utoronto.ca/%7Estake/ Principles.htm.

Dow, Gregory K. (2003), Governing the Firm Worker's Control in Theory and Practice, Cambridge: Cambridge University Press.

Drucker, Peter (1980), Managing in Turbulent Times, USA: Butterworth–Heinemann.

Ellerman, David P. (1990), The Democratic Workers-Owned Firm: A New Model for the East and West, USA: Unwin Hyman.

Evan, W. M. and Freeman, R. E. (1988), 'A Stakeholder Theory of the Modern Capitalism: Kantian Capitalism', in T. Beanchamp and N. Bowie (eds.), Ethical Theory and Business, Englewood Cliffs, NJ: Prentice Hall, pp. 75-93.

Freeman, R. E. (1984), Strategic Management: A Stakeholder Approach, Boston: Pitman.

Grossman, Stanford and Oliver Hart (1986), 'The Costs and Benefits of Ownership: A Theory of Vertical and Lateral Integration,' Journal of Political Economy, 94 (4), 691-719.

Lyon, Thomas P. and Maxwell, John W. (2011), 'Greenwash: Corporate Environmental Disclosure under Threat of Audit,' Journal of Economics and Management Strategy, 20 (1): 3-41.

Milgrom, Paul R. and John Roberts (1990), 'Bargaining Costs, Influence Costs, and the Organization of Economic Activity', in James E. Alt and Kenneth A. Shepsle (eds.), Perspectives on Political Economy, New York: Cambridge University Press.

Preston, L. E. and Sapienza, H. J. (1990), 'Stakeholder Management and Corporate Performance,' Journal of Behavioural Economics, 19: 361-375.

Shiva, Vandana (2006), Earth Democracy: Justice, Sustainability and Peace, London: Zed Books.

Society for Human Resource Management (SHRM) Survey Brief: Green Workplace. Available at www.shrm.org/research/surveyfindings/articles/documents/shrm%20green%20 workplace% 20 survey%20brief.pdf.

UN Global Compact. Available at https: //www.unglobalcompact.org/.

Williamson, Oliver E. (1985), The Economic Institutions of Capitalism, New York: Free Press.

# Index